# A TEXTBOOK OF ENGINEERING MATHEMATICS

A TEXTBOOK OF

# ENGINEERING MATHEMATICS

*For*

**B.Tech., (*IV Semester*)**
**Mahatma Gandhi University, Kerala**
**(Strictly according to the latest revised syllabus)**

*By*

**N.P. BALI**
*Formerly, Principal*
*S.B. College, Gurgaon*
Haryana

**Dr. A.J. GEORGE**
*HOD (Mathematics)*
*M.A. College of Engineering*
*(Mahatma Gandhi University)*
*Kothamangalan,*
Kerala

UNIVERSITY SCIENCE PRESS

(An Imprint of Laxmi Publications Pvt. Ltd.)

BANGALORE • CHENNAI • COCHIN • GUWAHATI • HYDERABAD
JALANDHAR • KOLKATA • LUCKNOW • MUMBAI • PATNA
RANCHI • NEW DELHI

*Published by :*

LAXMI PUBLICATIONS (P) LTD
113, Golden House, Daryaganj,
New Delhi-110002

*Phone* : 011-43 53 25 00
*Fax* : 011-43 53 25 28

www.laxmipublications.com
info@laxmipublications.com

*First Edition* : 2007 ; *Second Edition* : 2009
Reprint : 2010 ; *Third Edition* : 2012

**OFFICES**

| | | | |
|---|---|---|---|
| ✆ **Bangalore** | 080-26 75 69 30 | ✆ **Kolkata** | 033-22 27 43 84 |
| ✆ **Chennai** | 044-24 34 47 26 | ✆ **Lucknow** | 0522-220 99 16 |
| ✆ **Cochin** | 0484-237 70 04, 405 13 03 | ✆ **Mumbai** | 022-24 91 54 15, 24 92 78 69 |
| ✆ **Guwahati** | 0361-251 36 69, 251 38 81 | ✆ **Patna** | 0612-230 00 97 |
| ✆ **Hyderabad** | 040-24 65 23 33 | ✆ **Ranchi** | 0651-221 47 64 |
| ✆ **Jalandhar** | 0181-222 12 72 | | |

UEM-9496-125-ENGG MATH IV (KE)-BAL
*Typeset at* : Excellent Graphics, Delhi.

**C—**
*Printed at* : Repro Knowledgecast Limited, Thane

# CONTENTS

# PREFACE TO THE THIRD EDITION

This book is a part of the original book **"A Textbook of Engineering Mathematics"** by N.P. Bali running into seventh edition and very well received by the teachers and students of all Indian Universities. The rapid sale of the seventh edition bears testimony to the overwhelming response.

The present form of the book contains only five chapters and covers the entire syllabus for the students of *fourth semester of Mahatma Gandhi University*. More worked out problems were included in the third edition as examples. Problems collected from latest M.G. University Question papers were added in the exercise to increase the flavour of the book.

Appendix is attached. Problems in the statistics can be done with the help of the tables in the Appendix.

There is no dearth of books on Engineering Mathematics but the students find it difficult to solve most of the problems in the exercise in the absence of an adequate number of solved examples. An outstanding and distinguishing feature of the book is the large number of typical solved examples followed by well-graded problems. Many examples and problems have been selected from recent papers of various engineering examinations.

We have endeavoured to present the fundamental concepts in a comprehensive and lucid manner. We are indebted to all authors, Indian and Foreign, whose works we have frequently consulted.

All efforts have been made to keep the book free from errors. Answers to all exercises have been re-checked. All suggestions for improvement will be highly appreciated and gratefully acknowledged.

—Authors

# SYLLABUS

## ENGINEERING MATHEMATICS–III

**2-2-0** **(Common to all branches)** **credits 4**

**Module 1 : Fourier Seires** (12 hours)

Dirichlet conditions—Fourier series with period $2\pi$ and $2l$—Half range sine and cosine series—Harmonic Analysis—r.m.s. Value.

**Module 2 : Fourier Transform** (12 hours)

Statement of Fourier integral theorem—Fourier transforms—derivative of transforms-convolution theorem (no proof)—Parsevals identity.

**Module 3 : Partial Differential Equations** (12 hours)

Formation by eliminating arbitrary constants and arbitrary functions—solution of Lagrange's equation—Charpits method—solution of Homogeneous partial differential equations with constant coefficients.

**Module 4 : Probability Distribution** (12 hours)

Concept of random variable, probability distribution—Bernoulli'trial—Discrete distribution—Binomial distribution—its mean and variance-fitting of Binomial distribution—Poisson distribution as a limiting case of Binomial distribution—its mean and variance—fitting of Poisson distribution—continuous distribution—Uniform distribution—exponential distribution—its mean and variance—Normal distribution—Standard normal curve—its properties.

**Module 5 : Testing of Hypothesis** (12 hours)

Population and Samples—Hypothesis—level of significance—type I and type II error—Large samples tests—test of significance for single proportion, difference of proportion, single mean, difference of mean—chi—square test for variance—F test for equality of variances for small samples.

# Noticeable Concepts

- **Use of Greek Letters**

| | | | | | | | |
|---|---|---|---|---|---|---|---|
| $\alpha$ | alpha | $\phi$ | phi | $\kappa$ | kappa | $\tau$ | tau |
| $\beta$ | beta | $\psi$ | psi | $\mu$ | mu | $\chi$ | chi |
| $\gamma$ | gamma | $\xi$ | xi | $\nu$ | nu | $\omega$ | omega |
| $\delta$ | delta | $\eta$ | eta | $\pi$ | pi | $\Delta$ | cap. delta |
| $\varepsilon$ | epsilon | $\zeta$ | zeta | $\rho$ | rho | | |
| $i$ | iota | $\lambda$ | lambda | $\sigma$ | sigma | | |
| $\theta$ | theta | $\Gamma$ | cap. gamma | $\Sigma$ | cap. sigma | | |

- **Some Important Notations**

| | | | |
|---|---|---|---|
| $\in$ | belongs to | $\Leftrightarrow$ | implies and implied by |
| $\notin$ | does not belong to | iff | if and only if |
| $\Rightarrow$ | implies | $\cup$ | union |
| | | $\cap$ | intersection |

- **Useful Data**

| | | | |
|---|---|---|---|
| $\sqrt{2} = 1.4142$ | $\frac{1}{\pi} = 0.3183$ | 1 rad. = 57° 17′ 45″ | $\log_{10}e = 0.4343$ |
| $\sqrt{3} = 1.732$ | $e = 2.7183$ | 1° = 0.0174 rad. | $\log_e 2 = 0.6931$ |
| $\pi = 3.1416$ | $\frac{1}{e} = 0.3679$ | $\log_e 10 = 2.3026$ | $\log_e 3 = 1.0986$ |

- **Some Mathematical Symbols**

| | | | |
|---|---|---|---|
| $=$ | equals | $\sim$ | is of the order of magnitude of |
| $\approx$ | equals approximately | $\propto$ | is proportional to |
| $\neq$ | is not equal to | lim | the limit of |
| $\equiv$ | is identical to, is defined as | $\Sigma$ | the sum of |
| $>$ | is greater than | $\int$ | the integral of |
| $>>$ | is much greater than | $\Delta x$ | the change or difference in $x$ |
| $\geq$ | is greater than or equal to | $\lvert x \rvert$ | the absolute value or magnitude of $x$ |
| $<$ | is less than | | the average value of $x$ |
| $<<$ | is much less than | $df/dx$ | the derivative of $f$ with respect to $x$ |
| $\leq$ | is less than or equal to | $\partial f/\partial x$ | the partial derivative of $f$ with respect to $x$ |

# 1
# Fourier Series

## 1.1. PERIODIC FUNCTIONS

A function $f(x)$ which satisfies the relation $f(x + T) = f(x)$ for all $x$ is called a periodic function. The *smallest positive number* T, for which this relation holds, is called the **period** of $f(x)$.

If T is the period of $f(x)$, then $f(x) = f(x + T) = f(x + 2T) = ....... = f(x + nT) = ......$

Also $f(x) = f(x - T) = f(x - 2T) = ...... = f(x - nT) = ......$

$\therefore$ $f(x) = f(x \pm nT)$, where $n$ is a positive integer.

Thus, $f(x)$ repeats itself after periods of T.

For example, sin $x$, cos $x$, sec $x$ and cosec $x$ are periodic functions with period $2\pi$ while tan $x$ and cot $x$ are periodic functions with period $\pi$. The functions sin $nx$ and cos $nx$ are periodic with period $\frac{2\pi}{n}$.

The sum of a number of periodic functions is also periodic. If $T_1$ and $T_2$ are the periods of $f(x)$ and $g(x)$, then the period of $a\, f(x) + b\, g(x)$ is the least common multiple of $T_1$ and $T_2$.

For example, cos $x$, cos $2x$, cos $3x$ are periodic functions with periods $2\pi$, $\pi$ and $\frac{2\pi}{3}$ respectively.

$\therefore$ $f(x) = \cos x + \frac{1}{2}\cos 2x + \frac{1}{3}\cos 3x$ is also periodic with period $2\pi$, the L.C.M. of $2\pi$, $\pi$ and $\frac{2\pi}{3}$.

## 1.2. FOURIER SERIES

Periodic functions are of common occurrence in many physical and engineering problems ; for example, in conduction of heat and mechanical vibrations. It is useful to express these functions in a series of sines and cosines. Most of the single valued functions which occur in applied mathematics can be expressed in the form $\frac{a_0}{2} + a_1 \cos x + a_2 \cos 2x + a_3 \cos 3x + ......$
$+ b_1 \sin x + b_2 \sin 2x + b_3 \sin 3x + ......$
within a desired range of values of the variable. Such a series is known as *Fourier Series*. Thus, any function $f(x)$ defined in the interval $c_1 \le x \le c_2$ can be expressed in the Fourier Series

$$f(x) = \frac{a_0}{2} + \sum_{n=1}^{\infty} (a_n \cos nx + b_n \sin nx)$$

where $a_0, a_n, b_n$ $(n = 1, 2, 3, ......)$ are constants, called the Fourier co-efficients of $f(x)$.

**Note.** To determine $a_0$, $a_n$ and $b_n$, we shall need the following results : ($m$ and $n$ are integers)

(i) $\int_c^{c+2\pi} \sin nx\, dx = -\left[\frac{\cos nx}{n}\right]_c^{c+2\pi} = 0, \quad \int_c^{c+2\pi} \cos nx\, dx = \left[\frac{\sin nx}{n}\right]_c^{c+2\pi} = 0, n \neq 0$

(ii) $$\int_c^{c+2\pi} \sin mx \cos nx\, dx = \frac{1}{2}\int_c^{c+2\pi} [\sin (m+n)x + \sin (m-n)x]\, dx$$

$$= -\frac{1}{2}\left[\frac{\cos (m+n)x}{m+n} + \frac{\cos (m-n)x}{m-n}\right]_c^{c+2\pi} = 0, m \neq n$$

(iii) $$\int_c^{c+2\pi} \cos mx \cos nx\, dx = \frac{1}{2}\int_c^{c+2\pi} [\cos (m+n)x + \cos (m-n)x]\, dx$$

$$= \frac{1}{2}\left[\frac{\sin (m+n)x}{m+n} + \frac{\sin (m-n)x}{m-n}\right]_c^{c+2\pi} = 0, m \neq n$$

(iv) $$\int_c^{c+2\pi} \sin mx \sin nx\, dx = \frac{1}{2}\int_c^{c+2\pi} [\cos (m-n)x - \cos (m+n)x]\, dx$$

$$= \frac{1}{2}\left[\frac{\sin (m-n)x}{m-n} - \frac{\sin (m+n)x}{m+n}\right]_c^{c+2\pi} = 0, m \neq n$$

(v) $\int_c^{c+2\pi} \cos^2 nx\, dx = \left[\frac{x}{2} + \frac{\sin 2nx}{4n}\right]_c^{c+2\pi} = \pi, \quad \int_c^{c+2\pi} \sin^2 nx\, dx = \left[\frac{x}{2} - \frac{\sin 2nx}{4n}\right]_c^{c+2\pi} = \pi, n \neq 0$

(vi) $\int_c^{c+2\pi} \sin nx \cos nx\, dx = \frac{1}{2}\int_c^{c+2\pi} \sin 2nx\, dx = -\frac{1}{2}\left[\frac{\cos 2nx}{2n}\right]_c^{c+2\pi} = 0, n \neq 0$

(vii) To integrate the product of two functions, one of which is a positive integral power of $x$, we apply the *generalised rule of integration by parts.* If dashes denote differentiation and suffixes denote integration w.r.t. $x$, the rule can be stated as follows :

$\int uv\, dx = uv_1 - u'v_2 + u''v_3 - u'''v_4 + \ldots\ldots$ where $u$ and $v$ are functions of $x$. *i.e.,* Integral of the product of two functions

= 1st function × integral of 2nd – go on differentiating 1st, integrating 2nd, signs alternately + ve and – ve.

[Simplification should be done only when the integration is over.]

For example, $$\int x^3 e^{-2x}\, dx = x^3\left(\frac{e^{-2x}}{-2}\right) - 3x^2\left[\frac{e^{-2x}}{(-2)^2}\right] + 6x\left[\frac{e^{-2x}}{(-2)^3}\right] - 6\left[\frac{e^{-2x}}{(-2)^4}\right]$$

$$= e^{-2x}\left[-\frac{1}{2}x^3 - \frac{3}{4}x^2 - \frac{3}{4}x - \frac{3}{8}\right] = -\frac{1}{8}e^{-2x}(4x^3 + 6x^2 + 6x + 3)$$

$$\int x^2 \cos nx\, dx = x^2\left(\frac{\sin nx}{n}\right) - 2x\left(\frac{-\cos nx}{n^2}\right) + 2\left(-\frac{\sin nx}{n^3}\right)$$

$$= \frac{x^2}{n}\sin nx + \frac{2x}{n^2}\cos nx - \frac{2}{n^3}\sin nx.$$

(viii) $\sin n\pi = 0$ and $\cos n\pi = (-1)^n$

$\sin\left(n + \frac{1}{2}\right)\pi = (-1)^n$ and $\cos\left(n + \frac{1}{2}\right)\pi = 0$, where $n$ is an integer.

(*ix*) **Even and Odd Functions**

A function $f(x)$ is said to be *even* if $f(-x) = f(x)$ *e.g.*, $x^2$, $\cos x$, $\sin^2 x$ are even functions.

The graph of an even function is symmetrical about the $y$-axis.

A function $f(x)$ is said to be *odd* if $f(-x) = -f(x)$ *e.g.*, $x^3$, $\sin x$, $\tan^3 x$ are odd functions.

The graph of an odd function is symmetrical about the origin.

The product of two even functions or two odd functions is an even function while the product of an even function and an odd function is an odd function.

Also, $\int_{-c}^{c} f(x)\, dx = 0$, when $f(x)$ is an odd function

and $\int_{-c}^{c} f(x)\, dx = 2\int_{0}^{c} f(x)\, dx$, when $f(x)$ is an even function.

## 1.3. EULER'S FORMULAE

The Fourier series for the function $f(x)$ in the interval $c < x < c + 2\pi$ is given by

$$f(x) = \frac{a_0}{2} + \sum_{n=1}^{\infty} a_n \cos nx + \sum_{n=1}^{\infty} b_n \sin nx \qquad ...(1)$$

In finding the co-efficients $a_0$, $a_n$ and $b_n$, we assume that the series on the right hand side of (1) is uniformly convergent for $c < x < c + 2\pi$ and it can be integrated term by term in the given interval.

**To find $a_0$,** Integrate both sides of (1) w.r.t. $x$, between the limits $c$ to $c + 2\pi$.

$$\int_c^{c+2\pi} f(x)\, dx = \frac{a_0}{2}\int_c^{c+2\pi} dx + \int_c^{c+2\pi}\left(\sum_{n=1}^{\infty} a_n \cos nx\right) dx + \int_c^{c+2\pi}\left(\sum_{n=1}^{\infty} b_n \sin nx\right) dx$$

$$= \frac{a_0}{2}(c + 2\pi - c) + 0 + 0 \qquad \text{[by formulae } (i) \text{ above]}$$

$$= a_0\pi$$

$$\therefore \qquad \boxed{a_0 = \frac{1}{\pi}\int_c^{c+2\pi} f(x)\, dx}$$

**To find $a_n$,** multiply both sides of (1) by $\cos nx$ and integrate w.r.t. $x$, between the limits $c$ to $c + 2\pi$.

$$\int_c^{c+2\pi} f(x)\cos nx\, dx = \frac{a_0}{2}\int_c^{c+2\pi} \cos nx\, dx$$

$$+ \int_c^{c+2\pi}\left(\sum_{n=1}^{\infty} a_n \cos nx\right)\cos nx\, dx + \int_c^{c+2\pi}\left(\sum_{n=1}^{\infty} b_n \sin nx\right)\cos nx\, dx$$

$$= 0 + a_n\pi + 0 \qquad \text{[by formulae } (i), (v) \text{ and } (vi)\text{]}$$

$$= a_n\pi$$

$$\therefore \qquad \boxed{a_n = \frac{1}{\pi}\int_c^{c+2\pi} f(x)\cos nx\, dx}$$

**To find $b_n$,** multiply both sides of (1) by sin $nx$ and integrate w.r.t. $x$ between the limits $c$ to $c + 2\pi$.

$$\int_c^{c+2\pi} f(x)\sin nx\,dx = \frac{a_0}{2}\int_c^{c+2\pi} \sin nx\,dx + \int_c^{c+2\pi}\left(\sum_{n=1}^{\infty} a_n \cos nx\right)\sin nx\,dx$$

$$+ \int_c^{c+2\pi}\left(\sum_{n=1}^{\infty} b_n \sin nx\right)\sin nx\,dx$$

$$= 0 + 0 + b_n\pi \qquad \text{[by formulae } (i), (vi) \text{ and } (v)]$$

$$= b_n\pi$$

$$\therefore \qquad \boxed{b_n = \frac{1}{\pi}\int_c^{c+2\pi} f(x)\sin nx\,dx}$$

Hence $a_0 = \dfrac{1}{\pi}\displaystyle\int_c^{c+2\pi} f(x)\,dx\,;\ a_n = \dfrac{1}{\pi}\displaystyle\int_c^{c+2\pi} f(x)\cos nx\,dx\,;$ and $b_n = \dfrac{1}{\pi}\displaystyle\int_c^{c+2\pi} f(x)\sin nx\,dx$ ...(I)

These values of $a_0$, $a_n$ and $b_n$ are called Euler's formulae.

**Cor. 1.** *If c = 0, the interval becomes $0 < x < 2\pi$ and the formulae I reduce to*

$$a_0 = \frac{1}{\pi}\int_0^{2\pi} f(x)\,dx\,;\quad a_n = \frac{1}{\pi}\int_0^{2\pi} f(x)\cos nx\,dx\,;\quad b_n = \frac{1}{\pi}\int_0^{2\pi} f(x)\sin nx\,dx$$

**Cor. 2.** *If c = – π, the interval becomes $-\pi < x < \pi$, and the formulae I reduce to*

$$a_0 = \frac{1}{\pi}\int_{-\pi}^{\pi} f(x)\,dx\,;\ a_n = \frac{1}{\pi}\int_{-\pi}^{\pi} f(x)\cos nx\,dx\,;\ b_n = \frac{1}{\pi}\int_{-\pi}^{\pi} f(x)\sin nx\,dx$$

**Cor. 3.** *When f(x) is an odd function* $\quad a_0 = \dfrac{1}{\pi}\displaystyle\int_{-\pi}^{\pi} f(x)\,dx = 0$

Since cos $nx$ is an even function, therefore, $f(x)$ cos $nx$ is an odd function.

$$a_n = \frac{1}{\pi}\int_{-\pi}^{\pi} f(x)\cos nx\,dx = 0$$

Since sin $nx$ is an odd function, therefore, $f(x)$ sin $nx$ is an even function.

$$\therefore \qquad b_n = \frac{1}{\pi}\int_{-\pi}^{\pi} f(x)\sin nx\,dx = \frac{2}{\pi}\int_0^{\pi} f(x)\sin nx\,dx$$

Hence, if a periodic function $f(x)$ is odd, its Fourier expansion contains only sine terms,

*i.e.,* $$f(x) = \sum_{n=1}^{\infty} b_n \sin nx, \quad \text{where} \quad b_n = \frac{2}{\pi}\int_0^{\pi} f(x)\sin nx\,dx$$

*When f(x) is an even function* $\quad a_0 = \dfrac{1}{\pi}\displaystyle\int_{-\pi}^{\pi} f(x)\,dx = \dfrac{2}{\pi}\displaystyle\int_0^{\pi} f(x)\,dx$

Since cos $nx$ is an even function, therefore, $f(x)$ cos $nx$ is an even function.

$$\therefore \qquad a_n = \frac{1}{\pi}\int_{-\pi}^{\pi} f(x)\cos nx\,dx = \frac{2}{\pi}\int_0^{\pi} f(x)\cos nx\,dx$$

Since sin $nx$ is an odd function, therefore, $f(x)$ sin $nx$ is an odd function.

$$\therefore \qquad b_n = \frac{1}{\pi}\int_{-\pi}^{\pi} f(x)\sin nx\,dx = 0$$

Hence, if a periodic function $f(x)$ is even, its Fourier expansion contains only cosine terms,

*i.e.*, $$f(x) = \frac{a_0}{2} + \sum_{n=1}^{\infty} a_n \cos nx, \text{ where } a_0 = \frac{2}{\pi}\int_0^{\pi} f(x)\,dx \text{ and } a_0 = \frac{2}{\pi}\int_0^{\pi} f(x)\cos nx\,dx.$$

## ILLUSTRATIVE EXAMPLES

**Example 1.** *Obtain the Fourier series to represent* $f(x) = \frac{1}{4}(\pi - x)^2, 0 < x < 2\pi$.

*Hence obtain the following relations :*

(*i*) $\frac{1}{1^2} + \frac{1}{2^2} + \frac{1}{3^2} + \frac{1}{4^2} + \ldots\ldots = \sum_{n=1}^{\infty} \frac{1}{n^2} = \frac{\pi^2}{6}$

(*ii*) $\frac{1}{1^2} - \frac{1}{2^2} + \frac{1}{3^2} - \frac{1}{4^2} + \ldots\ldots = \sum_{n=1}^{\infty} \frac{(-1)^{n-1}}{n^2} = \frac{\pi^2}{12}$

(*iii*) $\frac{1}{1^2} + \frac{1}{3^2} + \frac{1}{5^2} + \ldots\ldots = \sum_{n=1}^{\infty} \frac{1}{(2n-1)^2} = \frac{\pi^2}{8}$.

**Sol.** Let $f(x) = \frac{1}{4}(\pi - x)^2 = \frac{a_0}{2} + \sum_{n=1}^{\infty} a_n \cos nx + \sum_{n=1}^{\infty} b_n \sin nx$

By Euler's formulae, we have

$$a_0 = \frac{1}{\pi}\int_0^{2\pi} f(x)\,dx = \frac{1}{\pi}\int_0^{2\pi} \frac{1}{4}(\pi - x)^2\,dx = \frac{1}{4\pi}\left[\frac{(\pi - x)^3}{-3}\right]_0^{2\pi} = -\frac{1}{12\pi}[-\pi^3 - \pi^3] = \frac{\pi^2}{6}$$

$$a_n = \frac{1}{\pi}\int_0^{2\pi} f(x)\cos nx\,dx = \frac{1}{\pi}\int_0^{2\pi} \frac{1}{4}(\pi - x)^2 \cos nx\,dx$$

$$= \frac{1}{4\pi}\left[(\pi - x)^2 \frac{\sin nx}{n} - \{-2(\pi - x)\}\left(-\frac{\cos nx}{n^2}\right) + 2\left(-\frac{\sin nx}{n^3}\right)\right]_0^{2\pi}$$

$$= \frac{1}{4\pi}\left[\left(0 + \frac{2\pi\cos 2n\pi}{n^2} + 0\right) - \left(0 - \frac{2\pi\cos 0}{n^2} + 0\right)\right] = \frac{1}{4\pi}\left[\frac{2\pi}{n^2} + \frac{2\pi}{n^2}\right] = \frac{1}{n^2}$$

$$b_n = \frac{1}{\pi}\int_0^{2\pi} f(x)\sin nx\,dx = \frac{1}{\pi}\int_0^{2\pi} \frac{1}{4}(\pi - x)^2 \sin nx\,dx$$

$$= \frac{1}{4\pi}\left[(\pi - x)^2\left(-\frac{\cos nx}{n}\right) - \{-2(\pi - x)\}\left(-\frac{\sin nx}{n^2}\right) + 2\left(\frac{\cos nx}{n^3}\right)\right]_0^{2\pi}$$

$$= \frac{1}{4\pi}\left[\left(-\frac{\pi^2\cos 2n\pi}{n} - 0 + \frac{2\cos 2n\pi}{n^3}\right) - \left(-\frac{\pi^2}{n} - 0 + \frac{2\cos 0}{n^3}\right)\right]$$

$$= \frac{1}{4\pi}\left[\left(-\frac{\pi^2}{n}+\frac{2}{n^3}\right)-\left(-\frac{\pi^2}{n}+\frac{2}{n^3}\right)\right] = 0$$

$$\therefore \quad f(x) = \frac{\pi^2}{12} + \sum_{n=1}^{\infty} \frac{\cos nx}{n^2} = \frac{\pi^2}{12} + \frac{\cos x}{1^2} + \frac{\cos 2x}{2^2} + \frac{\cos 3x}{3^2} + \ldots\ldots \qquad \ldots(1)$$

**Deductions**

(*i*) Putting $x = 0$ in equation (1), we get

$$f(0) = \frac{\pi^2}{12} + \left(\frac{1}{1^2}+\frac{1}{2^2}+\frac{1}{3^2}+\frac{1}{4^2}+\ldots\ldots\right)$$

$$\Rightarrow \quad \frac{\pi^2}{4} = \frac{\pi^2}{12} + \left(\frac{1}{1^2}+\frac{1}{2^2}+\frac{1}{3^2}+\frac{1}{4^2}+\ldots\ldots\right)$$

$$\Rightarrow \quad \frac{1}{1^2}+\frac{1}{2^2}+\frac{1}{3^2}+\frac{1}{4^2}+\ldots\ldots = \frac{\pi^2}{6} \qquad \ldots(2)$$

(*ii*) Putting $x = \pi$ in equation (1), we get

$$f(\pi) = \frac{\pi^2}{12} + \left[\left(\frac{-1}{1^2}\right)+\frac{1}{2^2}+\left(\frac{-1}{3^2}\right)+\frac{1}{4^2}+\ldots\ldots\right]$$

$$\Rightarrow \quad 0 = \frac{\pi^2}{12} - \frac{1}{1^2}+\frac{1}{2^2}-\frac{1}{3^2}+\frac{1}{4^2}+\ldots\ldots$$

$$\Rightarrow \quad \frac{1}{1^2}-\frac{1}{2^2}+\frac{1}{3^2}-\frac{1}{4^2}+\ldots\ldots = \frac{\pi^2}{12} \qquad \ldots(3)$$

(*iii*) Adding (2) and (3), we get

$$2\left(\frac{1}{1^2}+\frac{1}{3^2}+\frac{1}{5^2}+\ldots\ldots\right) = \frac{\pi^2}{6}+\frac{\pi^2}{12}$$

$$\Rightarrow \quad \frac{1}{1^2}+\frac{1}{3^2}+\frac{1}{5^2}+\ldots\ldots = \frac{1}{2}\left(\frac{\pi^2}{4}\right) = \frac{\pi^2}{8}.$$

**Example 2.** *Expand $f(x) = x \sin x$, $0 < x < 2\pi$ as a Fourier series.*

**Sol.** Let $f(x) = x \sin x = \frac{a_0}{2} + \sum_{n=1}^{\infty} a_n \cos nx + \sum_{n=1}^{\infty} b_n \sin nx$

By Euler's formulae, we have $a_0 = \frac{1}{\pi}\int_0^{2\pi} f(x)\, dx = \frac{1}{\pi}\int_0^{2\pi} x \sin x\, dx$

$$= \frac{1}{\pi}\Big[x(-\cos x) - 1.(-\sin x)\Big]_0^{2\pi} = \frac{1}{\pi}[-2\pi] = -2$$

$$a_n = \frac{1}{\pi}\int_0^{2\pi} f(x)\cos nx\, dx = \frac{1}{\pi}\int_0^{2\pi} x \sin x \cos nx\, dx = \frac{1}{2\pi}\int_0^{2\pi} x(2\cos nx \sin x)\, dx$$

$$= \frac{1}{2\pi}\int_0^{2\pi} x[\sin(n+1)x - \sin(n-1)x]\,dx$$

$$= \frac{1}{2\pi}\left[x\left\{-\frac{\cos(n+1)x}{n+1} + \frac{\cos(n-1)x}{n-1}\right\} - 1.\left\{-\frac{\sin(n+1)x}{(n+1)^2} + \frac{\sin(n-1)x}{(n-1)^2}\right\}\right]_0^{2\pi}$$

$$= \frac{1}{2\pi}\left[2\pi\left\{-\frac{\cos 2(n+1)\pi}{n+1} + \frac{\cos 2(n-1)\pi}{n-1}\right\}\right]$$

$$= -\frac{1}{n+1} + \frac{1}{n-1} = \frac{2}{n^2-1},\ n \neq 1$$

When $n = 1$, we have $a_1 = \frac{1}{\pi}\int_0^{2\pi} x\sin x\cos x\,dx = \frac{1}{2\pi}\int_0^{2\pi} x\sin 2x\,dx$

$$= \frac{1}{2\pi}\left[x\left(-\frac{\cos 2x}{2}\right) - 1.\left(-\frac{\sin 2x}{4}\right)\right]_0^{2\pi} = \frac{1}{2\pi}[-\pi] = -\frac{1}{2}$$

$$b_n = \frac{1}{\pi}\int_0^{2\pi} f(x)\sin nx\,dx = \frac{1}{\pi}\int_0^{2\pi} x\sin x\sin nx\,dx$$

$$= \frac{1}{2\pi}\int_0^{2\pi} x(2\sin nx\sin x)\,dx = \frac{1}{2\pi}\int_0^{2\pi} x\,[\cos(n-1)x - \cos(n+1)x]\,dx$$

$$= \frac{1}{2\pi}\left[x\left\{\frac{\sin(n-1)x}{n-1} - \frac{\sin(n+1)x}{n+1}\right\} - 1.\left\{-\frac{\cos(n-1)x}{(n-1)^2} + \frac{\cos(n+1)x}{(n+1)^2}\right\}\right]_0^{2\pi}$$

$$= \frac{1}{2\pi}\left[\frac{\cos 2(n-1)\pi}{(n-1)^2} - \frac{\cos 2(n+1)\pi}{(n+1)^2} - \frac{1}{(n-1)^2} + \frac{1}{(n+1)^2}\right]$$

$$= \frac{1}{2\pi}\left[\frac{1}{(n-1)^2} - \frac{1}{(n+1)^2} - \frac{1}{(n-1)^2} + \frac{1}{(n+1)^2}\right] = 0,\ n \neq 1$$

When $n = 1$, we have $b_1 = \frac{1}{\pi}\int_0^{2\pi} x\sin x\sin x\,dx = \frac{1}{2\pi}\int_0^{2\pi} x(1-\cos 2x)\,dx$

$$= \frac{1}{2\pi}\left[x\left(x - \frac{\sin 2x}{2}\right) - 1.\left(\frac{x^2}{2} + \frac{\cos 2x}{4}\right)\right]_0^{2\pi}$$

$$= \frac{1}{2\pi}\left[2\pi(2\pi) - \frac{4\pi^2}{2} - \frac{1}{4} + \frac{1}{4}\right] = \frac{1}{2\pi}(2\pi^2) = \pi$$

$$\therefore \qquad f(x) = \frac{a_0}{2} + a_1\cos x + b_1\sin x + \sum_{n=2}^{\infty} a_n\cos nx + \sum_{n=2}^{\infty} b_n\sin nx$$

$$= -1 - \frac{1}{2}\cos x + \pi\sin x + \sum_{n=2}^{\infty}\frac{2}{n^2-1}\cos nx + 0$$

$$= -1 + \pi\sin x - \frac{1}{2}\cos x + \frac{2}{2^2-1}\cos 2x + \frac{2}{3^2-1}\cos 3x + \ldots\ldots$$

**Example 3.** *Find a Fourier series to represent $x - x^2$ from $x = -\pi$ to $x = \pi$. Hence show that*

$$\frac{1}{1^2} - \frac{1}{2^2} + \frac{1}{3^2} - \frac{1}{4^2} + \ldots\ldots = \frac{\pi^2}{12}.$$

**Sol.** Let $x - x^2 = \dfrac{a_0}{2} + \displaystyle\sum_{n=1}^{\infty} a_n \cos nx + \sum_{n=1}^{\infty} b_n \sin nx$

By Euler's formulae, we have $a_0 = \dfrac{1}{\pi}\displaystyle\int_{-\pi}^{\pi} (x - x^2)\, dx = \frac{1}{\pi}\left[\frac{x^2}{2} - \frac{x^3}{3}\right]_{-\pi}^{\pi}$

$$= \frac{1}{\pi}\left[\left(\frac{\pi^2}{2} - \frac{\pi^3}{3}\right) - \left(\frac{\pi^2}{2} + \frac{\pi^3}{3}\right)\right] = -\frac{2\pi^2}{3}$$

$$a_n = \frac{1}{\pi}\int_{-\pi}^{\pi} (x - x^2) \cos nx \, dx$$

$$= \frac{1}{\pi}\left[(x - x^2)\frac{\sin nx}{n} - (1 - 2x)\left(-\frac{\cos nx}{n^2}\right) + (-2)\left(-\frac{\sin nx}{n^3}\right)\right]_{-\pi}^{\pi}$$

$$= \frac{1}{\pi}\left[(1 - 2\pi)\frac{\cos n\pi}{n^2} - (1 + 2\pi)\frac{\cos n\pi}{n^2}\right] = \frac{1}{\pi}\left(-4\pi \, . \frac{\cos n\pi}{n^2}\right)$$

$$= -4\frac{(-1)^n}{n^2} \qquad [\because \cos n\pi = (-1)^n]$$

$$b_n = \frac{1}{\pi}\int_{-\pi}^{\pi} (x - x^2) \sin nx \, dx$$

$$= \frac{1}{\pi}\left[(x - x^2)\left(-\frac{\cos nx}{n}\right) - (1 - 2x)\left(-\frac{\sin nx}{n^2}\right) + (-2)\left(\frac{\cos nx}{n^3}\right)\right]_{-\pi}^{\pi}$$

$$= \frac{1}{\pi}\left[(\pi^2 - \pi)\frac{\cos n\pi}{n} - 2\frac{\cos n\pi}{n^3} + (-\pi - \pi^2)\frac{\cos n\pi}{n} + 2\frac{\cos n\pi}{n^3}\right]$$

$$= \frac{1}{\pi}\left[-2\pi \, . \frac{\cos n\pi}{n}\right] = -2\frac{(-1)^n}{n}$$

$$\therefore \quad x - x^2 = -\frac{\pi^2}{3} - 4\sum_{n=1}^{\infty} \frac{(-1)^n}{n^2} \cos nx - 2\sum_{n=1}^{\infty} \frac{(-1)^n}{n} \sin nx$$

$$= -\frac{\pi^2}{3} - 4\left[-\frac{\cos x}{1^2} + \frac{\cos 2x}{2^2} - \frac{\cos 3x}{3^2} + \ldots\ldots\right] - 2\left[\frac{-\sin x}{1} + \frac{\sin 2x}{2} - \frac{\sin 3x}{3} + \ldots\ldots\right]$$

$$= -\frac{\pi^2}{3} + 4\left[\frac{\cos x}{1^2} - \frac{\cos 2x}{2^2} + \frac{\cos 3x}{3^2} - \ldots\ldots\right] + 2\left[\frac{\sin x}{1} - \frac{\sin 2x}{2} + \frac{\sin 3x}{3} - \ldots\ldots\right]$$

Putting $x = 0$, we get $0 = -\dfrac{\pi^2}{3} + 4\left(\dfrac{1}{1^2} - \dfrac{1}{2^2} + \dfrac{1}{3^2} - \dfrac{1}{4^2} + \ldots\ldots\right)$

$$\Rightarrow \quad \frac{1}{1^2} - \frac{1}{2^2} + \frac{1}{3^2} - \frac{1}{4^2} + \ldots.. = \frac{\pi^2}{12}.$$

**Example 4.** *Obtain the Fourier series for the function $f(x) = x^2$, $-\pi < x < \pi$. Hence show that*

$$(i)\ \frac{1}{1^2}+\frac{1}{2^2}+\frac{1}{3^2}+\frac{1}{4^2}+\ldots\ldots=\sum_{n=1}^{\infty}\frac{1}{n^2}=\frac{\pi^2}{6}$$

$$(ii)\ \frac{1}{1^2}-\frac{1}{2^2}+\frac{1}{3^2}-\frac{1}{4^2}+\ldots\ldots=\sum_{n=1}^{\infty}\frac{(-1)^{n-1}}{n^2}=\frac{\pi^2}{12}$$

$$(iii)\ \frac{1}{1^2}+\frac{1}{3^2}+\frac{1}{5^2}+\ldots\ldots=\sum_{n=1}^{\infty}\frac{1}{(2n-1)^2}=\frac{\pi^2}{8}.$$

**Sol.** Since $f(-x) = (-x)^2 = x^2 = f(x)$.

$\therefore$ $f(x)$ is an even function and hence $b_n = 0$

Let $$f(x) = x^2 = \frac{a_0}{2}+\sum_{n=1}^{\infty} a_n \cos nx$$

Then $$a_0 = \frac{2}{\pi}\int_0^{\pi} f(x)\, dx = \frac{2}{\pi}\int_0^{\pi} x^2\, dx = \frac{2}{\pi}\left[\frac{x^3}{3}\right]_0^{\pi} = \frac{2}{3}\pi^2$$

$$a_n = \frac{2}{\pi}\int_0^{\pi} f(x)\cos nx\, dx = \frac{2}{\pi}\int_0^{\pi} x^2 \cos nx\, dx$$

$$= \frac{2}{\pi}\left[x^2\left(\frac{\sin nx}{n}\right) - 2x\left(-\frac{\cos nx}{n^2}\right) + 2\left(-\frac{\sin nx}{n^3}\right)\right]_0^{\pi} = \frac{2}{\pi}\left[2\pi \,.\, \frac{\cos n\pi}{n^2}\right] = 4\frac{(-1)^n}{n^2}$$

$$\therefore \quad x^2 = \frac{\pi^2}{3} + 4\sum_{n=1}^{\infty}\frac{(-1)^n}{n^2}\cos nx$$

$$= \frac{\pi^2}{3} - 4\left(\frac{\cos x}{1^2} - \frac{\cos 2x}{2^2} + \frac{\cos 3x}{3^2} - \frac{\cos 4x}{4^2} + \ldots\ldots\right) \qquad \ldots(1)$$

Putting $x = \pi$ in (1), we get

$$\pi^2 = \frac{\pi^2}{3} - 4\left(-\frac{1}{1^2} - \frac{1}{2^2} - \frac{1}{3^2} - \frac{1}{4^2} + \ldots\ldots\right) \Rightarrow \frac{2\pi^2}{3} = 4\left(\frac{1}{1^2}+\frac{1}{2^2}+\frac{1}{3^2}+\frac{1}{4^2}+\ldots\ldots\right)$$

$$\therefore \quad \frac{1}{1^2}+\frac{1}{2^2}+\frac{1}{3^2}+\frac{1}{4^2}+\ldots\ldots=\frac{\pi^2}{6} \qquad \text{[Result } (i)]$$

Putting $x = 0$ in (1), we get $0 = \dfrac{\pi^2}{3} - 4\left(\dfrac{1}{1^2}-\dfrac{1}{2^2}+\dfrac{1}{3^2}-\dfrac{1}{4^2}+\ldots\ldots\right)$

$$\therefore \quad \frac{1}{1^2}-\frac{1}{2^2}+\frac{1}{3^2}-\frac{1}{4^2}+\ldots\ldots=\frac{\pi^2}{12} \qquad \text{[Result } (ii)]$$

Adding (*i*) and (*ii*), we get $2\left(\dfrac{1}{1^2}+\dfrac{1}{3^2}+\dfrac{1}{5^2}+\ldots\ldots\right)=\dfrac{\pi^2}{4}$

$$\therefore \quad \frac{1}{1^2}+\frac{1}{3^2}+\frac{1}{5^2}+\ldots\ldots=\frac{\pi^2}{8}. \qquad \text{[Result } (iii)]$$

**Example 5.** *Obtain the Fourier series for $f(x) = e^{-x}$ in the interval $0 < x < 2\pi$.*

**Sol.** Let $$f(x) = e^{-x} = \frac{a_0}{2} + \sum_{n=1}^{\infty} a_n \cos nx + \sum_{n=1}^{\infty} b_n \sin nx$$

Then $$a_0 = \frac{1}{\pi}\int_0^{2\pi} f(x)\,dx = \frac{1}{\pi}\int_0^{2\pi} e^{-x}\,dx = \frac{1}{\pi}\Big[-e^{-x}\Big]_0^{2\pi} = \frac{1-e^{-2\pi}}{\pi}$$

$$a_n = \frac{1}{\pi}\int_0^{2\pi} f(x)\cos nx\,dx = \frac{1}{\pi}\int_0^{2\pi} e^{-x}\cos nx\,dx$$

$$= \frac{1}{\pi}\left[\frac{e^{-x}}{1+n^2}(-\cos nx + n\sin nx)\right]_0^{2\pi}$$

$$\left[\because \int e^{ax}\cos bx\,dx = \frac{e^{ax}}{a^2+b^2}(a\cos bx + b\sin bx)\right]$$

$$= \frac{1-e^{-2\pi}}{\pi(1+n^2)}$$

$$b_n = \frac{1}{\pi}\int_0^{2\pi} f(x)\sin nx\,dx = \frac{1}{\pi}\int_0^{2\pi} e^{-x}\sin nx\,dx$$

$$= \frac{1}{\pi}\left[\frac{e^{-x}}{1+n^2}(-\sin nx - n\cos nx)\right]_0^{2\pi} = \frac{1-e^{-2\pi}}{\pi}\cdot\frac{n}{1+n^2}$$

$$\left[\because \int e^{ax}\sin bx\,dx = \frac{e^{ax}}{a^2+b^2}(a\sin bx - b\cos bx)\right]$$

$\therefore$ $$e^{-x} = \frac{1-e^{-2\pi}}{2\pi} + \frac{1-e^{-2\pi}}{\pi}\sum_{n=1}^{\infty}\frac{\cos nx}{1+n^2} + \frac{1-e^{-2\pi}}{\pi}\sum_{n=1}^{\infty}\frac{n\sin nx}{1+n^2}$$

$$= \frac{1-e^{-2\pi}}{\pi}\left[\frac{1}{2} + \left(\frac{1}{2}\cos x + \frac{1}{5}\cos 2x + \frac{1}{10}\cos 3x + \ldots\ldots\right) + \left(\frac{1}{2}\sin x + \frac{2}{5}\sin 2x + \frac{3}{10}\sin 3x + \ldots\ldots\right)\right]$$

**Example 6.** *Find the Fourier series to represent $e^{ax}$ in the interval $-\pi < x < \pi$. Hence derive series for $\frac{\pi}{\sinh \pi}$.*

**Sol.** Let $f(x) = e^{ax} = \frac{a_0}{2} + \sum_{n=1}^{\infty} a_n \cos nx + \sum_{n=1}^{\infty} b_n \sin nx$

Then $$a_0 = \frac{1}{\pi}\int_{-\pi}^{\pi} f(x)\,dx = \frac{1}{\pi}\int_{-\pi}^{\pi} e^{ax}\,dx = \frac{1}{\pi}\left[\frac{e^{ax}}{a}\right]_{-\pi}^{\pi} = \frac{1}{a\pi}(e^{a\pi} - e^{-a\pi}) = \frac{2\sinh a\pi}{a\pi}$$

$$a_n = \frac{1}{\pi}\int_{-\pi}^{\pi} f(x)\cos nx\,dx = \frac{1}{\pi}\int_{-\pi}^{\pi} e^{ax}\cos nx\,dx$$

$$= \frac{1}{\pi}\left[\frac{e^{ax}}{a^2+n^2}(a\cos nx + n\sin nx)\right]_{-\pi}^{\pi} = \frac{1}{\pi(a^2+n^2)}[ae^{a\pi}\cos n\pi - ae^{-a\pi}\cos n\pi]$$

$$= \frac{a\cos n\pi\,(e^{a\pi} - e^{-a\pi})}{\pi(a^2+n^2)} = \frac{2a(-1)^n\sinh a\pi}{\pi(a^2+n^2)}$$

Similarly, $b_n = \dfrac{2n(-1)^n \sinh a\pi}{\pi(a^2+n^2)}$

$$\therefore \quad e^{ax} = \frac{\sinh a\pi}{a\pi} + \sum_{n=1}^{\infty} \frac{2a(-1)^n \sinh a\pi}{\pi(a^2+n^2)} \cos nx + \sum_{n=1}^{\infty} \frac{2n(-1)^n \sinh a\pi}{\pi(a^2+n^2)} \sin nx$$

$$= \frac{2\sinh a\pi}{\pi}\left[\frac{1}{2a} - a\left(\frac{\cos x}{a^2+1^2} - \frac{\cos 2x}{a^2+2^2} + \frac{\cos 3x}{a^2+3^2} - \ldots\ldots\right) - \left(\frac{\sin x}{a^2+1^2} - \frac{2\sin 2x}{a^2+2^2} + \frac{3\sin 3x}{a^2+3^2} - \ldots\ldots\right)\right]$$

**Deduction.** Putting $x = 0$ and $a = 1$, we get

$$1 = \frac{2\sinh \pi}{\pi}\left[\frac{1}{2} - \left(\frac{1}{1+1^2} - \frac{1}{1+2^2} + \frac{1}{1+3^2} - \frac{1}{1+4^2} + \ldots\ldots\right)\right]$$

$$\Rightarrow \quad \frac{\pi}{\sinh \pi} = 2\left(\frac{1}{1+2^2} - \frac{1}{1+3^2} + \frac{1}{1+4^2} - \ldots\ldots\right)$$

**Example 7.** *Express $f(x) = |x|, -\pi < x < \pi$, as Fourier series.* *(M.G.U. Dec. 2007)*

**Sol.** Since $f(-x) = |-x| = |x| = f(x)$

$\therefore$ $f(x)$ is an even function and hence $b_n = 0$

Let
$$f(x) = |x| = \frac{a_0}{2} + \sum_{n=1}^{\infty} a_n \cos nx$$

Then
$$a_0 = \frac{2}{\pi}\int_0^{\pi} f(x)\,dx = \frac{2}{\pi}\int_0^{\pi} |x|\,dx = \frac{2}{\pi}\int_0^{\pi} x\,dx = \frac{2}{\pi}\left[\frac{x^2}{2}\right]_0^{\pi} = \pi$$

$$a_n = \frac{2}{\pi}\int_0^{\pi} f(x)\cos nx\,dx = \frac{2}{\pi}\int_0^{\pi} |x|\cos nx\,dx = \frac{2}{\pi}\int_0^{\pi} x\cos nx\,dx$$

$$= \frac{2}{\pi}\left[x\left(\frac{\sin nx}{n}\right) - 1.\left(-\frac{\cos nx}{n^2}\right)\right]_0^{\pi}$$

$$= \frac{2}{\pi}\left[\frac{\cos n\pi}{n^2} - \frac{1}{n^2}\right] = \frac{2}{\pi n^2}[(-1)^n - 1] = \begin{cases} 0, & \text{if } n \text{ is even} \\ \dfrac{-4}{\pi n^2}, & \text{if } n \text{ is odd} \end{cases}$$

$$\therefore \quad |x| = \frac{\pi}{2} - \frac{4}{\pi}\left(\cos x + \frac{\cos 3x}{3^2} + \frac{\cos 5x}{5^2} + \ldots\ldots\right)$$

**Note.** Putting $x = 0$ in the above result, we get $\dfrac{1}{1^2} + \dfrac{1}{3^2} + \dfrac{1}{5^2} + \ldots\ldots = \dfrac{\pi^2}{8}$.

**Example 8.** *Expand the function $f(x) = x \sin x$ as a Fourier series in the interval $-\pi \le x \le \pi$.*

*Deduce that* $\dfrac{1}{1.3} - \dfrac{1}{3.5} + \dfrac{1}{5.7} - \dfrac{1}{7.9} + \ldots\ldots = \dfrac{\pi - 2}{4}$.

**Sol.** Since $x \sin x$ is an even function of $x$, $b_n = 0$

Let $$f(x) = x \sin x = \frac{a_0}{2} + \sum_{n=1}^{\infty} a_n \cos nx$$

Then $$a_0 = \frac{2}{\pi}\int_0^{\pi} x \sin x \, dx = \frac{2}{\pi}\Big[x(-\cos x) - 1.(-\sin x)\Big]_0^{\pi} = \frac{2}{\pi}(-\pi \cos \pi) = 2$$

$$a_n = \frac{2}{\pi}\int_0^{\pi} x \sin x \cos nx \, dx = \frac{1}{\pi}\int_0^{\pi} x(2 \cos nx \sin x)\, dx$$

$$= \frac{1}{\pi}\int_0^{\pi} x[\sin (n+1)x - \sin (n-1)x]\, dx$$

$$= \frac{1}{\pi}\left[x\left\{-\frac{\cos (n+1)x}{n+1} + \frac{\cos (n-1)x}{n-1}\right\} - 1.\left\{-\frac{\sin (n+1)x}{(n+1)^2} + \frac{\sin (n-1)x}{(n-1)^2}\right\}\right]_0^{\pi}$$

$$= \frac{1}{\pi}\left[\pi\left\{-\frac{\cos (n+1)\pi}{n+1} + \frac{\cos (n-1)\pi}{n-1}\right\}\right], \; n \neq 1$$

$$= \frac{\cos (n-1)\pi}{n-1} - \frac{\cos (n+1)\pi}{n+1}$$

When $n$ is odd, $n \neq 1$, $n - 1$ and $n + 1$ are even

$$\therefore \quad a_n = \frac{1}{n-1} - \frac{1}{n+1} = \frac{2}{n^2 - 1}$$

When $n$ is even, $n - 1$ and $n + 1$ are odd

$$\therefore \quad a_n = \frac{-1}{n-1} + \frac{1}{n+1} = \frac{-2}{n^2 - 1}$$

When $n = 1$, we have $$a_1 = \frac{2}{\pi}\int_0^{\pi} x \sin x \cos x \, dx = \frac{1}{\pi}\int_0^{\pi} x \sin 2x \, dx$$

$$= \frac{1}{\pi}\left[x\left(-\frac{\cos 2x}{2}\right) - 1.\left(-\frac{\sin 2x}{4}\right)\right]_0^{\pi} = \frac{1}{\pi}\left[-\frac{\pi \cos 2\pi}{2}\right] = -\frac{1}{2}$$

$$\therefore \quad x \sin x = 1 - \frac{1}{2}\cos x - 2\left(\frac{\cos 2x}{2^2 - 1} - \frac{\cos 3x}{3^2 - 1} + \frac{\cos 4x}{4^2 - 1} - \frac{\cos 5x}{5^2 - 1} + \ldots\ldots\right)$$

Putting $x = \frac{\pi}{2}$, we get $$\frac{\pi}{2} = 1 - 2\left(\frac{-1}{2^2 - 1} + \frac{1}{4^2 - 1} - \frac{1}{6^2 - 1} + \ldots\ldots\right)$$

$$\Rightarrow \quad \frac{\pi}{2} - 1 = 2\left(\frac{1}{2^2 - 1} - \frac{1}{4^2 - 1} + \frac{1}{6^2 - 1} - \ldots\ldots\right) \quad \Rightarrow \quad \frac{\pi - 2}{4} = \frac{1}{1.3} - \frac{1}{3.5} + \frac{1}{5.7} - \ldots\ldots$$

**Example 9.** *Show that for* $-\pi < x < \pi$, (M.G.U. May 2009)

$$\sin ax = \frac{2 \sin a\pi}{\pi}\left(\frac{\sin x}{1^2 - a^2} - \frac{2 \sin 2x}{2^2 - a^2} + \frac{3 \sin 3x}{3^2 - a^2} - \ldots\ldots\right).$$

**Sol.** Since $\sin ax$ is an odd function of $x$, $a_0 = 0$ and $a_n = 0$

Let $$\sin ax = \sum_{n=1}^{\infty} b_n \sin nx$$

Then $$b_n = \frac{2}{\pi}\int_0^{\pi} \sin ax \sin nx \, dx = \frac{1}{\pi}\int_0^{\pi} [\cos (n-a)x - \cos (n+a)x]\, dx$$

$$= \frac{1}{\pi}\left[\frac{\sin (n-a)x}{n-a} - \frac{\sin (n+a)x}{n+a}\right]_0^{\pi} = \frac{1}{\pi}\left[\frac{\sin (n-a)\pi}{n-a} - \frac{\sin (n+a)\pi}{n+a}\right]$$

$$= \frac{1}{\pi}\left[\frac{(-1)^n(-\sin a\pi)}{n-a} - \frac{(-1)^n \sin a\pi}{n+a}\right] = -\frac{(-1)^n \sin a\pi}{\pi}\left[\frac{1}{n-a} + \frac{1}{n+a}\right]$$

$$= (-1)^{n+1} \cdot \frac{2n \sin a\pi}{\pi(n^2 - a^2)}$$

$$\therefore \quad \sin ax = \frac{2 \sin a\pi}{\pi} \sum_{n=1}^{\infty} \frac{(-1)^{n+1}}{n^2 - a^2} \sin nx$$

$$= \frac{2 \sin a\pi}{\pi}\left(\frac{\sin x}{1^2 - a^2} - \frac{2 \sin 2x}{2^2 - a^2} + \frac{3 \sin 3x}{3^2 - a^2} - \ldots\ldots\right).$$

**Example 10.** *Obtain Fourier series for the function f(x) given by*

$$f(x) = \begin{cases} 1 + \dfrac{2x}{\pi}, & -\pi \le x \le 0 \\ 1 - \dfrac{2x}{\pi}, & 0 \le x \le \pi \end{cases}$$

*Hence deduce that* $\dfrac{1}{1^2} + \dfrac{1}{3^2} + \dfrac{1}{5^2} + \ldots\ldots = \dfrac{\pi^2}{8}$.

**Sol.** When $-\pi \le x \le 0, \qquad 0 \le -x \le \pi$

$$\therefore \quad f(-x) = 1 - \frac{2(-x)}{\pi} = 1 + \frac{2x}{\pi} = f(x)$$

When $0 \le x \le \pi, \qquad -\pi \le -x \le 0$

$$\therefore \quad f(-x) = 1 + \frac{2(-x)}{\pi} = 1 - \frac{2x}{\pi} = f(x)$$

$\Rightarrow$ $f(x)$ is an even function of $x$ in $[-\pi, \pi]$. This is also clear from its graph which is symmetrical above the $y$-axis.

$$\therefore \quad b_n = 0$$

Let $$f(x) = \frac{a_0}{2} + \sum_{n=1}^{\infty} a_n \cos nx$$

then $$a_0 = \frac{2}{\pi}\int_0^{\pi} f(x)\, dx = \frac{2}{\pi}\int_0^{\pi} \left(1 - \frac{2x}{\pi}\right) dx = \frac{2}{\pi}\left[x - \frac{x^2}{\pi}\right]_0^{\pi} = 0$$

$$a_n = \frac{2}{\pi}\int_0^{\pi} f(x) \cos nx\, dx = \frac{2}{\pi}\int_0^{\pi} \left(1 - \frac{2x}{\pi}\right) \cos nx\, dx$$

$$= \frac{2}{\pi}\left[\left(1 - \frac{2x}{\pi}\right)\frac{\sin nx}{n} - \left(-\frac{2}{\pi}\right)\left(-\frac{\cos nx}{n^2}\right)\right]_0^{\pi}$$

$$= \frac{2}{\pi}\left[-\frac{2\cos n\pi}{\pi n^2} + \frac{2}{\pi n^2}\right] = \frac{4}{\pi^2 n^2}[1-(-1)^n]$$

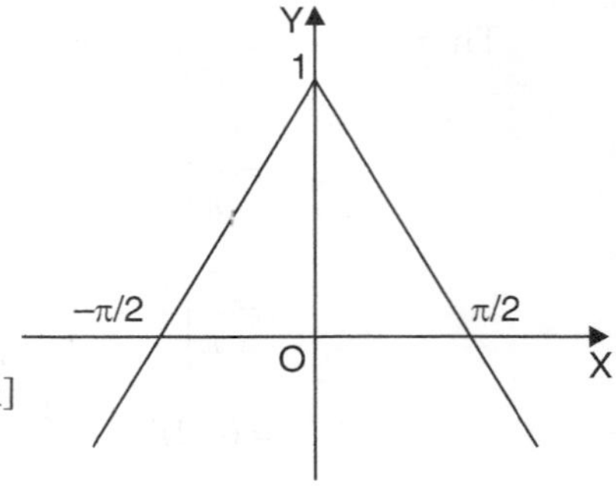


$$\therefore \quad f(x) = \frac{4}{\pi^2}\sum_{n=1}^{\infty}[1-(-1)^n]\frac{\cos nx}{n^2}$$

$$= \frac{4}{\pi^2}\left(\frac{2\cos x}{1^2} + \frac{2\cos 3x}{3^2} + \frac{2\cos 5x}{5^2} + \ldots\ldots\right)$$

[$\because$ $1 - (-1)^n = 0$ when $n$ is even]

$$= \frac{8}{\pi^2}\left(\frac{\cos x}{1^2} + \frac{\cos 3x}{3^2} + \frac{\cos 5x}{5^2} + \ldots\ldots\right)$$

Putting $x = 0$, we get $\frac{1}{1^2} + \frac{1}{3^2} + \frac{1}{5^2} + \ldots\ldots = \frac{\pi^2}{8}$, since $f(0) = 1$.

## TEST YOUR KNOWLEDGE

1. Expand in a Fourier series the function $f(x) = x$ in the interval $0 < x < 2\pi$.
2. Express $f(x) = \frac{1}{2}(\pi - x)$ in a Fourier series in the interval $0 < x < 2\pi$.
3. Find the Fourier series for the function $f(x) = x + x^2$ in the interval $-\pi < x < \pi$. Hence show that

   (*i*) $\frac{1}{1^2} - \frac{1}{2^2} + \frac{1}{3^2} - \frac{1}{4^2} + \ldots\ldots = \frac{\pi^2}{12}$. (*ii*) $1 + \frac{1}{2^2} + \frac{1}{3^2} + \frac{1}{4^2} + \ldots\ldots = \frac{\pi^2}{6}$

4. If $f(x) = \left(\frac{\pi - x}{2}\right)^2$ in the interval $0 < x < 2\pi$, show that $f(x) = \frac{\pi^2}{12} + \sum_{n=1}^{\infty}\frac{\cos nx}{n^2}$

   Hence obtain the following relations :

   (*i*) $\frac{1}{1^2} + \frac{1}{2^2} + \frac{1}{3^2} + \frac{1}{4^2} + \ldots\ldots = \frac{\pi^2}{6}$ (*ii*) $\frac{1}{1^2} - \frac{1}{2^2} + \frac{1}{3^2} - \frac{1}{4^2} + \ldots.. = \frac{\pi^2}{12}$

   (*iii*) $\frac{1}{1^2} + \frac{1}{3^2} + \frac{1}{5^2} + \ldots\ldots = \frac{\pi^2}{8}$.

5. Prove that for all values of $x$ between $-\pi$ and $\pi$, $\frac{1}{2}x = \sin x - \frac{1}{2}\sin 2x + \frac{1}{3}\sin 3x - \frac{1}{4}\sin 4x + \ldots\ldots$
6. Obtain the Fourier series to represent $e^x$ in the interval $0 < x < 2\pi$.
7. Find the Fourier series to represent $e^x$ in the interval $-\pi < x < \pi$.
8. Find the Fourier series to represent the function $f(x) = |\sin x|, -\pi < x < \pi$.
9. Expand $f(x) = |\cos x|$ as a Fourier series in the interval $-\pi < x < \pi$.
10. Prove that in the interval $-\pi < x < \pi$, $x\cos x = -\frac{1}{2}\sin x + 2\sum_{n=2}^{\infty}\frac{(-1)^n}{n^2-1}\sin nx$.
11. Prove that for $-\pi < x < \pi$, $\frac{x(\pi^2 - x^2)}{12} = \frac{\sin x}{1^3} - \frac{\sin 2x}{2^3} + \frac{\sin 3x}{3^3} - \frac{\sin 4x}{4^3} + \ldots\ldots$
12. (*a*) Obtain a Fourier expansion for $\sqrt{1-\cos x}$ in the interval $-\pi < x < \pi$.

   [**Hint.** For all integral values of $n$, $\cos\left(n + \frac{1}{2}\right)\pi = 0 = \cos\left(n - \frac{1}{2}\right)\pi$.]

(*b*) Obtain a Fourier series for $\sqrt{1-\cos x}$ in the interval $(0, 2\pi)$ and hence find the value of

$$\frac{1}{1.3}+\frac{1}{3.5}+\frac{1}{5.7}+\ldots\ldots$$

**13.** Express $f(x) = \cos wx, -\pi < x < \pi$, where $w$ is a fraction, as a Fourier series. Hence prove that

$$\cot\theta = \frac{1}{\theta}+\frac{2\theta}{\theta^2-\pi^2}+\frac{2\theta}{\theta^2-4\pi^2}+\ldots\ldots$$

**14.** Find the Fourier series for $f(x)$ in the interval $(-\pi, \pi)$ when

$$f(x) = \pi + x, \qquad -\pi < x < 0$$
$$= \pi - x, \qquad 0 < x < \pi .$$

**15.** Obtain a Fourier series to represent $e^{-ax}$ from $x = -\pi$ to $x = \pi$. Hence derive series for $\dfrac{\pi}{\sinh \pi}$.

**16.** Prove that in the range $-\pi < x < \pi$, $\cosh ax = \dfrac{2a}{\pi}\sinh a\pi\left[\dfrac{1}{2a^2}+\displaystyle\sum_{n=1}^{\infty}\frac{(-1)^n}{n^2+a^2}\cos nx\right]$.

**17.** Given $f(x) = \begin{cases} -x+1 & \text{for} \quad -\pi \le x \le 0 \\ x+1 & \text{for} \quad 0 \le x \le \pi \end{cases}$

Is the function even or odd ? Find the Fourier series for $f(x)$ and deduce the value of

$$\frac{1}{1^2}+\frac{1}{3^2}+\frac{1}{5^2}+\ldots\ldots$$

**18.** Find the Fourier series for $f(x) = x + x^2 ; -\pi < x < \pi$.

**19.** Obtain the F.S. of the function $f(x) = x ; -\pi < x < \pi$ and deduce that

$$\frac{\pi}{4} = 1-\frac{1}{3}+\frac{1}{5}-\frac{1}{7}+\ldots$$

## Answers

**1.** $f(x) = \pi - 2\displaystyle\sum_{n=1}^{\infty}\frac{\sin nx}{n}$ **2.** $f(x) = \displaystyle\sum_{n=1}^{\infty}\frac{\sin nx}{n}$

**3.** $f(x) = \dfrac{\pi^2}{3} - 4\left(\dfrac{\cos x}{1^2}-\dfrac{\cos 2x}{2^2}+\dfrac{\cos 3x}{3^2}-\ldots\ldots\right)+2\left(\dfrac{\sin x}{1}-\dfrac{\sin 2x}{2}+\dfrac{\sin 3x}{3}-\ldots\ldots\right)$

**6.** $e^x = \dfrac{e^{2\pi}-1}{2\pi}+\dfrac{e^{2\pi}-1}{\pi}\displaystyle\sum_{n=1}^{\infty}\left(\frac{\cos nx}{1+n^2}-\frac{n}{1+n^2}\sin nx\right)$

**7.** $e^x = \dfrac{2\sinh\pi}{\pi}$

$$\left[\frac{1}{2}-\left(\frac{1}{2}\cos x-\frac{1}{5}\cos 2x+\frac{1}{10}\cos 3x-\ldots\ldots\right)-\left(\frac{1}{2}\sin x-\frac{2}{5}\sin 2x+\frac{3}{10}\sin 3x-\ldots\ldots\right)\right]$$

**8.** $|\sin x| = \dfrac{2}{\pi}-\dfrac{4}{\pi}\left(\dfrac{\cos 2x}{3}+\dfrac{\cos 4x}{15}+\ldots\ldots+\dfrac{\cos 2nx}{4n^2-1}+\ldots\ldots\right)$

**9.** $|\cos x| = \dfrac{2}{\pi}+\dfrac{4}{\pi}\left(\dfrac{\cos 2x}{3}-\dfrac{\cos 4x}{15}+\ldots\ldots\right)$

**12.** (*a*) $\sqrt{1-\cos x} = \dfrac{2\sqrt{2}}{\pi}-\dfrac{4\sqrt{2}}{\pi}\displaystyle\sum_{n=1}^{\infty}\frac{\cos nx}{4n^2-1}$ (*b*) Same as in part (*a*) ; $\dfrac{1}{2}$

**13.** $\cos wx = \dfrac{2w \sin w\pi}{\pi}\left(\dfrac{1}{2w^2} + \dfrac{\cos x}{1^2 - w^2} - \dfrac{\cos 2x}{2^2 - w^2} + \dfrac{\cos 3x}{3^2 - w^2} - \ldots\ldots\right)$

**14.** $f(x) = \dfrac{\pi}{2} + \dfrac{4}{\pi}\left(\dfrac{\cos x}{1^2} + \dfrac{\cos 3x}{3^2} + \dfrac{\cos 5x}{5^2} + \ldots\ldots\right)$

**15.** $e^{-ax} = \dfrac{2 \sinh a\pi}{\pi}\left[\left(\dfrac{1}{2a} - \dfrac{a \cos x}{1^2 + a^2} + \dfrac{a \cos 2x}{2^2 + a^2} - \ldots\ldots\right) - \left(\dfrac{\sin x}{1^2 + a^2} - \dfrac{2 \sin 2x}{2^2 + a^2} + \dfrac{3 \sin 3x}{3^2 + a^2} - \ldots\ldots\right)\right]$

$\dfrac{\pi}{\sinh \pi} = 2\left[\dfrac{1}{2^2 + 1} - \dfrac{1}{3^2 + 1} + \dfrac{1}{4^2 + 1} - \ldots\ldots\right]$

**17.** Even $f(x) = \dfrac{\pi}{2} + 1 - \dfrac{4}{\pi}\left(\cos x + \dfrac{\cos 3x}{3^2} + \dfrac{\cos 5x}{5^2} + \ldots\ldots\right)$; $\dfrac{\pi^2}{8}$

**18.** $\dfrac{\pi^2}{3} + \displaystyle\sum_{n=1}^{\infty} \dfrac{4(-1)^n}{n^2} \cos nx + \sum_{n=1}^{\infty} \dfrac{2}{n}(-1)^{n+1} \sin nx$ **19.** $x = \displaystyle\sum_{n=1}^{\infty} \dfrac{2(-1)^{n+1}}{n} \sin nx$.

## 1.4. DIRICHLET'S CONDITIONS

The sufficient conditions for the uniform convergence of a Fourier series are called Dirichlet's conditions (after Dirichlet, a German mathematician). All the functions that normally arise in engineering problems satisfy these conditions and hence they can be expressed as a Fourier series.

*Any function f(x) can be expressed as a Fourier series* $\dfrac{a_0}{2} + \displaystyle\sum_{n=1}^{\infty} a_n \cos nx + \sum_{n=1}^{\infty} b_n \sin nx$

*where $a_0$, $a_n$, $b_n$ are constants, provided*

*(i) f(x) is periodic, single valued and finite*

*(ii) f(x) has a finite number of finite discontinuities in any one period.*

*(iii) f(x) has a finite number of maxima and minima.*

When these conditions are satisfied, the Fourier series converges to $f(x)$ at every point of continuity. At a point of discontinuity, the sum of the series is equal to the mean of the limits on the right and left

*i.e.,* $\frac{1}{2}[f(x + 0) + f(x - 0)]$

where $f(x + 0)$ and $f(x - 0)$ denote the limit on the right and the limit on the left respectively.

## 1.5. FOURIER SERIES FOR DISCONTINUOUS FUNCTIONS

In 1.3, we derived Euler's formulae for $a_0$, $a_n$, $b_n$ on the assumption that $f(x)$ is continous in $(c, c + 2\pi)$. However, if $f(x)$ has finitely many points of finite discontinuity, even then it can be expressed as a Fourier series. The integrals for $a_0$, $a_n$, $b_n$ are to be evaluated by breaking up the range of integration.

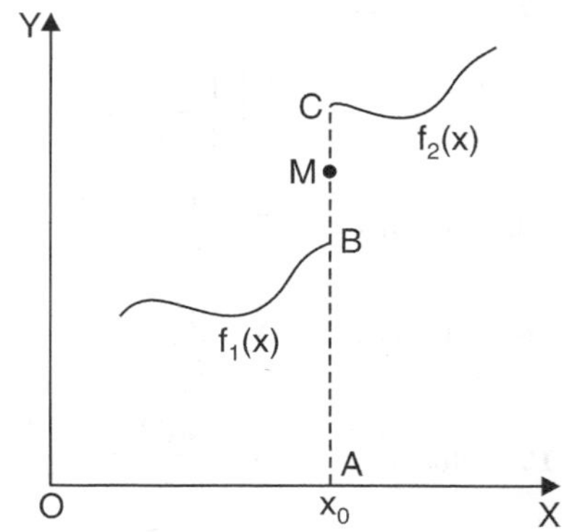


Let $f(x)$ be defined by $f(x) = f_1(x),\ c < x < x_0$

$= f_2(x),\ x_0 < x < c + 2\pi$

where $x_0$ is the point of finite discontinuity in the interval $(c, c + 2\pi)$.

The values of $a_0$, $a_n$, $b_n$ are given by

$$a_0 = \frac{1}{\pi}\left[\int_c^{x_0} f_1(x)\,dx + \int_{x_0}^{c+2\pi} f_2(x)\,dx\right]$$

$$a_n = \frac{1}{\pi}\left[\int_c^{x_0} f_1(x)\cos nx\,dx + \int_{x_0}^{c+2\pi} f_2(x)\cos nx\,dx\right]$$

$$b_n = \frac{1}{\pi}\left[\int_c^{x_0} f_1(x)\sin nx\,dx + \int_{x_0}^{c+2\pi} f_2(x)\sin nx\,dx\right]$$

At $x = x_0$, there is a finite jump in the graph of the function. Both the limits $f(x_0 - 0)$ and $f(x_0 + 0)$ exist but are unequal. The sum of the Fourier series $= \frac{1}{2}[f(x_0 - 0) + f(x_0 + 0)] = \frac{1}{2}$ (AB + AC) = AM, where M is the mid-point of BC.

## ILLUSTRATIVE EXAMPLES

**Example 1.** *Find the Fourier series to represent the function f(x) given by*

$$f(x) = x \quad \text{for} \quad 0 \le x \le \pi$$

*and*

$$= 2\pi - x \quad \text{for} \quad \pi \le x \le 2\pi.$$

*Deduce that* $\frac{1}{1^2} + \frac{1}{3^2} + \frac{1}{5^2} + \ldots\ldots = \frac{\pi^2}{8}$. (M.G.U. June 2006)

**Sol.** Let $f(x) = \frac{a_0}{2} + \sum_{n=1}^{\infty} a_n \cos nx + \sum_{n=1}^{\infty} b_n \sin nx$

Then $$a_0 = \frac{1}{\pi}\int_0^{2\pi} f(x)\,dx = \frac{1}{\pi}\left[\int_0^{\pi} x\,dx + \int_{\pi}^{2\pi} (2\pi - x)\,dx\right]$$

$$= \frac{1}{\pi}\left[\left|\frac{x^2}{2}\right|_0^{\pi} + \left|2\pi x - \frac{x^2}{2}\right|_{\pi}^{2\pi}\right] = \frac{1}{\pi}\left[\frac{\pi^2}{2} + (4\pi^2 - 2\pi^2) - \left(2\pi^2 - \frac{\pi^2}{2}\right)\right] = \pi$$

$$a_n = \frac{1}{\pi}\int_0^{2\pi} f(x)\cos nx\,dx = \frac{1}{\pi}\left[\int_0^{\pi} x\cos nx\,dx + \int_{\pi}^{2\pi} (2\pi - x)\cos nx\,dx\right]$$

$$= \frac{1}{\pi}\left[\left|x\,.\frac{\sin nx}{n} - 1.\left(-\frac{\cos nx}{n^2}\right)\right|_0^{\pi} + \left|(2\pi - x)\left(\frac{\sin nx}{n}\right) - (-1)\left(-\frac{\cos nx}{n^2}\right)\right|_{\pi}^{2\pi}\right]$$

$$= \frac{1}{\pi}\left[\left(\frac{\cos n\pi}{n^2} - \frac{1}{n^2}\right) + \left(-\frac{\cos 2n\pi}{n^2} + \frac{\cos n\pi}{n^2}\right)\right]$$

$$= \frac{1}{\pi n^2}[(-1)^n - 1 - 1 + (-1)^n] = \frac{2}{\pi n^2}[(-1)^n - 1] = \begin{cases} -\frac{4}{\pi n^2}, & \text{if } n \text{ is odd} \\ 0, & \text{if } n \text{ is even} \end{cases}$$

$$b_n = \frac{1}{\pi}\int_0^{2\pi} f(x)\sin nx\,dx = \frac{1}{\pi}\left[\int_0^{\pi} x\sin nx\,dx + \int_{\pi}^{2\pi} (2\pi - x)\sin nx\,dx\right]$$

$$= \frac{1}{\pi}\left[\left| x\left(-\frac{\cos nx}{n}\right) - 1.\left(-\frac{\sin nx}{n^2}\right)\right|_0^{\pi} + \left| (2\pi - x)\times\left(-\frac{\cos nx}{n}\right) - 1.\left(-\frac{\sin nx}{n^2}\right)\right|_{\pi}^{2\pi}\right]$$

$$= \frac{1}{\pi}\left[-\frac{\pi\cos n\pi}{n} + \frac{\pi\cos n\pi}{n}\right] = 0$$

$$\therefore \qquad f(x) = \frac{\pi}{2} - \frac{4}{\pi}\left(\frac{\cos x}{1^2} + \frac{\cos 3x}{3^2} + \frac{\cos 5x}{5^2} + \ldots\ldots\right)$$

Putting $x = 0$, we get $0 = \frac{\pi}{2} - \frac{4}{\pi}\left(\frac{1}{1^2} + \frac{1}{3^2} + \frac{1}{5^2} + \ldots\ldots\right) \Rightarrow \frac{\pi^2}{8} = \frac{1}{1^2} + \frac{1}{3^2} + \frac{1}{5^2} + \ldots\ldots$

**Example 2.** *If* $\quad f(x) = 0, \quad -\pi \le x \le 0$

$\qquad\qquad = \sin x, \quad 0 \le x \le \pi,$

*prove that* $f(x) = \frac{1}{\pi} + \frac{1}{2}\sin x - \frac{2}{\pi}\sum_{n=1}^{\infty}\frac{\cos 2nx}{4n^2 - 1}$.

*Hence show that*

(i) $\frac{1}{1.3} + \frac{1}{3.5} + \frac{1}{5.7} + \ldots\ldots = \frac{1}{2}$ $\qquad$ (ii) $\frac{1}{1.3} - \frac{1}{3.5} + \frac{1}{5.7} - \ldots\ldots = \frac{\pi - 2}{4}$.

**Sol.** Let $\quad f(x) = \frac{a_0}{2} + \sum_{n=1}^{\infty} a_n \cos nx + \sum_{n=1}^{\infty} b_n \sin nx$

Then $\quad a_0 = \frac{1}{\pi}\int_{-\pi}^{\pi} f(x)\,dx = \frac{1}{\pi}\left[\int_{-\pi}^{0} 0\,dx + \int_0^{\pi}\sin x\,dx\right] = \frac{2}{\pi}$

$$a_n = \frac{1}{\pi}\int_{-\pi}^{\pi} f(x)\cos nx\,dx = \frac{1}{\pi}\left[\int_{-\pi}^{0} 0\,dx + \int_0^{\pi}\sin x\cos nx\,dx\right]$$

$$= \frac{1}{2\pi}\int_0^{\pi} 2\cos nx\sin x\,dx = \frac{1}{2\pi}\int_0^{\pi}[\sin(n+1)x - \sin(n-1)x]\,dx$$

$$= \frac{1}{2\pi}\left[-\frac{\cos(n+1)x}{n+1} + \frac{\cos(n-1)x}{n-1}\right]_0^{\pi}, \; n \ne 1$$

$$= \frac{1}{2\pi}\left[-\frac{\cos(n+1)\pi}{n+1} + \frac{\cos(n-1)\pi}{n-1} + \frac{1}{n+1} - \frac{1}{n-1}\right]$$

$$= \frac{1}{2\pi}\left[-\frac{(-1)^{n+1}}{n+1} + \frac{(-1)^{n-1}}{n-1} + \frac{1}{n+1} - \frac{1}{n-1}\right]$$

$$= \begin{cases} \frac{1}{2\pi}\left(-\frac{1}{n+1} + \frac{1}{n-1} + \frac{1}{n+1} - \frac{1}{n-1}\right), & \text{when } n \text{ is odd} \\ \frac{1}{2\pi}\left(\frac{1}{n+1} - \frac{1}{n-1} + \frac{1}{n+1} - \frac{1}{n-1}\right), & \text{when } n \text{ is even} \end{cases}$$

$$= \begin{cases} 0, \text{ when } n \text{ is odd, } i.e., n = 3, 5, 7, \ldots.. \\ -\dfrac{2}{\pi(n^2-1)}, \text{ when } n \text{ is even} \end{cases}$$

When $n = 1$, we have $a_1 = \dfrac{1}{\pi}\displaystyle\int_0^{\pi} \sin x \cos x \, dx = \dfrac{1}{2\pi}\int_0^{\pi} \sin 2x \, dx = \dfrac{1}{2\pi}\left[-\dfrac{\cos 2x}{2}\right]_0^{\pi} = 0$

$$b_n = \frac{1}{\pi}\int_{-\pi}^{\pi} f(x) \sin nx \, dx = \frac{1}{\pi}\left[\int_{-\pi}^{0} 0 \, dx + \int_0^{\pi} \sin x \sin nx \, dx\right]$$

$$= \frac{1}{2\pi}\int_0^{\pi} 2 \sin nx \sin x \, dx = \frac{1}{2\pi}\int_0^{\pi} [\cos (n-1)x - \cos (n+1)x] \, dx$$

$$= \frac{1}{2\pi}\left[\frac{\sin (n-1)x}{n-1} - \frac{\sin (n+1)x}{n+1}\right]_0^{\pi} = 0, n \neq 1$$

When $n = 1$, we have

$$b_1 = \frac{1}{\pi}\int_0^{\pi} \sin x \sin x \, dx = \frac{1}{2\pi}\int_0^{\pi}(1 - \cos 2x) \, dx = \frac{1}{2\pi}\left[x - \frac{\sin 2x}{2}\right]_0^{\pi} = \frac{1}{2}$$

$$\therefore \quad f(x) = \frac{1}{\pi} - \frac{2}{\pi}\left[\frac{\cos 2x}{2^2-1} + \frac{\cos 4x}{4^2-1} + \frac{\cos 6x}{6^2-1} + \ldots\ldots\right] + \frac{1}{2}\sin x$$

$$= \frac{1}{\pi} + \frac{1}{2}\sin x - \frac{2}{\pi}\sum_{n=1}^{\infty} \frac{\cos 2nx}{(2n)^2 - 1} \qquad \ldots(1)$$

Putting $x = 0$ in (1), we have $0 = \dfrac{1}{\pi} - \dfrac{2}{\pi}\displaystyle\sum_{n=1}^{\infty} \dfrac{1}{4n^2-1}$

$$\Rightarrow \quad \frac{1}{2} = \sum_{n=1}^{\infty} \frac{1}{4n^2-1} = \sum_{n=1}^{\infty} \frac{1}{(2n-1)(2n+1)} = \frac{1}{1.3} + \frac{1}{3.5} + \frac{1}{5.7} + \ldots\ldots$$

Putting $x = \dfrac{\pi}{2}$ in (1), we have $1 = \dfrac{1}{\pi} + \dfrac{1}{2} - \dfrac{2}{\pi}\displaystyle\sum_{n=1}^{\infty} \dfrac{\cos n\pi}{4n^2-1}$

$$\Rightarrow \quad \frac{1}{2} - \frac{1}{\pi} = -\frac{2}{\pi}\sum_{n=1}^{\infty} \frac{(-1)^n}{4n^2-1}$$

$$\Rightarrow \quad \frac{\pi-2}{4} = -\sum_{n=1}^{\infty} \frac{(-1)^n}{(2n-1)(2n+1)} = -\left(-\frac{1}{1.3} + \frac{1}{3.5} - \frac{1}{5.7} + \ldots\ldots\right)$$

$$\Rightarrow \quad \frac{1}{1.3} - \frac{1}{3.5} + \frac{1}{5.7} - \ldots\ldots = \frac{\pi-2}{4}.$$

## TEST YOUR KNOWLEDGE

1. Find the Fourier series to represent the function

$$f(x) = -k \quad \text{when} \quad -\pi < x < 0$$
$$= k \quad \text{when} \quad 0 < x < \pi$$

Also deduce that $\dfrac{\pi}{4} = 1 - \dfrac{1}{3} + \dfrac{1}{5} - \dfrac{1}{7} + \ldots\ldots$

**2.** Develop $f(x)$ in a Fourier series in the interval $(-\pi, \pi)$ if $f(x) = 0$ when $-\pi < x < 0$
$= 1$ when $0 < x < \pi$.

**3.** Find the Fourier series expansion for $f(x)$, if $f(x) = -\pi, -\pi < x < 0$
$= x, \quad 0 < x < \pi$

Deduce that $\frac{1}{1^2} + \frac{1}{3^2} + \frac{1}{5^2} + \ldots\ldots = \frac{\pi^2}{8}$.

[**Hint.** For the deduction, put $x = 0$ in the expansion of $f(x)$.

$$f(0-0) = -\pi \text{ and } f(0+0) = 0 \quad \therefore \quad f(0) = \frac{1}{2}[f(0-0) + f(0+0)] = -\frac{\pi}{2}\Big]$$

**4.** Find the Fourier expansion of the function defined in one period by the relations

$$f(x) = 1 \text{ for } 0 < x < \pi$$
$$= 2 \text{ for } \pi < x < 2\pi$$

and deduce that $\frac{\pi}{4} = 1 - \frac{1}{3} + \frac{1}{5} - \frac{1}{7} + \ldots\ldots$

**5.** Find the Fourier series of the following function :

$$f(x) = x^2, \qquad 0 \le x \le \pi$$
$$= -x^2, \qquad -\pi \le x \le 0.$$

**6.** An alternating current after passing through a rectifier has the form

$$i = I_0 \sin x \quad \text{for} \quad 0 \le x \le \pi$$
$$= 0 \quad \text{for} \quad \pi \le x \le 2\pi$$

where $I_0$ is the maximum current and the period is $2\pi$. Express $i$ as a Fourier series.

**7.** Obtain Fourier series for the function

$$f(x) = \begin{cases} x & \text{for} \quad -\pi < x < 0 \\ -x & \text{for} \quad 0 < x < \pi \end{cases}$$

and hence show that

$$\frac{1}{1^2} + \frac{1}{3^2} + \frac{1}{5^2} + \ldots\ldots = \frac{\pi^2}{8}$$

**8.** Find the Fourier series for the function

$$f(x) = \begin{cases} -1 & \text{for } -\pi < x < -\frac{\pi}{2} \\ 0 & \text{for } -\frac{\pi}{2} < x < \frac{\pi}{2} \\ 1 & \text{for } \frac{\pi}{2} < x < \pi \end{cases}$$

## Answers

**1.** $f(x) = \frac{4k}{\pi}\left(\sin x + \frac{\sin 3x}{3} + \frac{\sin 5x}{5} + \ldots\ldots\right)$ **2.** $f(x) = \frac{1}{2} + \frac{2}{\pi}\left(\sin x + \frac{\sin 3x}{3} + \frac{\sin 5x}{5} + \ldots\ldots\right)$

**3.** $f(x) = -\frac{\pi}{4} - \frac{2}{\pi}\left(\cos x + \frac{\cos 3x}{3^2} + \frac{\cos 5x}{5^2} + \ldots\ldots\right) + \left(3 \sin x - \frac{\sin 2x}{2} + \sin 3x - \frac{\sin 4x}{4} + \ldots\ldots\right)$

**4.** $f(x) = \frac{3}{2} - \frac{2}{\pi}\left(\sin x + \frac{\sin 3x}{3} + \frac{\sin 5x}{5} + \ldots\ldots\right)$

**5.** $f(x) = 2\left(\pi - \frac{4}{\pi}\right)\sin x - \pi \sin 2x + \frac{2}{3}\left(\pi - \frac{4}{9\pi}\right)\sin 3x - \frac{\pi}{2}\sin 4x + \ldots\ldots$

**6.** $i = \frac{I_0}{2} + \frac{I_0}{2}\sin x - \frac{2I_0}{\pi}\left(\frac{\cos 2x}{2^2 - 1} + \frac{\cos 4x}{4^2 - 1} + \frac{\cos 6x}{6^2 - 1} + \ldots\ldots\right)$

**7.** $f(x) = -\frac{\pi}{2} + \frac{4}{\pi}\left(\frac{\cos x}{1^2} + \frac{\cos 3x}{3^2} + \frac{\cos 5x}{5^2} + \ldots\ldots\right)$

**8.** $f(x) = \frac{2}{\pi}\left(\sin x - \sin 2x + \frac{\sin 3x}{3} - \ldots\ldots\right)$

## 1.6. CHANGE OF INTERVAL

In many engineering problems, it is desired to expand a function in a Fourier series over an interval of length $2l$ and not $2\pi$. In order to apply foregoing theory, this interval must be transformed into an interval of length $2\pi$. This can be achieved by a transformation of the variable.

Consider a periodic function $f(x)$ defined in the interval $c < x < c + 2l$. To change the interval into one of length $2\pi$, we put

$$\frac{x}{l} = \frac{z}{\pi} \quad \text{or} \quad z = \frac{\pi x}{l} \quad \text{so that when } x = c,\ z = \frac{\pi c}{l} = d \text{ (say)}$$

and when $x = c + 2l,\quad z = \frac{\pi(c + 2l)}{l} = \frac{\pi c}{l} + 2\pi = d + 2\pi.$

Thus the function $f(x)$ of period $2l$ in $(c, c + 2l)$ is transformed to the function $f\left(\frac{lz}{\pi}\right) = F(z)$, say, of period $2\pi$ in $(d, d + 2\pi)$ and the latter function can be expressed as the Fourier series

$$F(z) = \frac{a_0}{2} + \sum_{n=1}^{\infty} a_n \cos nz + \sum_{n=1}^{\infty} b_n \sin nz \quad \ldots(1)$$

where $a_0 = \frac{1}{\pi}\int_d^{d+2\pi} F(z)\, dz$ ; $a_n = \frac{1}{\pi}\int_d^{d+2\pi} F(z)\cos nz\, dz$ ; and $b_n = \frac{1}{\pi}\int_d^{d+2\pi} F(z)\sin nz\, dz$ ...(2)

Now making the inverse substitution $z = \frac{\pi x}{l},\ dz = \frac{\pi}{l}\, dx$

When $z = d,\ x = c$ and when $z = d + 2\pi,\ x = c + 2l.$

The expression (1) becomes $F(z) = F\left(\frac{\pi x}{l}\right) = f(x) = \frac{a_0}{2} + \sum_{n=1}^{\infty} a_n \cos \frac{n\pi x}{l} + \sum_{n=1}^{\infty} b_n \sin \frac{n\pi x}{l}$ and the co-efficients $a_0, a_n, b_n$ from (2) reduce to

$$a_0 = \frac{1}{l}\int_c^{c+2l} f(x)\, dx\ ; \quad a_n = \frac{1}{l}\int_c^{c+2l} f(x)\cos\frac{n\pi x}{l}\, dx\ ; \quad \text{and} \quad b_n = \frac{1}{l}\int_c^{c+2l} f(x)\sin\frac{n\pi x}{l}\, dx$$

**Hence the Fourier series for f(x) in the interval c < x < c + 2l is given by**

$$f(x) = \frac{a_0}{2} + \sum_{n=1}^{\infty} a_n \cos\frac{n\pi x}{l} + \sum_{n=1}^{\infty} b_n \sin\frac{n\pi x}{l}$$

where $a_0 = \int_c^{c+2l} f(x)\,dx, \quad a_n = \frac{1}{l}\int_c^{c+2l} f(x)\cos\frac{n\pi x}{l}\,dx$ and $b_n = \frac{1}{l}\int_c^{c+2l} f(x)\sin\frac{n\pi x}{l}\,dx.$

**Cor. 1.** If we put $c = 0$, the interval becomes $0 < x < 2l$ and the above results reduce to

$$a_0 = \frac{1}{l}\int_0^{2l} f(x)\,dx\,; \quad a_n = \frac{1}{l}\int_0^{2l} f(x)\cos\frac{n\pi x}{l}\,dx\,; \quad \text{and} \quad a_n = \frac{1}{l}\int_0^{2l} f(x)\sin\frac{n\pi x}{l}\,dx.$$

**Cor. 2.** If we put $c = -l$, the interval becomes $-l < x < l$ and the above results reduce to

$$a_0 = \frac{1}{l}\int_{-l}^{l} f(x)\,dx, \quad a_n = \frac{1}{l}\int_{-l}^{l} f(x)\cos\frac{n\pi x}{l}\,dx \quad \text{and} \quad b_n = \frac{1}{l}\int_{-l}^{l} f(x)\sin\frac{n\pi x}{l}\,dx.$$

**If f(x) is an even function,** we have

$$a_0 = \frac{2}{l}\int_0^{l} f(x)\,dx, \quad a_n = \frac{2}{l}\int_0^{l} f(x)\cos\frac{n\pi x}{l}\,dx \quad \text{and} \quad b_n = 0$$

**If f(x) is an odd function,** we have $a_0 = 0, \quad a_n = 0$

and $$b_n = \frac{2}{l}\int_0^{l} f(x)\sin\frac{n\pi x}{l}\,dx.$$

## ILLUSTRATIVE EXAMPLES

**Example 1.** *Find Fourier expansion for the function $f(x) = x - x^2, -1 < x < 1$.*

**Sol.** Let $f(x) = \frac{a_0}{2} + \sum_{n=1}^{\infty} a_n \cos n\pi x + \sum_{n=1}^{\infty} b_n \sin n\pi x$

Then $$a_0 = \int_{-1}^{1}(x - x^2)\,dx = \int_{-1}^{1} x\,dx - \int_{-1}^{1} x^2\,dx = 0 - 2\int_0^1 x^2\,dx = -2\left[\frac{x^3}{3}\right]_0^1 = -\frac{2}{3}$$

$$a_n = \int_{-1}^{1}(x - x^2)\cos n\pi x\,dx = \int_{-1}^{1} x\cos n\pi x\,dx - \int_{-1}^{1} x^2\cos n\pi x\,dx$$

$$= 0 - 2\int_0^1 x^2\cos n\pi x\,dx = -2\left[x^2\cdot\frac{\sin n\pi x}{n\pi} - 2x\left(-\frac{\cos n\pi x}{n^2\pi^2}\right) + 2\left(-\frac{\sin n\pi x}{n^3\pi^3}\right)\right]_0^1$$

$$= -2\left[\frac{2\cos n\pi}{n^2\pi^2}\right] = \frac{-4(-1)^n}{n^2\pi^2} = \frac{4(-1)^{n+1}}{n^2\pi^2}$$

$$b_n = \int_{-1}^{1}(x - x^2)\sin n\pi x\,dx = \int_{-1}^{1} x\sin n\pi x\,dx - \int_{-1}^{1} x^2\sin n\pi x\,dx$$

$$= 2\int_0^1 x\sin n\pi x\,dx - 0 = 2\left[x\left(-\frac{\cos n\pi x}{n\pi}\right) - 1.\left(-\frac{\sin n\pi x}{n^2\pi^2}\right)\right]_0^1$$

$$= 2\left[-\frac{\cos n\pi}{n\pi}\right] = \frac{-2(-1)^n}{n\pi} = \frac{2(-1)^{n+1}}{n\pi}$$

$$\therefore \qquad x - x^2 = -\frac{1}{3} + \frac{4}{\pi^2}\left(\frac{\cos \pi x}{1^2} - \frac{\cos 2\pi x}{2^2} + \frac{\cos 3\pi x}{3^2} - \ldots\ldots\right)$$

$$+ \frac{2}{\pi}\left(\frac{\sin \pi x}{1} - \frac{\sin 2\pi x}{2} + \frac{\sin 3\pi x}{3^2} - \ldots\ldots\right)$$

**Example 2.** *Find the Fourier series to represent* $f(x) = x^2 - 2$, *when* $-2 \le x \le 2$.

**Sol.** Since $f(x)$ is an even function, $b_n = 0$.

Let $$f(x) = x^2 - 2 = \frac{a_0}{2} + \sum_{n=1}^{\infty} a_n \cos \frac{n\pi x}{2}$$

Then $$a_0 = \frac{2}{2}\int_0^2 (x^2 - 2)\, dx = \left[\frac{x^3}{3} - 2x\right]_0^2 = \frac{8}{3} - 4 = -\frac{4}{3}$$

$$a_n = \frac{2}{2}\int_0^2 (x^2 - 2) \cos \frac{n\pi x}{2}\, dx$$

$$= \left[(x^2 - 2) \cdot \frac{\sin \frac{n\pi x}{2}}{\frac{n\pi}{2}} - 2x\left(-\frac{\cos \frac{n\pi x}{2}}{\frac{n^2\pi^2}{4}}\right) + 2\left(-\frac{\sin \frac{n\pi x}{2}}{\frac{n^3\pi^3}{8}}\right)\right]_0^2$$

$$= \frac{16 \cos n\pi}{n^2\pi^2} = \frac{16(-1)^n}{n^2\pi^2}$$

$$\therefore \qquad x^2 - 2 = -\frac{2}{3} - \frac{16}{\pi^2}\left(\cos \frac{\pi x}{2} - \frac{1}{4}\cos \pi x + \frac{1}{9}\cos \frac{3\pi x}{2} - \ldots\ldots\right).$$

**Example 3.** *Expand* $f(x) = e^{-x}$ *as a Fourier series in the interval* $(-l, l)$.

**Sol.** Let $$f(x) = e^{-x} = \frac{a_0}{2} + \sum_{n=1}^{\infty} a_n \cos \frac{n\pi x}{l} + \sum_{n=1}^{\infty} b_n \sin \frac{n\pi x}{l}$$

Then $$a_0 = \frac{1}{l}\int_{-l}^{l} e^{-x}\, dx = \frac{1}{l}\left[-e^{-x}\right]_{-l}^{l} = \frac{1}{l}(e^l - e^{-l}) = \frac{2 \sinh l}{l}$$

$$a_n = \frac{1}{l}\int_{-l}^{l} e^{-x} \cos \frac{n\pi x}{l}\, dx = \frac{1}{l}\left[\frac{e^{-x}}{1 + \left(\frac{n\pi}{l}\right)^2}\left(-\cos \frac{n\pi x}{l} + \frac{n\pi}{l}\sin \frac{n\pi x}{l}\right)\right]_{-l}^{l}$$

$$\left[\because \int e^{ax} \cos bx\, dx = \frac{e^{ax}}{a^2 + b^2}(a \cos bx + b \sin bx)\right]$$

$$= \frac{l}{l^2 + (n\pi)^2}[-e^{-l} \cos n\pi + e^l \cos n\pi] = -\frac{2l \cos n\pi}{l^2 + (n\pi)^2}\left(\frac{e^l - e^{-l}}{2}\right) = \frac{2l(-1)^n \sinh l}{l^2 + (n\pi)^2}$$

$$b_n = \frac{1}{l}\int_{-l}^{l} e^{-x} \sin \frac{n\pi x}{l}\, dx$$

$$= \frac{1}{l}\left[\frac{e^{-x}}{1+\left(\frac{n\pi}{l}\right)^2}\left(-\sin\frac{n\pi x}{l} - \frac{n\pi}{l}\cos\frac{n\pi x}{l}\right)\right]_{-l}^{l}$$

$$\left[\because \int e^{ax}\sin bx\, dx = \frac{e^{ax}}{a^2+b^2}(a\sin bx - b\cos bx)\right]$$

$$= -\frac{1}{l^2+(n\pi)^2}\left[\frac{n\pi}{l}(e^{-l}-e^{l})\cos n\pi\right] = \frac{2n\pi\cos n\pi}{l^2+(n\pi)^2}\left(\frac{e^{l}-e^{-l}}{2}\right) = \frac{2n\pi\,(-1)^n\sinh l}{l^2+(n\pi)^2}$$

$$\therefore \quad e^{-x} = \sinh l\left[\frac{1}{l} - 2l\left(\frac{1}{l^2+\pi^2}\cos\frac{\pi x}{l} - \frac{1}{l^2+2^2\pi^2}\cos\frac{2\pi x}{l} + \frac{1}{l^2+3^2\pi^2}\cos\frac{3\pi x}{l} - \ldots\ldots\right)\right.$$

$$\left. - 2\pi\left(\frac{1}{l^2+\pi^2}\sin\frac{\pi x}{l} - \frac{2}{l^2+2^2\pi^2}\sin\frac{2\pi x}{l} + \frac{3}{l^2+3^2\pi^2}\sin\frac{3\pi x}{l} - \ldots\ldots\right)\right].$$

**Example 4.** *Obtain Fourier series for the function* $f(x) = \pi x, \quad 0 \le x \le 1$
$= \pi(2-x), \quad 1 \le x \le 2.$

(M.G.U. June 2006)

**Sol.** Let $f(x) = \frac{a_0}{2} + \sum_{n=1}^{\infty} a_n \cos n\pi x + \sum_{n=1}^{\infty} b_n \sin n\pi x$

Then $a_0 = \int_0^2 f(x)\,dx = \int_0^1 \pi x\,dx + \int_1^2 \pi(2-x)\,dx = \pi\left[\frac{x^2}{2}\right]_0^1 + \pi\left[2x - \frac{x^2}{2}\right]_1^2$

$$= \pi\left(\frac{1}{2}\right) + \pi\left[(4-2) - \left(2-\frac{1}{2}\right)\right] = \pi$$

$$a_n = \int_0^2 f(x)\cos n\pi x\,dx = \int_0^1 \pi x\cos n\pi x\,dx + \int_1^2 \pi(2-x)\cos n\pi x\,dx$$

$$= \left[\pi x\,.\frac{\sin n\pi x}{n\pi} - \pi\left(-\frac{\cos n\pi x}{n^2\pi^2}\right)\right]_0^1 + \left[\pi(2-x)\,.\frac{\sin n\pi x}{n\pi} - (-\pi)\left(-\frac{\cos n\pi x}{n^2\pi^2}\right)\right]_1^2$$

$$= \left[\frac{\cos n\pi}{n^2\pi} - \frac{1}{n^2\pi}\right] + \left[-\frac{\cos 2n\pi}{n^2\pi} + \frac{\cos n\pi}{n^2\pi}\right] = \frac{2}{n^2\pi}(\cos n\pi - 1) = \frac{2}{n^2\pi}[(-1)^n - 1]$$

$= 0$ or $-\frac{4}{n^2\pi}$ according as $n$ is even or odd.

$$b_n = \int_0^2 f(x)\sin n\pi x\,dx = \int_0^1 \pi x\sin n\pi x\,dx + \int_1^2 \pi(2-x)\sin n\pi x\,dx$$

$$= \left[\pi x\left(-\frac{\cos n\pi x}{n\pi}\right) - \pi\left(-\frac{\sin n\pi x}{n^2\pi^2}\right)\right]_0^1 + \left[\pi(2-x)\left(-\frac{\cos n\pi x}{n\pi}\right) - (-\pi)\left(-\frac{\sin n\pi x}{n^2\pi^2}\right)\right]_1^2$$

$$= \left[-\frac{\cos n\pi}{n}\right] + \left[\frac{\cos n\pi}{n}\right] = 0$$

$$\therefore \quad f(x) = \frac{\pi}{2} - \frac{4}{\pi}\left(\frac{\cos \pi x}{1^2} + \frac{\cos 3\pi x}{3^2} + \frac{\cos 5\pi x}{5^2} + \ldots\ldots\right).$$

**Note.** Putting $x = 0$, we have $f(0) = \frac{\pi}{2} - \frac{4}{\pi}\left(\frac{1}{1^2} + \frac{1}{3^2} + \frac{1}{5^2} + \ldots\ldots\right)$

or
$$0 = \frac{\pi}{2} - \frac{4}{\pi}\left(\frac{1}{1^2} + \frac{1}{3^2} + \frac{1}{5^2} + \ldots\ldots\right)$$

$$\therefore \quad \frac{1}{1^2} + \frac{1}{3^2} + \frac{1}{5^2} + \ldots\ldots = \frac{\pi^2}{8}.$$

## TEST YOUR KNOWLEDGE

1. Find a Fourier series for $f(t) = 1 - t^2$ when $-1 \le t \le 1$.
2. Expand $f(x)$ in Fourier series in the interval $(-2, 2)$ when $f(x) = 0, \quad -2 < x < 0$
   $= 1, \quad 0 < x < 2.$
3. Develop $f(x)$ in a Fourier series in the interval $(0, 2)$ if $f(x) = x, \quad 0 < x < 1$
   $= 0, \quad 1 < x < 2.$
4. Find the Fourier expansion for $f(x) = \pi x$ from $x = -c$ to $x = c$.
5. Find the Fourier expansion for the function $f(x) = x - x^3$ in the interval $-1 < x < 1$.
6. Find the Fourier series for the function given by $f(t) = t, \quad 0 < t < 1$
   $= 1 - t, \quad 1 < t < 2.$
7. Find a Fourier series to represent $x^2$ in the interval $(-l, l)$. *(M.G.U., May 2009)*
8. Expand $f(x) = e^{-x}$ as a Fourier series in the interval $(-2, 2)$.
9. Expand : $$f(x) = \begin{cases} \frac{1}{4} - x, & 0 < x < \frac{1}{2} \\ x - \frac{3}{4}, & \frac{1}{2} < x < 1 \\ 1, & 1 < x < \frac{3}{2} \\ x - 1, & \frac{3}{2} < x < 2 \end{cases}$$
   as a Fourier series.
10. Find the Fourier series for the function $f(x) = \begin{cases} 0 & \text{when} \quad -2 < x < -1 \\ k & \text{when} \quad -1 < x < 1 \\ 0 & \text{when} \quad 1 < x < 2. \end{cases}$
11. A sinusoidal voltage E sin $\omega t$ is passed through a half-wave rectifier which clips the negative portion of the wave.

    Expand the resulting periodic function $u(t) = \begin{cases} 0 & \text{when } -\frac{T}{2} < t < 0 \\ E \sin \omega t & \text{when } 0 < t < \frac{T}{2} \end{cases}$

    and $T = \frac{2\pi}{\omega}$, in a Fourier series.

## Answers

**1.** $1 - t^2 = \frac{2}{3} + \frac{4}{\pi^2}\left(\cos \pi t - \frac{\cos 2\pi t}{2^2} + \frac{\cos 3\pi t}{3^2} - \ldots\ldots\right)$

**2.** $f(x) = \frac{1}{2} + \frac{2}{\pi}\left(\sin \frac{\pi x}{2} + \frac{1}{3}\sin \frac{3\pi x}{2} + \frac{1}{5}\sin \frac{5\pi x}{2} + \ldots\ldots\right)$

**3.** $f(x) = \frac{1}{4} - \frac{2}{\pi^2}\left(\cos \pi x + \frac{\cos 3\pi x}{3^2} + \frac{\cos 5\pi x}{5^2} + \ldots\ldots\right) + \frac{1}{\pi}\left(\sin \pi x + \frac{\sin 2\pi x}{2} + \frac{\sin 3\pi x}{3} + \ldots\ldots\right)$

**4.** $f(x) = 2c\left[\sin\left(\frac{\pi x}{c}\right) - \frac{1}{2}\sin\left(\frac{2\pi x}{c}\right) + \frac{1}{3}\sin\left(\frac{3\pi x}{c}\right) - \ldots\ldots\right]$

**5.** $f(x) = \frac{12}{\pi^3}\left(\sin \pi x - \frac{\sin 2\pi x}{2^3} + \frac{\sin 3\pi x}{3^3} - \ldots\ldots\right)$

**6.** $f(t) = -\frac{4}{\pi^2}\left(\cos \pi t + \frac{\cos 3\pi t}{3^2} + \frac{\cos 5\pi t}{5^3} + \ldots\ldots\right) + \frac{2}{\pi}\left(\sin \pi t + \frac{\sin 3\pi t}{3} + \ldots\ldots\right)$

**7.** $x^2 = \frac{l^2}{3} - \frac{4l^2}{\pi^2}\left(\frac{\cos \pi x/l}{1^2} - \frac{\cos 2\pi x/l}{2^2} + \frac{\cos 3\pi x/l}{3^2} - \frac{\cos 4\pi x/l}{4^2} + \ldots\ldots\right)$

**8.** $$e^{-x} = \sinh 2\left[\frac{1}{2} - 4\left(\frac{1}{2^2+\pi^2}\cos\frac{\pi x}{2} - \frac{1}{2^2+2^2\pi^2}\cos \pi x + \frac{1}{2^2+3^2\pi^2}\cos\frac{3\pi x}{2} - \ldots\ldots\right)\right.$$
$$\left. - 2\pi\left(\frac{1}{2^2+\pi^2}\sin\frac{\pi x}{2} - \frac{2}{2^2+2^2\pi^2}\sin \pi x + \frac{3}{2^2+3^2\pi^2}\sin\frac{3\pi x}{2} - \ldots\ldots\right)\right]$$

**9.** $f(x) = \frac{7}{16} + \frac{1}{\pi}\left(\frac{1}{\pi} + \frac{1}{4}\right)\cos \pi x - \frac{3}{\pi}\left(\frac{1}{\pi} + \frac{1}{2}\right)\sin \pi x + \ldots\ldots$

**10.** $f(x) = \frac{k}{2} + \frac{2k}{\pi}\left(\cos\frac{\pi t}{2} - \frac{1}{3}\cos\frac{3\pi t}{2} + \frac{1}{5}\cos\frac{5\pi t}{2} - \ldots\ldots\right)$

**11.** $u(t) = \frac{E}{\pi} + \frac{E}{2}\sin \omega t - \frac{2E}{\pi}\left(\frac{\cos 2\omega t}{1.3} + \frac{\cos 4\omega t}{3.5} + \frac{\cos 6\omega t}{5.7} + \ldots\ldots\right)$

### 1.7. HALF RANGE SERIES

Sometimes it is required to expand a function $f(x)$ in the range $(0, \pi)$ in a Fourier series of period $2\pi$ or more generally in the range $(0, l)$ in a Fourier series of period $2l$.

If it is required to expand $f(x)$ in the interval $(0, l)$, then it is immaterial what the function may be outside the range $0 < x < l$. We are free to choose it arbitrarily in the interval $(-l, 0)$.

If we extend the function $f(x)$ by reflecting it in the $y$-axis so that $f(-x) = f(x)$, then the extended function is even for which $b_n = 0$. The Fourier expansion of $f(x)$ will contain only cosine terms.

If we extend the function $f(x)$ by reflecting it in the origin so that $f(-x) = -f(x)$, then the extended function is odd for which $a_0 = a_n = 0$. The Fourier expansion of $f(x)$ will contain only sine terms.

For example, consider the function

$$f(x) = x, \qquad 0 < x < \frac{\pi}{2}$$

$$= \pi - x \qquad \frac{\pi}{2} < x < \pi$$

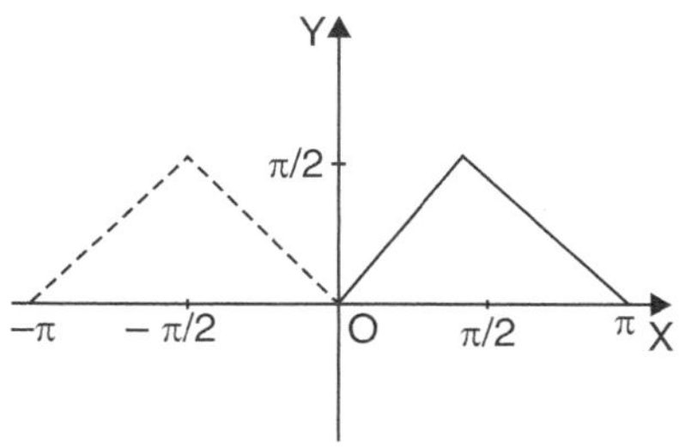


(Reflection in the $y$-axis)

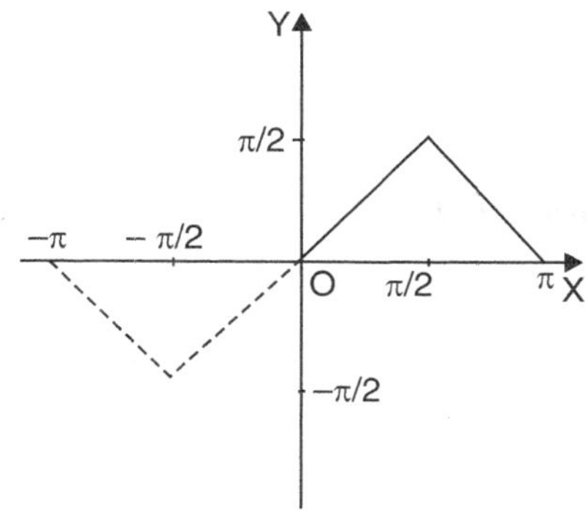


(Reflection in the origin)

Hence a function $f(x)$ defined over the interval $0 < x < l$ is capable of two distinct half-range series.

The half-range cosine series is $f(x) = \dfrac{a_0}{2} + \sum_{n=1}^{\infty} a_n \cos \dfrac{n\pi x}{l}$

where $a_0 = \dfrac{2}{l}\int_0^l f(x)\, dx$ ; $a_n = \dfrac{2}{l}\int_0^l f(x) \cos \dfrac{n\pi x}{l}\, dx$.

The half-range sine series is $f(x) = \sum_{n=1}^{\infty} b_n \sin \dfrac{n\pi x}{l}$, where $b_n = \dfrac{2}{l}\int_0^l f(x) \sin \dfrac{n\pi x}{l}\, dx$.

**Cor.** If the range is $0 < x < \pi$, then

(*i*) The half-range cosine series is $f(x) = \dfrac{a_0}{2} + \sum_{n=1}^{\infty} a_n \cos nx$

where $a_0 = \dfrac{2}{\pi}\int_0^{\pi} f(x)\, dx$ ; $a_n = \dfrac{2}{\pi}\int_0^{\pi} f(x) \cos nx\, dx$.

(*ii*) The half-range sine series is $f(x) = \sum_{n=1}^{\infty} b_n \sin nx$, where $b_n = \dfrac{2}{\pi}\int_0^{\pi} f(x) \sin nx\, dx$.

## ILLUSTRATIVE EXAMPLES

**Example 1.** *Expand $\pi x - x^2$ in a half-range sine series in the interval $(0, \pi)$ upto the first three terms.*

**Sol.** Let $\pi x - x^2 = \sum_{n=1}^{\infty} b_n \sin nx$, then

$$b_n = \frac{2}{\pi}\int_0^{\pi} (\pi x - x^2) \sin nx\, dx$$

$$= \frac{2}{\pi}\left[(\pi x - x^2)\left(-\frac{\cos nx}{n}\right) - (\pi - 2x)\left(-\frac{\sin nx}{n^2}\right) + (-2)\left(\frac{\cos nx}{n^3}\right)\right]_0^\pi$$

$$= \frac{2}{\pi}\left[-\frac{2\cos n\pi}{n^3} + \frac{2}{n^3}\right] = \frac{4}{\pi n^3}\,[1 - (-1)^n]$$

$$= 0 \quad \text{or} \quad \frac{8}{\pi n^3} \text{ according as } n \text{ is even or odd.}$$

$$\therefore \qquad \pi x - x^2 = \frac{8}{\pi}\left(\sin x + \frac{\sin 3x}{3^3} + \frac{\sin 5x}{5^3} + \ldots\ldots\right).$$

**Example 2.** *If* $f(x) = x, \quad 0 < x < \frac{\pi}{2}$

$$= \pi - x, \quad \frac{\pi}{2} < x < \pi$$

*show that (i)* $f(x) = \frac{4}{\pi}\left[\sin x - \frac{\sin 3x}{3^2} + \frac{\sin 5x}{5^2} - \ldots\ldots\right]$

*(ii)* $f(x) = \frac{\pi}{4} - \frac{2}{\pi}\left[\frac{\cos 2x}{1^2} + \frac{\cos 6x}{3^2} + \frac{\cos 10x}{5^2} + \ldots\ldots\right].$

**Sol.** (*i*) **For the half-range sine series.**

Let $f(x) = \sum_{n=1}^{\infty} b_n \sin nx$

Then $b_n = \frac{2}{\pi}\int_0^\pi f(x)\sin nx\,dx = \frac{2}{\pi}\left[\int_0^{\pi/2} x\sin nx\,dx + \int_{\pi/2}^{\pi}(\pi - x)\sin nx\,dx\right]$

$$= \frac{2}{\pi}\left[x\left(-\frac{\cos nx}{n}\right) - 1.\left(-\frac{\sin nx}{n^2}\right)\right]_0^{\pi/2} + \frac{2}{\pi}\left[(\pi - x)\left(-\frac{\cos nx}{n}\right) - (-1)\left(-\frac{\sin nx}{n^2}\right)\right]_0^\pi$$

$$= \frac{2}{\pi}\left[-\frac{\pi}{2n}\cos\frac{n\pi}{2} + \frac{1}{n^2}\sin\frac{n\pi}{2}\right] + \frac{2}{\pi}\left[\frac{\pi}{2n}\cos\frac{n\pi}{2} + \frac{1}{n^2}\sin\frac{n\pi}{2}\right]$$

$$= \frac{2}{\pi}\left[\frac{2}{n^2}\sin\frac{n\pi}{2}\right] = \frac{4}{\pi n^2}\sin\frac{n\pi}{2}$$

When $n$ is even, $b_n = 0$.

$$\therefore \quad f(x) = \frac{4}{\pi}\left[\sin x - \frac{\sin 3x}{3^2} + \frac{\sin 5x}{5^2} - \ldots\ldots\right]$$

(*ii*) **For the half-range cosine series.**

Let $f(x) = \frac{a_0}{2} + \sum_{n=1}^{\infty} a_n \cos nx$

Then $a_0 = \frac{2}{\pi}\int_0^\pi f(x)\,dx = \frac{2}{\pi}\left[\int_0^{\pi/2} x\,dx + \int_{\pi/2}^{\pi}(\pi - x)\,dx\right]$

$$= \frac{2}{\pi}\left[\left|\frac{x^2}{2}\right|_0^{\pi/2} + \left|\pi x - \frac{x^2}{2}\right|_{\pi/2}^{\pi}\right]$$

$$= \frac{2}{\pi}\left[\frac{\pi^2}{8} + \left(\pi^2 - \frac{\pi^2}{2}\right) - \left(\frac{\pi^2}{2} - \frac{\pi^2}{8}\right)\right] = \frac{2}{\pi}\left[\frac{\pi^2}{4}\right] = \frac{\pi}{2}$$

$$a_n = \frac{2}{\pi}\int_0^{\pi} f(x)\cos nx\,dx = \frac{2}{\pi}\left[\int_0^{\pi/2} x\cos nx\,dx + \int_{\pi/2}^{\pi} (\pi - x)\cos nx\,dx\right]$$

$$= \frac{2}{\pi}\left[x\,.\,\frac{\sin nx}{n} - 1.\left(-\frac{\cos nx}{n^2}\right)\right]_0^{\pi/2} + \frac{2}{\pi}\left[(\pi - x)\,.\,\frac{\sin nx}{n} - (-1)\left(-\frac{\cos nx}{n^2}\right)\right]_{\pi/2}^{\pi}$$

$$= \frac{2}{\pi}\left[\frac{\pi}{2n}\sin\frac{n\pi}{2} + \frac{1}{n^2}\cos\frac{n\pi}{2} - \frac{1}{n^2}\right] + \frac{2}{\pi}\left[-\frac{\cos n\pi}{n^2} - \frac{\pi}{2n}\sin\frac{n\pi}{2} + \frac{1}{n^2}\cos\frac{n\pi}{2}\right]$$

$$= \frac{2}{\pi}\left[\frac{2}{n^2}\cos\frac{n\pi}{2} - \frac{\cos n\pi}{n^2} - \frac{1}{n^2}\right] = \frac{2}{\pi n^2}\left[2\cos\frac{n\pi}{2} - \cos n\pi - 1\right]$$

$$\therefore \quad a_1 = 0,\ a_2 = \frac{2}{\pi\,.\,2^2}(2\cos\pi - \cos 2\pi - 1) = \frac{-2}{\pi\,.\,1^2},$$

$$a_3 = 0,\ a_4 = 0,\ a_5 = 0,\ a_6 = \frac{2}{\pi\,.\,6^2}(2\cos 3\pi - \cos 6\pi - 1) = \frac{-2}{\pi\,.\,3^2},$$

$$a_7 = 0,\ a_8 = 0,\ a_9 = 0,\ a_{10} = \frac{2}{\pi\,.\,10^2}(2\cos 5\pi - \cos 10\pi - 1) = \frac{-2}{\pi\,.\,5^2},\ \ldots\ldots$$

Hence $f(x) = \frac{\pi}{4} - \frac{2}{\pi}\left[\frac{\cos 2x}{1^2} + \frac{\cos 6x}{3^2} + \frac{\cos 10x}{5^2} + \ldots\ldots\right].$

**Example 3.** *Find a series of cosines of multiples of x which will represent x sin x in the interval (0, π) and show that* $\frac{1}{1.3} - \frac{1}{3.5} + \frac{1}{5.7} - \ldots\ldots = \frac{\pi - 2}{4}$.

**Sol.** Since $x \sin x$ is an even function of $x$, $b_n = 0$

Let $x\sin x = \frac{a_0}{2} + \sum_{n=1}^{\infty} a_n \cos nx$

Then $a_0 = \frac{2}{\pi}\int_0^{\pi} x\sin x\,dx = \frac{2}{\pi}\left[x(-\cos x) - 1.(-\sin x)\right]_0^{\pi} = \frac{2}{\pi}[-\pi\cos\pi] = 2$

$$a_n = \frac{2}{\pi}\int_0^{\pi} x\sin x\cos nx\,dx = \frac{1}{\pi}\int_0^{\pi} x\,(2\cos nx\sin x)\,dx$$

$$= \frac{1}{\pi}\int_0^{\pi} x\,[\sin(n+1)x - \sin(n-1)x]\,dx$$

$$= \frac{1}{\pi}\left[x\left\{-\frac{\cos(n+1)x}{n+1} + \frac{\cos(n-1)x}{n-1}\right\} - 1.\left\{-\frac{\sin(n+1)x}{(n+1)^2} - \frac{\sin(n-1)x}{(n-1)^2}\right\}\right]_0^{\pi}$$

$$= \frac{1}{\pi}\left[-\frac{\pi\cos(n+1)\pi}{n+1} + \frac{\pi\cos(n-1)\pi}{n-1}\right], \quad \text{when } n \neq 1$$

$$= -\frac{(-1)^{n+1}}{n+1} + \frac{(-1)^{n-1}}{n-1} = (-1)^{n-1}\left[\frac{1}{n-1} - \frac{1}{n+1}\right] = \frac{2(-1)^{n-1}}{(n-1)(n+1)}$$

When $n = 1$, we have

$$a_1 = \frac{2}{\pi}\int_0^{\pi} x \sin x \cos x \, dx = \frac{1}{\pi}\int_0^{\pi} x \sin 2x \, dx = \frac{1}{\pi}\left[x\left(-\frac{\cos 2x}{2}\right) - 1.\left(-\frac{\sin 2x}{2^2}\right)\right]_0^{\pi}$$

$$= \frac{1}{\pi}\left[-\frac{\pi \cos 2\pi}{2}\right] = -\frac{1}{2}$$

$$\therefore \quad x \sin x = 1 - \frac{1}{2}\cos x - 2\left(\frac{\cos 2x}{1.3} - \frac{\cos 3x}{2.4} + \frac{\cos 4x}{3.5} - \ldots\ldots\right).$$

Putting $x = \frac{\pi}{2}$, we get $\frac{\pi}{2} = 1 - 2\left(\frac{-1}{1.3} + \frac{1}{3.5} + \frac{-1}{5.7} - \ldots\ldots\right)$

$$\Rightarrow \quad 1 + \frac{2}{1.3} - \frac{2}{3.5} + \frac{2}{5.7} - \ldots\ldots = \frac{\pi}{2}$$

$$\Rightarrow \quad \frac{2}{1.3} - \frac{2}{3.5} + \frac{2}{5.7} - \ldots\ldots = \frac{\pi}{2} - 1$$

Hence $$\frac{1}{1.3} - \frac{1}{3.5} + \frac{1}{5.7} - \ldots\ldots = \frac{\pi - 2}{4}.$$

**Example 4.** *Obtain the half-range sine series for $e^x$ in $0 < x < 1$.*

**Sol.** Let $e^x = \sum_{n=1}^{\infty} b_n \sin n\pi x$, (since $l = 1$)

Then $b_n = 2\int_0^1 e^x \sin n\pi x \, dx = 2\left[\frac{e^x}{1+(n\pi)^2}(\sin n\pi x - n\pi \cos n\pi x)\right]_0^1$

$$\left[\because \int e^{ax} \sin bx \, dx = \frac{e^{ax}}{a^2+b^2}(a \sin bx - b \cos bx)\right]$$

$$= 2\left[\frac{e}{1+(n\pi)^2}(-n\pi \cos n\pi) - \frac{1}{1+(n\pi)^2}(-n\pi)\right]$$

$$= \frac{2}{1+n^2\pi^2}\,[-en\pi\,(-1)^n + n\pi] = \frac{2n\pi}{1+n^2\pi^2}\,[1 - e\,(-1)^n]$$

Hence $e^x = 2\pi \sum_{n=1}^{\infty} \frac{n[1-e(-1)^n]}{1+n^2\pi^2}$

$$= 2\pi\left[\frac{1+e}{1+\pi^2}\sin \pi x + \frac{2(1-e)}{1+4\pi^2}\sin 2\pi x + \frac{3(1+e)}{1+9\pi^2}\sin 3\pi x + \ldots\ldots\right].$$

**Example 5.** *Develop $\sin\left(\frac{\pi x}{l}\right)$ in half-range cosine series in the range $0 < x < l$.*

(M.G.U. May 2009)

**Sol.** Let $\sin\left(\frac{\pi x}{l}\right) = \frac{a_0}{2} + \sum_{n=1}^{\infty} a_n \cos \frac{n\pi x}{l}$

then $$a_0 = \frac{2}{l}\int_0^l \sin\frac{\pi x}{l}\,dx = \frac{2}{l}\left[-\frac{\cos\frac{\pi x}{l}}{\frac{\pi}{l}}\right]_0^l = -\frac{2}{\pi}[\cos\pi - 1] = \frac{4}{\pi}$$

$$a_n = \frac{2}{l}\int_0^l \sin\frac{\pi x}{l}\cos\frac{n\pi x}{l}\,dx$$

$$= \frac{1}{l}\int_0^l \left[\sin(n+1)\frac{\pi x}{l} - \sin(n-1)\frac{\pi x}{l}\right]dx$$

$$= \frac{1}{l}\left[-\frac{\cos(n+1)\frac{\pi x}{l}}{(n+1)\frac{\pi}{l}} + \frac{\cos(n-1)\frac{\pi x}{l}}{(n-1)\frac{\pi}{l}}\right]_0^l$$

$$= \frac{1}{\pi}\left[\left\{-\frac{\cos(n+1)\pi}{n+1} + \frac{\cos(n-1)\pi}{n-1}\right\} - \left\{-\frac{1}{n+1} + \frac{1}{n-1}\right\}\right]$$

$$= \frac{1}{\pi}\left[-\frac{(-1)^{n+1}}{n+1} + \frac{(-1)^{n-1}}{n-1} + \frac{1}{n+1} - \frac{1}{n-1}\right]$$

When $n$ is odd, $$a_n = \frac{1}{\pi}\left[-\frac{1}{n+1} + \frac{1}{n-1} + \frac{1}{n+1} - \frac{1}{n-1}\right] = 0$$

When $n$ is even, $$a_n = \frac{1}{\pi}\left[\frac{1}{n+1} - \frac{1}{n-1} + \frac{1}{n+1} - \frac{1}{n-1}\right]$$

$$= \frac{2}{\pi}\left[\frac{1}{n+1} - \frac{1}{n-1}\right] = -\frac{4}{\pi(n+1)(n-1)}$$

$$\therefore \quad \sin\left(\frac{\pi x}{l}\right) = \frac{2}{\pi} - \frac{4}{\pi}\left[\frac{\cos\frac{2\pi x}{l}}{1.3} + \frac{\cos\frac{4\pi x}{l}}{3.5} + \frac{\cos\frac{6\pi x}{l}}{5.7} + \ldots\ldots\right].$$

**Example 6.** *Obtain a half-range cosine series for*

$$f(x) = kx \qquad \text{for} \quad 0 \le x \le \frac{l}{2}$$

$$= k(l-x) \qquad \text{for} \quad \frac{l}{2} \le x \le l.$$

*Deduce the sum of the series* $\frac{1}{1^2} + \frac{1}{3^2} + \frac{1}{5^2} + \ldots\ldots$

**Sol.** Let $$f(x) = \frac{a_0}{2} + \sum_{n=1}^{\infty} a_n \cos\frac{n\pi x}{l}$$

then $$a_0 = \frac{2}{l}\int_0^l f(x)\,dx = \frac{2}{l}\left[\int_0^{l/2} kx\,dx + \int_{l/2}^l k(l-x)\,dx\right]$$

$$= \frac{2}{l}\left[\left|\frac{kx^2}{2}\right|_0^{l/2} + \left|k\left(lx - \frac{x^2}{2}\right)\right|_{l/2}^{l}\right]$$

$$= \frac{2}{l}\left[\frac{kl^2}{8} + k\left(l^2 - \frac{l^2}{2}\right) - k\left(\frac{l^2}{2} - \frac{l^2}{8}\right)\right] = \frac{2}{l}\left(\frac{kl^2}{4}\right) = \frac{kl}{2}$$

$$a_n = \frac{2}{l}\int_0^l f(x)\cos\frac{n\pi x}{l}\,dx = \frac{2}{l}\left[\int_0^{l/2} kx\,.\cos\frac{n\pi x}{l}\,dx + \int_{l/2}^{l} k(l-x)\,.\cos\frac{n\pi x}{l}\,dx\right]$$

$$= \frac{2}{l}\left[\left|kx\,.\frac{1}{n\pi}\sin\frac{n\pi x}{l} + k\,.\frac{l^2}{n^2\pi^2}\cos\frac{n\pi x}{l}\right|_0^{l/2}\right.$$

$$\left. + \left|k(l-x)\,.\frac{1}{n\pi}\sin\frac{n\pi x}{l} - k\,.\frac{l^2}{n^2\pi^2}\cos\frac{n\pi x}{l}\right|_{l/2}^{l}\right]$$

$$= \frac{2}{l}\left[\left|\frac{kl^2}{2n\pi}\sin\frac{n\pi}{2} + \frac{kl^2}{n^2\pi^2}\left(\cos\frac{n\pi}{2} - 1\right)\right|\right.$$

$$\left. + \left|\frac{-kl^2}{n^2\pi^2}\cos n\pi - \frac{kl^2}{2n\pi}\sin\frac{n\pi}{2} + \frac{kl^2}{n^2\pi^2}\cos\frac{n\pi}{2}\right|\right]$$

$$= \frac{2}{l}\left[\frac{2kl^2}{n^2\pi^2}\cos\frac{n\pi}{2} - \frac{kl^2}{n^2\pi^2} - \frac{kl^2}{n^2\pi^2}\cos n\pi\right] = \frac{2kl}{n^2\pi^2}\left[2\cos\frac{n\pi}{2} - 1 - \cos n\pi\right]$$

**When n is odd,** $\cos\frac{n\pi}{2} = 0$ and $\cos n\pi = -1$ $\quad\therefore\quad a_n = 0 \Rightarrow a_1 = a_3 = a_5 = \ldots\ldots = 0$

**When n is even,** $a_2 = \frac{2kl}{2^2\pi^2}[2\cos\pi - 1 - \cos 2\pi] = -\frac{8kl}{2^2\pi^2}$ ;

$$a_4 = \frac{2kl}{4^2\pi^2}[2\cos 2\pi - 1 - \cos 4\pi] = 0$$

$$a_6 = \frac{2kl}{6^2\pi^2}[2\cos 3\pi - 1 - \cos 6\pi]$$

$$= \frac{2kl}{6^2\pi^2}(-2-1-1) = -\frac{8kl}{6^2\pi^2} \text{ and so on.}$$

$$\therefore \quad f(x) = \frac{kl}{4} - \frac{8kl}{\pi^2}\left(\frac{1}{2^2}\cos\frac{2\pi x}{l} + \frac{1}{6^2}\cos\frac{6\pi x}{l} + \ldots\ldots\right) \quad \ldots(1)$$

Putting $\quad x = l,\ f(l) = 0$

$\therefore$ From (1), we have $\quad 0 = \frac{kl}{4} - \frac{8kl}{\pi^2}\left(\frac{1}{2^2} + \frac{1}{6^2} + \ldots\ldots\right)$

$$\Rightarrow \quad \frac{1}{2^2} + \frac{1}{6^2} + \ldots\ldots = \frac{\pi^2}{32} \Rightarrow \frac{1}{2^2}\left[\frac{1}{1^2} + \frac{1}{3^2} + \ldots\ldots\right] = \frac{\pi^2}{32}$$

Hence $\quad \frac{1}{1^2} + \frac{1}{3^2} + \ldots\ldots = \frac{\pi^2}{8}$ .

**Example 7.** *Express $f(x) = x(\pi - x)$ ; $0 < x < \pi$ as Fourier sine series in period $2\pi$.*
(M.G.U. Dec., 2007)

**Sol.** The Fourier sine series expansion of $f(x)$ is $f(x) = \sum_{n=1}^{\infty} b_n \sin nx$

where $$b_n = \frac{2}{\pi}\int_0^{\pi} f(x) \sin nx\, dx.$$

Now, $$b_n = \frac{2}{\pi}\int_0^{\pi} (\pi x - x^2) \sin nx\, dx$$

$$= \frac{2}{\pi}\left[(\pi x - x^2)\frac{-\cos nx}{n} - (\pi - 2x)\frac{-\sin nx}{n^2} + (-2)\frac{\cos nx}{n^3}\right]_0^{\pi}$$

$$= \frac{2}{\pi}\frac{(-2)\cos n\pi}{n^3} - \frac{2}{\pi}\frac{(-2)}{n^3}$$

$$= \frac{-4}{\pi n^3}(\cos n\pi - 1)$$

$$= \frac{-4}{n^3\pi}[(-1)^n - 1]$$

Therefore the series expansion is $f(x) = \sum_{n=1}^{\infty} \frac{-4}{n^3\pi}[(-1)^n - 1] \sin nx.$

Hence the result.

**Example 8.** *Find Fourier cosine series of* $f(x) = \begin{cases} x^2 & in \quad 0 < x < 1 \\ 2 - x & in \quad 1 < x < 2 \end{cases}$
(M.G.U. Dec., 2007)

**Sol.** Let $$f(x) = \frac{a_0}{2} + \sum_{n=1}^{\infty} a_n \cos\frac{n\pi x}{2}$$

where $$a_n = \frac{2}{2}\int_0^2 f(x) \cos\frac{n\pi x}{2}\, dx.$$

$$a_0 = \frac{2}{2}\int_0^2 f(x)\, dx$$

Now $$a_0 = \int_0^2 f(x)\, dx = \int_0^1 x^2\, dx + \int_1^2 (2 - x)\, dx$$

$$= \left(\frac{x^3}{3}\right)_0^1 + \left(2x - \frac{x^2}{2}\right)_1^2 = \frac{1}{3} + \left(2 - \frac{3}{2}\right) = \frac{5}{6}$$

$$a_n = \int_0^2 f(x) \cos\frac{n\pi x}{2}\, dx$$

$$= \int_0^1 x^2 \cos\frac{n\pi x}{2}\, dx + \int_1^2 (2 - x) \cos\frac{n\pi x}{2}\, dx$$

$$= \left[ x^2 \frac{\sin \frac{n\pi}{2} x}{\frac{n\pi}{2}} - 2x \frac{-\cos \frac{n\pi}{2} x}{\left(\frac{n\pi}{2}\right)^2} + 2 \frac{-\sin \frac{n\pi}{2} x}{\left(\frac{n\pi}{2}\right)^3} \right]_0^1$$

$$+ \left[ (2-x) \frac{\sin \frac{n\pi}{2} x}{\left(\frac{n\pi}{2}\right)} + \frac{-\cos \frac{n\pi}{2} x}{\left(\frac{n\pi}{2}\right)^2} \right]_1^2$$

$$= \frac{8}{n^3\pi^3} \sin\left(\frac{n\pi}{2}\right) + \frac{12}{n^2\pi^2} \cos\left(\frac{n\pi}{2}\right) - \frac{4}{n^2\pi^2} \cos(n\pi).$$

Hence the half range cosine series of $f(x)$ is

$$f(x) = \frac{5}{12} + \sum_{n=1}^{\infty} a_n \cos \frac{n\pi x}{2}$$

$$= \frac{5}{12} + \sum_{n=1}^{\infty} \left[ \frac{8}{n^3\pi^3} \sin\left(\frac{n\pi}{2}\right) + \frac{12}{n^2\pi^2} \cos\left(\frac{n\pi}{2}\right) - \frac{4}{n^2\pi^2} \cos(n\pi) \right] \cos\left(\frac{n\pi x}{2}\right).$$

## TEST YOUR KNOWLEDGE

1. (a) Obtain cosine and sine series for $f(x) = x$ in the interval $0 \le x \le \pi$. Hence show that $\frac{1}{1^2} + \frac{1}{3^2} + \frac{1}{5^2} + \ldots\ldots = \frac{\pi^2}{8}$. *(M.G.U. May 2009)*

   (b) Prove that for $0 < x < l$

   $$x = \frac{l}{2} - \frac{4l}{\pi^2} \left( \cos \frac{\pi x}{l} + \frac{1}{3^2} \cos \frac{3\pi x}{l} + \frac{1}{5^2} \cos \frac{5\pi x}{l} + \ldots\ldots \right)$$

2. Find the half-range cosine series for the function $f(x) = x^2$ in the range $0 \le x \le \pi$.
3. Find the half-range cosine series for the function $f(x) = (x-1)^2$ in the interval $0 < x < 1$. *(M.G.U. May 2009 ; M.D.U.)*

   Hence show that

   (i) $\frac{1}{1^2} + \frac{1}{2^2} + \frac{1}{3^2} + \frac{1}{4^2} + \ldots\ldots = \frac{\pi^2}{6}$ (ii) $\frac{1}{1^2} - \frac{1}{2^2} + \frac{1}{3^2} - \frac{1}{4^2} + \ldots\ldots = \frac{\pi^2}{12}$

   (iii) $\frac{1}{1^2} + \frac{1}{3^2} + \frac{1}{5^2} + \frac{1}{7^2} + \ldots\ldots = \frac{\pi^2}{8}$.
4. (a) Express $\sin x$ as a cosine series in $0 < x < \pi$.

   (b) Show that a constant function $c$ can be expanded in an infinite series

   $\frac{4}{\pi} \left( \sin x + \frac{\sin 3x}{3} + \frac{\sin 5x}{5} + \ldots\ldots \right)$ in the range $0 < x < \pi$.

**5.** If
$$f(x) = \frac{\pi}{3}, \qquad 0 \le x \le \frac{\pi}{3}$$
$$= 0, \qquad \frac{\pi}{3} \le x \le \frac{2\pi}{3}$$
$$= -\frac{\pi}{3}, \qquad \frac{2\pi}{3} \le x \le \pi$$
then show that $f(x) = \frac{2}{\sqrt{3}}\left[\cos x - \frac{\cos 5x}{5} + \frac{\cos 7x}{7} - \ldots\ldots\right]$

**6.** If
$$f(x) = mx, \qquad 0 \le x \le \frac{\pi}{2}$$
$$= m(\pi - x), \qquad \frac{\pi}{2} \le x \le \pi$$
then show that $f(x) = \frac{4m}{\pi}\left[\frac{\sin x}{1^2} - \frac{\sin 3x}{3^2} + \frac{\sin 5x}{5^2} - \ldots\ldots\right]$

**7.** Express $f(x) = x$ as a half-range.
(*i*) sine series in $0 < x < 2$. (*ii*) cosine series in $0 < x < 2$.

**8.** Show that the series $\frac{1}{\pi}\sum_{n=1}^{\infty}\frac{1}{n}\sin\frac{2n\pi x}{l}$ represents $\frac{1}{2}l - x$ when $0 < x < l$.

**9.** Find the half-range sine series for $f(x) = \frac{1}{4} - x, \quad 0 < x < \frac{1}{2}$
$$= x - \frac{3}{4}, \qquad \frac{1}{2} < x < 1.$$

**10.** Represent the following function by Fourier sine series
$$f(x) = 1 \quad \text{when} \quad 0 < x < \frac{l}{2}$$
$$= 0 \quad \text{when} \quad \frac{l}{2} < x < l.$$

**11.** Find the half-range sine series for the function $f(t) = t - t^2$, $0 < t < 1$.

**12.** Prove that for $0 < x < \pi$,
$$x(\pi - x) = \frac{\pi^2}{6} - \left(\frac{\cos 2x}{1^2} + \frac{\cos 4x}{2^2} + \frac{\cos 6x}{3^2} + \ldots\ldots\right)$$

**13.** Let $f(x) = \begin{cases} \omega x, & \text{when } 0 \le x \le \frac{l}{2} \\ \omega(l - x), & \text{when } \frac{l}{2} \le x \le l \end{cases}$

Show that $f(x) = \frac{4\omega l}{\pi^2}\sum_{n=0}^{\infty}\frac{(-1)^n}{(2n+1)^2}\sin\frac{(2n+1)\pi x}{l}$

Hence obtain the sum of the series
$$1 + \frac{1}{3^2} + \frac{1}{5^2} + \ldots\ldots$$

**14.** If $f(x) = \begin{cases} \sin x, & \text{for } 0 \le x < \dfrac{\pi}{4} \\ \cos x, & \text{for } \dfrac{\pi}{4} \le x \le \dfrac{\pi}{2} \end{cases}$ expand $f(x)$ in a series of sines.

**15.** For the function defined by the graph OAB, find the half-range Fourier sine series.

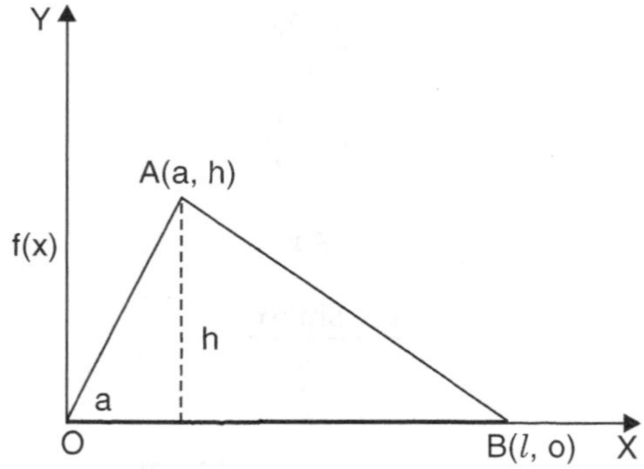


**16.** Find the half-range sine series for $f(x) = \dfrac{l}{2} - x, \quad 0 < x < l.$ *(M.G.U. June 2006)*

**17.** Find the half-range cosine series for $f(x) = x \sin x,\ 0 < x < \pi.$ *(M.G.U. June 2006)*

## Answers

**1.** (*a*) $\dfrac{\pi}{2} - \dfrac{4}{\pi}\left(\cos x + \dfrac{\cos 3x}{3^2} + \dfrac{\cos 5x}{5^2} + \ldots\ldots\right)$; $2\left(\sin x - \dfrac{\sin 2x}{2} + \dfrac{\sin 3x}{3} - \dfrac{\sin 4x}{4} + \ldots\ldots\right)$

**2.** $\dfrac{\pi^2}{3} - 4\left[\cos x - \dfrac{\cos 2x}{2^2} + \dfrac{\cos 3x}{3^2} - \dfrac{\cos 4x}{4^2} + \ldots\ldots\right]$

**3.** $\dfrac{1}{3} + \dfrac{1}{\pi^2}\left(\cos \pi x + \dfrac{\cos 2\pi x}{2^2} + \dfrac{\cos 3\pi x}{3^2} + \ldots\ldots\right)$ **4.** (*a*) $\dfrac{2}{\pi} - \dfrac{4}{\pi}\left[\dfrac{\cos 2x}{1.3} + \dfrac{\cos 4x}{3.5} + \dfrac{\cos 6x}{5.7} + \ldots\ldots\right]$

**7.** (*i*) $\dfrac{4}{\pi}\left(\sin \dfrac{\pi x}{2} - \dfrac{1}{2}\sin \dfrac{2\pi x}{2} + \dfrac{1}{3}\sin \dfrac{3\pi x}{2} - \dfrac{1}{4}\sin \dfrac{4\pi x}{2} + \ldots\ldots\right)$

(*ii*) $1 - \dfrac{8}{\pi^2}\left[\cos \dfrac{\pi x}{2} + \dfrac{1}{3^2}\cos \dfrac{3\pi x}{2} + \dfrac{1}{5^2}\cos \dfrac{5\pi x}{2} + \ldots\ldots\right]$

**9.** $f(x) = \left(\dfrac{1}{\pi} - \dfrac{4}{\pi^2}\right)\sin \pi x + \left(\dfrac{1}{3\pi} - \dfrac{4}{3^2\pi^2}\right)\sin 3\pi x + \left(\dfrac{1}{5\pi} - \dfrac{4}{5^2\pi^2}\right)\sin 5\pi x + \ldots$

**10.** $f(x) = \dfrac{2}{\pi}\left[\sin \dfrac{\pi x}{l} + \sin \dfrac{2\pi x}{l} + \dfrac{1}{3}\sin \dfrac{3\pi x}{l} + \dfrac{1}{5}\sin \dfrac{5\pi x}{l} + \ldots\ldots\right]$

**11.** $\dfrac{8}{\pi^3}\left(\dfrac{\sin \pi t}{1^3} + \dfrac{\sin 3\pi t}{3^3} + \dfrac{\sin 5\pi t}{5^3} + \ldots\ldots\right)$ **14.** $\dfrac{4\sqrt{2}}{\pi}\left(\dfrac{\sin 2x}{1.3} - \dfrac{\sin 6x}{5.7} + \dfrac{\sin 10x}{9.11} \ldots\ldots\right)$

**15.** $\dfrac{2l^2h}{a(l-a)\pi^2}\sum_{n=1}^{\infty}\dfrac{1}{n^2}\sin\dfrac{n\pi a}{l}\sin\dfrac{n\pi x}{l}.$

**16.** $f(x)=\sum_{n=1}^{\infty}\dfrac{l}{n\pi}\left[(-1)^n+1\right]\sin\left(\dfrac{n\pi x}{l}\right)$

**17.** $f(x)=1+\left(-\dfrac{1}{2}\right)\cos x+\sum_{n=2}^{\infty}\dfrac{2(-1)^{n+1}}{n^2-1}\cos nx.$

## 1.8. PARSEVAL'S THEOREM ON FOURIER CONSTANTS

**If the Fourier series of f(x) over an interval c < x < c + 2*l* is given as**

$$\mathbf{f(x)}=\frac{\mathbf{a_0}}{\mathbf{2}}+\sum_{\mathbf{n=1}}^{\infty}\left\{\mathbf{a_n}\cos\frac{\mathbf{n\pi x}}{l}+\mathbf{b_n}\sin\frac{\mathbf{n\pi x}}{l}\right\}$$

**then**
$$\frac{1}{2l}\int_c^{c+2l}[f(x)]^2\,dx=\frac{a_0^2}{4}+\frac{1}{2}\sum_{n=1}^{\infty}(a_n^2+b_n^2).$$

**Proof.** The Fourier series of $f(x)$ in $c < x < c + 2l$ is given as

$$f(x)=\frac{a_0}{2}+\sum_{n=1}^{\infty}\left\{a_n\cos\frac{n\pi x}{l}+b_n\sin\frac{n\pi x}{l}\right\} \qquad ...(1)$$

where $a_0=\dfrac{1}{l}\displaystyle\int_c^{c+2l}f(x)\,dx$ ; $a_n=\dfrac{1}{l}\displaystyle\int_c^{c+2l}f(x)\cos\dfrac{n\pi x}{l}\,dx$ ; $b_n=\dfrac{1}{l}\displaystyle\int_c^{c+2l}f(x)\sin\dfrac{n\pi x}{l}\,dx$ ...(2)

Multiplying both sides of (1) by $f(x)$, we have

$$[f(x)]^2=\frac{a_0}{2}f(x)+\sum_{n=1}^{\infty}a_nf(x)\cos\frac{n\pi x}{l}+\sum_{n=1}^{\infty}b_nf(x)\sin\frac{n\pi x}{l}$$

Integrating both sides w.r.t. $x$, between the limits $c$ to $c + 2l$, we have

$$\int_c^{c+2l}[f(x)]^2\,dx=\frac{a_0}{2}\int_c^{c+2l}f(x)\,dx+\sum_{n=1}^{\infty}a_n\int_c^{c+2l}f(x)\cos\frac{n\pi x}{l}\,dx$$
$$+\sum_{n=1}^{\infty}b_n\int_c^{c+2l}f(x)\sin\frac{n\pi x}{l}\,dx$$
$$=\frac{a_0}{2}.\,la_0+\sum_{n=1}^{\infty}a_n(la_n)+\sum_{n=1}^{\infty}b_n(lb_n) \qquad \text{[Using (2)]}$$

$$\Rightarrow \int_c^{c+2l}[f(x)]^2\,dx=\frac{la_0^2}{2}+l\sum_{n=1}^{\infty}(a_n^2+b_n^2)$$

$$\therefore \frac{1}{2l}\int_c^{c+2l}[f(x)]^2\,dx=\frac{1}{2l}\left\{\frac{la_0^2}{2}+l\sum_{n=1}^{\infty}(a_n^2+b_n^2)\right\}$$

or $$\frac{1}{2l}\int_{c}^{c+2l}[f(x)]^2\,dx = \frac{a_0^{\,2}}{4} + \frac{1}{2}\sum_{n=1}^{\infty}(a_n^{\,2} + b_n^{\,2})$$ (Parseval's identity)

Hence the proof.

**Note.** *Parseval's identities in different cases :*

(*i*) If $c = 0$, the interval becomes $0 < x < 2l$ and Parseval's identity reduces to

$$\frac{1}{2l}\int_{0}^{2l}[f(x)]^2\,dx = \frac{a_0^{\,2}}{4} + \frac{1}{2}\sum_{n=1}^{\infty}(a_n^{\,2} + b_n^{\,2})$$

If $c = -l$, the interval becomes $-l < x < l$ and Parseval's identity reduces to

$$\frac{1}{2l}\int_{-l}^{l}[f(x)]^2\,dx = \frac{a_0^{\,2}}{4} + \frac{1}{2}\sum_{n=1}^{\infty}(a_n^{\,2} + b_n^{\,2}).$$

(*ii*) If $f(x)$ is an even function in $(-l, l)$ then $\frac{2}{l}\int_{0}^{l}[f(x)]^2\,dx = \frac{a_0^{\,2}}{2} + \sum_{n=1}^{\infty} a_n^{\,2}$

(*iii*) If $f(x)$ is an odd function in $(-l, l)$ then $\frac{2}{l}\int_{0}^{l}[f(x)]^2\,dx = \sum_{n=1}^{\infty} b_n^{\,2}$

(*iv*) If $f(x) = \frac{a_0}{2} + \sum_{n=1}^{\infty} a_n \cos\frac{n\pi x}{l}$ in $(0, l)$ then $\frac{2}{l}\int_{0}^{l}[f(x)]^2\,dx = \frac{a_0^{\,2}}{2} + \sum_{n=1}^{\infty} a_n^{\,2}$

(*v*) If $f(x) = \sum_{n=1}^{\infty} b_n \sin\frac{n\pi x}{l}$ in $(0, l)$ then $\frac{2}{l}\int_{0}^{l}[f(x)]^2\,dx = \sum_{n=1}^{\infty} b_n^{\,2}$.

## 1.9. ROOT MEAN SQUARE (R.M.S.) VALUVE

The root mean square value of the function $f(x)$ over an interval $(a, b)$ is defined as

$$\Big[f(x)\Big]_{\text{r.m.s.}} = \sqrt{\frac{\int_a^b [f(x)]^2\,dx}{b-a}}$$

The r.m.s. value of a function is also known as the effective value of the function.

## ILLUSTRATIVE EXAMPLES

**Example 1.** *Find the Fourier sine series for unity in $0 < x < \pi$ and hence show that*

$$1 + \frac{1}{3^2} + \frac{1}{5^2} + \frac{1}{7^2} + \ldots\ldots = \frac{\pi^2}{8}.$$

**Sol.** We require half-range Fourier sine series for 1 in $(0, \pi)$

Let $$1 = \sum_{n=1}^{\infty} b_n \sin nx \qquad ...(1)$$

Then $$b_n = \frac{2}{\pi}\int_0^{\pi} (1) \sin nx\, dx = \frac{2}{\pi}\left[-\frac{\cos nx}{n}\right]_0^{\pi} = -\frac{2}{n\pi}(\cos n\pi - 1)$$

$$= \frac{2}{n\pi}[1-(-1)^n] \qquad [\because \quad \cos n\pi = (-1)^n]$$

Now $b_n = 0$ when $n$ is even ; and $b_n = \dfrac{4}{n\pi}$ when $n$ is odd.

Substituting in (1), we get

$$\therefore \quad 1 = \sum_{m=1}^{\infty} \frac{4}{(2m-1)\pi} \sin (2m-1)x \quad \text{or} \quad 1 = \frac{4}{\pi}\left(\sin x + \frac{\sin 3x}{3} + \frac{\sin 5x}{5} + \ldots\ldots\right) \qquad ...(2)$$

Now from Parseval's theorem on Fourier constants

$$\int_c^{c+2l} [f(x)]^2\, dx = 2l\left[\frac{a_0^{\,2}}{4} + \frac{l}{2}\sum_{n=1}^{\infty} (a_n^{\,2} + b_n^{\,2})\right] \qquad ...(3)$$

Applying (3) to half-range sine series for 1 in $(0, \pi)$

$$c = 0,\ 2l = \pi,\ f(x) = 1,\ a_0 = 0,\ a_n = 0, \text{ and } b_n = \frac{4}{(2m-1)\pi},\ m = 1, 2 \ldots\ldots$$

We get, $$\int_0^{\pi} (1)^2\, dx = \pi \cdot \frac{1}{2}\sum_{m=1}^{\infty} \frac{16}{(2m-1)^2} \cdot \pi^2$$

$$\Rightarrow \qquad \Big[x\Big]_0^{\pi} = \frac{8}{\pi}\left\{\frac{1}{1^2} + \frac{1}{3^2} + \frac{1}{5^2} + \ldots\ldots\right\} \quad \text{or} \quad \frac{\pi^2}{8} = 1 + \frac{1}{3^2} + \frac{1}{5^2} + \ldots\ldots$$

Hence the result.

**Example 2.** *Find Fourier series of $x^2$ in $(-\pi, \pi)$. Use Parseval's identity to prove that*

$$\frac{\pi^4}{90} = 1 + \frac{1}{2^4} + \frac{1}{3^4} + \ldots\ldots.$$

**Sol.** The Fourier series of $x^2$ in $(-\pi, \pi)$ is

$$x^2 = \frac{\pi^2}{3} + \sum_{n=1}^{\infty} \frac{4(-1)^n}{n^2} \cos nx \qquad ...(1)$$

Here $$a_0 = \frac{2\pi^2}{3},\ a_n = \frac{4(-1)^n}{n^2},\ b_n = 0,\ f(x) = x^2$$

Now by Parseval's identity from (1), we get

$$\int_{-\pi}^{\pi} (x^2)^2\, dx = 2\pi\left[\frac{\pi^4}{9} + \frac{1}{2}\sum_{n=1}^{\infty}\frac{16}{n^4}\right]$$

$$\Rightarrow \qquad \left[\frac{x^5}{5}\right]_{-\pi}^{\pi} = \frac{2\pi^5}{9} + \pi\sum_{n=1}^{\infty}\frac{16}{n^4} \quad \text{or} \quad \frac{2\pi^5}{5} - \frac{2\pi^5}{9} = \pi\sum_{n=1}^{\infty}\frac{16}{n^4}$$

or $$\frac{\pi^4}{90} = \sum_{n=1}^{\infty}\frac{1}{n^4} \quad \text{or} \quad 1 + \frac{1}{2^4} + \frac{1}{3^4} + \ldots\ldots = \frac{\pi^4}{90}.$$

## TEST YOUR KNOWLEDGE

**1.** If $f(x)$ has the Fourier series expansion

$$\frac{a_0}{2} + \sum_{n=1}^{\infty}\left(a_n \cos\frac{n\pi x}{l} + b_n \sin\frac{n\pi x}{l}\right) \text{ in } a \le x \le a + 2l$$

show that $\displaystyle\int_a^{a+2l} [f(x)]^2\, dx = 2l\left[\frac{{a_0}^2}{4} + \frac{1}{2}\sum_{n=1}^{\infty}({a_n}^2 + {b_n}^2)\right].$

**2.** If $f(x) = \dfrac{a_0}{2} + \displaystyle\sum_{n=1}^{\infty} a_n \cos\frac{n\pi x}{l}$ in $0 < x < l$, then show that

$$\int_0^l [f(x)]^2\, dx = \frac{l}{2}\left[\frac{{a_0}^2}{2} + \sum_{n=1}^{\infty}{a_n}^2\right].$$

**3.** If $f(x) = \displaystyle\sum_{n=1}^{\infty} b_n \sin\frac{n\pi x}{l}$ in $(0, l)$, then show that $\displaystyle\int_0^l [f(x)]^2\, dx = \frac{l}{2}\sum_{n=1}^{\infty}{b_n}^2.$

**4.** Prove that in the range $(0, l)$, $x = \dfrac{l}{2} - \dfrac{4l}{\pi^2}\displaystyle\sum_{n=1}^{\infty}\frac{1}{(2m-1)^2}\cos\frac{(2m-1)\pi x}{l}$ and deduce that

$$\frac{1}{1^4} + \frac{1}{3^4} + \frac{1}{5^4} + \ldots\ldots = \frac{\pi^4}{96}.$$

**5.** Show that for $0 < x < \pi$,

$$x(\pi - x) = \frac{\pi^2}{6} - \left(\frac{\cos 2x}{1^2} + \frac{\cos 4x}{2^2} + \frac{\cos 6x}{3^2} + \ldots\ldots\right)$$

and hence evaluate $\displaystyle\sum_{n=1}^{\infty}\frac{1}{n^4}$.

## 1.10. TYPICAL WAVEFORMS

A periodic waveform is a waveform that repeats a basic pattern. It is a single-valued periodic function. Therefore it can be developed as a Fourier series.

We give below some typical waveforms usually met with in communication engineering and also the corresponding Fourier series. The student is urged to construct the Fourier series in each case.

### I. Square (or Rectangular) Waveform

It is a periodic function of the form given below.

(*i*)
$$f(x) = \begin{cases} -k & \text{for } -\pi < x < 0 \\ k & \text{for } \quad 0 < x < \pi \end{cases}, \; f(x + 2\pi) = f(x)$$

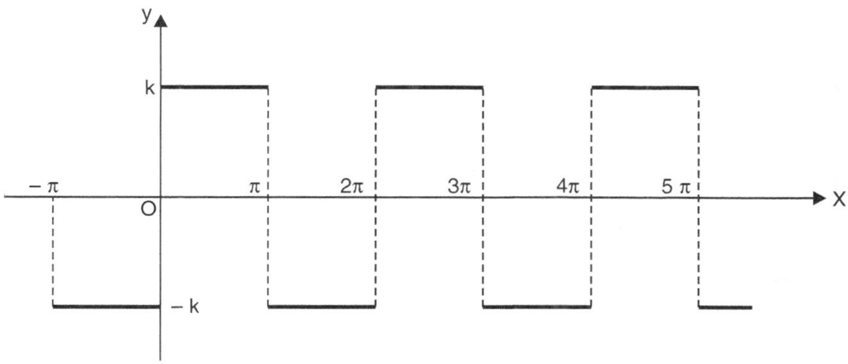


Its Fourier expansion is

$$f(x) = \frac{4k}{\pi}\left[\frac{\sin x}{1} + \frac{\sin 3x}{3} + \frac{\sin 5x}{5} + \ldots\ldots\right]$$

[See Question 1 in Test Your Knowledge on Page No. 19]

(*ii*)
$$f(x) = \begin{cases} 1 & \text{when } \; 0 < x < \pi \\ 0 & \text{when } \pi < x < 2\pi \end{cases}, \; f(x + 2\pi) = f(x)$$

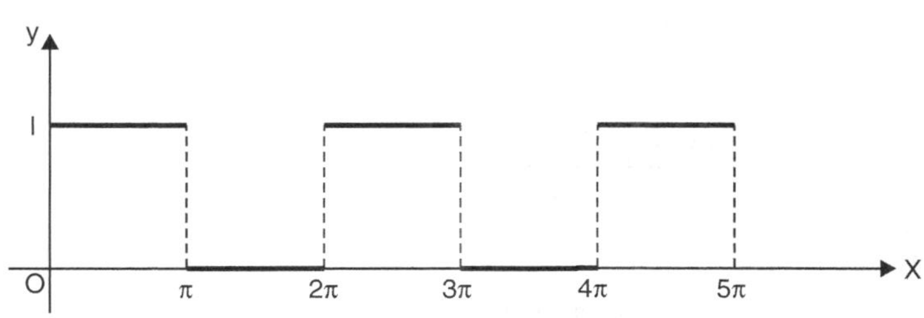

Its Fourier expansion is

$$f(x) = \frac{1}{2} + \frac{2}{\pi}\left(\frac{\sin x}{1} + \frac{\sin 3x}{3} + \frac{\sin 5x}{5} + \ldots\ldots\right)$$

*(iii)* $$f(x) = \begin{cases} 0 & \text{for } -\pi < x < 0 \\ 1 & \text{for } \quad 0 < x < \pi \end{cases}, f(x + 2\pi) = f(x)$$

Its Fourier expansion is

$$f(x) = \frac{1}{2} + \frac{2}{\pi}\left(\frac{\sin x}{1} + \frac{\sin 3x}{3} + \frac{\sin 5x}{5} + \ldots\ldots\right)$$

[See Question 2 in Test Your Knowledge on Page 20]

*(iv)* $$f(x) = \begin{cases} 1 & \text{for } 0 < x < \pi \\ 2 & \text{for } \pi < x < 2\pi \end{cases}, f(x + 2\pi) = f(x)$$

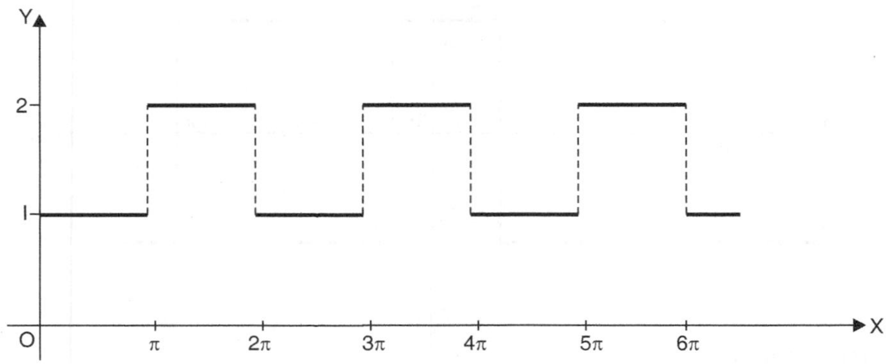


Its Fourier expansion is

$$f(x) = \frac{3}{2} - \frac{2}{\pi}\left(\frac{\sin x}{1} + \frac{\sin 3x}{3} + \frac{\sin 5x}{5} + \ldots\ldots\right)$$

*(v)* $$f(x) = \begin{cases} -\dfrac{\pi}{4} & \text{for } -\pi < x < 0 \\ \dfrac{\pi}{4} & \text{for } 0 < x < \pi \end{cases}, f(x + 2\pi) = f(x)$$

Its Fourier expansion is

$$f(x) = \frac{\sin x}{1} + \frac{\sin 3x}{3} + \frac{\sin 5x}{5} + \ldots\ldots$$

**II. Saw-toothed Waveform**

It is a periodic function of the form given below.

*(i)* $f(x) = x, -\pi < x < \pi$ and $f(x + 2\pi) = f(x)$

Its Fourier expansion is

$$f(x) = 2\left(\frac{\sin x}{1} - \frac{\sin 2x}{2} + \frac{\sin 3x}{3} - \frac{\sin 4x}{4} + \ldots\ldots\right)$$

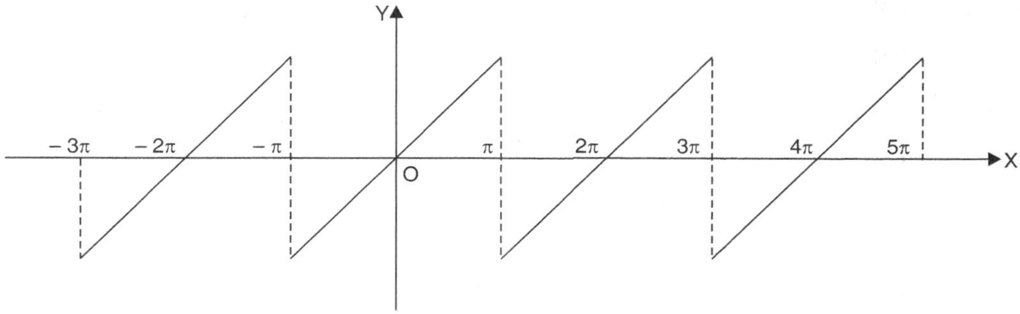


*(ii)* $$f(x) = \frac{1}{T}x \quad \text{when} \quad 0 < x < T \quad \text{and} \quad f(x + T) = f(x)$$

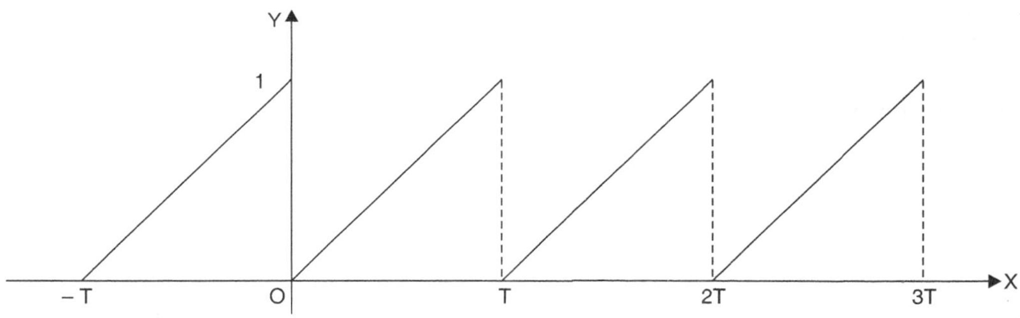


Its Fourier expansion is

$$f(x) = \frac{1}{2} - \frac{1}{\pi}\sum_{n=1}^{\infty} \frac{\sin n\omega x}{n}, \qquad \text{where } \omega = \frac{2\pi}{T}.$$

**III. Modified Saw-toothed Waveform**

It is a periodic function of the form given below.

$$f(x) = \begin{cases} \pi + x & \text{for } -\pi < x < 0 \\ 0 & \text{for } \ \ 0 \le x < \pi \end{cases}, f(x + 2\pi) = f(x)$$

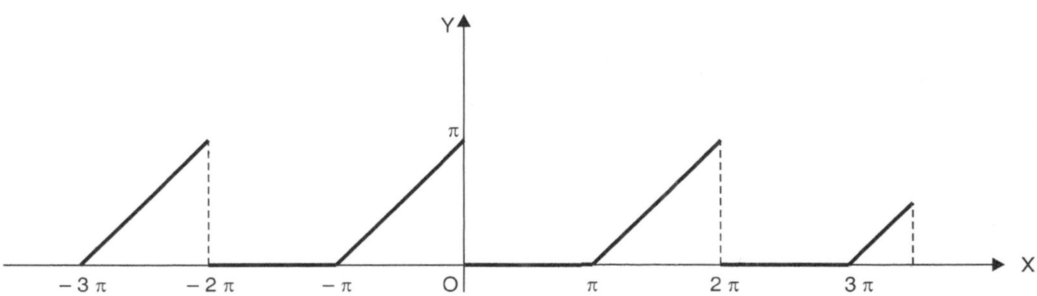

Its Fourier expansion is

$$f(x) = \frac{\pi}{4} + \frac{2}{\pi}\left(\frac{\cos x}{1^2} + \frac{\cos 3x}{3^2} + \ldots\ldots\right) - \left(\frac{\sin x}{1} + \frac{\sin 2x}{2} + \ldots\ldots\right)$$

## IV. Triangular Waveform

It is a periodic function of the form given below.

(*i*)
$$f(x) = \begin{cases} 2 + x & \text{for } -2 \le x \le 0 \\ 2 - x & \text{for } \quad 0 < x \le 2 \end{cases}, \; f(x+4) = f(x)$$

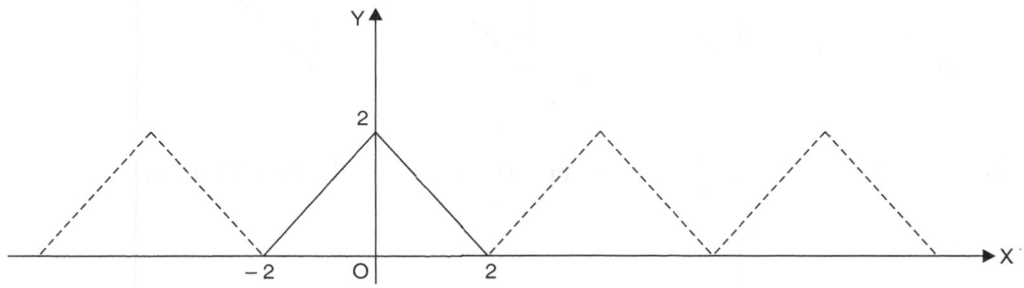


Its Fourier expansion is

$$f(x) = 1 + \frac{8}{\pi^2}\sum_{n=1}^{\infty} \frac{1}{n^2}\cos\left[(2n-1)\frac{\pi x}{2}\right]$$

(*ii*)
$$f(x) = \begin{cases} 1 + \dfrac{2x}{\pi} & \text{for } -\pi \le x \le 0 \\ 1 - \dfrac{2x}{\pi} & \text{for } \quad 0 < x \le \pi \end{cases}, \; f(x + 2\pi) = f(x)$$

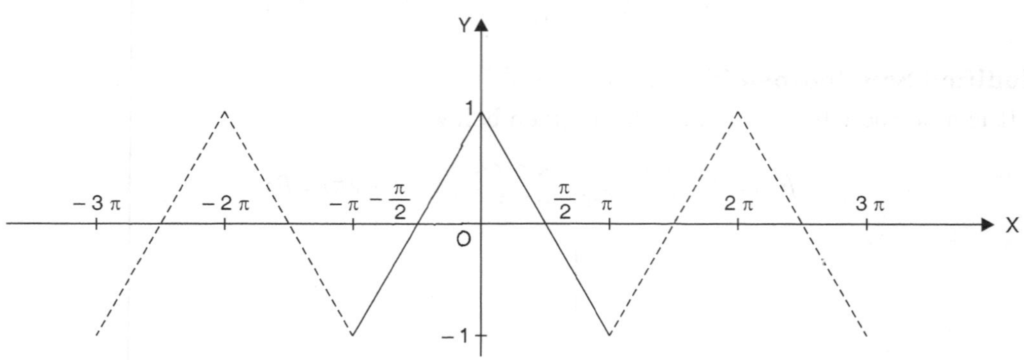

Its Fourier expansion is

$$f(x) = \frac{8}{\pi^2}\left(\frac{\cos x}{1^2} + \frac{\cos 3x}{3^2} + \frac{\cos 5x}{5^2} + \ldots\ldots\right)$$

[See Example 10 before Test Your Knowledge on Page 14]

**V. Half Rectified Waveform**

It is a periodic function of the form given below.

(*i*)
$$f(x) = \begin{cases} 0 & \text{for } -\pi \le x \le 0 \\ \sin x & \text{for } \ 0 \le x \le \pi \end{cases}$$

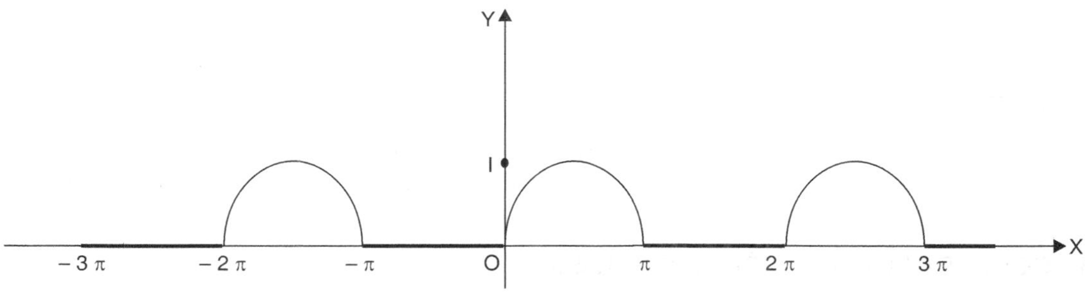


Its Fourier expansion is

$$f(x) = \frac{1}{\pi} + \frac{1}{2}\sin x - \frac{2}{\pi}\sum_{n=1}^{\infty} \frac{\cos 2nx}{4n^2 - 1}$$

(*ii*)
$$f(x) = \begin{cases} I_0 \sin x & \text{for } \ 0 \le x \le \pi \\ 0 & \text{for } \pi \le x \le 2\pi \end{cases}, f(x + 2\pi) = f(x)$$

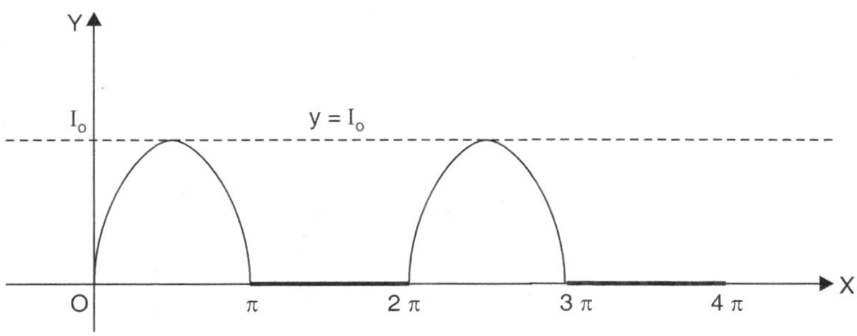


Its Fourier expansion is

$$f(x) = \frac{I_0}{\pi} + \frac{1}{2} I_0 \sin x - \frac{2I_0}{\pi}\sum_{n=1}^{\infty} \frac{\cos 2nx}{4n^2 - 1}$$

[See Question 6 in Test Your Knowledge on Page 19]

### VI. Full Rectified Waveform

It is a periodic function of the form given below.

$$f(x) = a \sin x \text{ for } 0 \le x \le \pi,\ f(x + \pi) = f(x)$$

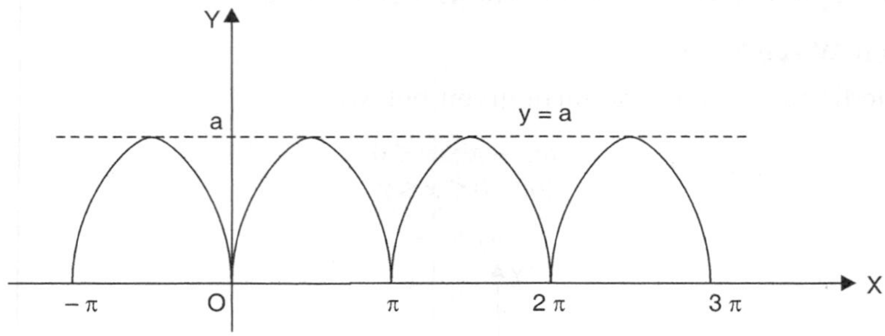


Its Fourier expansion is

$$f(x) = \frac{4a}{\pi}\left[\frac{1}{2} - \frac{\cos 2x}{1.3} - \frac{\cos 4x}{3.5} - \frac{\cos 6x}{5.7} - \ldots\ldots\right]$$

## 1.11. COMPLEX FORM OF FOURIER SERIES

We know that in the interval $c < x < c + 2l$, the Fourier series expansion of $f(x)$ can be written as

$$f(x) = \frac{a_0}{2} + \sum_{n=1}^{\infty}\left(a_n \cos\frac{n\pi x}{l} + b_n \sin\frac{n\pi x}{l}\right) \qquad \ldots(1)$$

We also know that $\cos\theta = \frac{1}{2}(e^{i\theta} + e^{-i\theta})$ and $\sin\theta = \frac{1}{2i}(e^{i\theta} - e^{-i\theta})$

Substituting the exponential equivalents for the trigonometric terms in (1), we get

$$f(x) = \frac{a_0}{2} + \sum_{n=1}^{\infty} a_n\left(\frac{e^{\frac{in\pi x}{l}} + e^{-\frac{in\pi x}{l}}}{2}\right) + \sum_{n=1}^{\infty} b_n\left(\frac{e^{\frac{in\pi x}{l}} - e^{-\frac{in\pi x}{l}}}{2i}\right)$$

$$= \frac{a_0}{2} + \sum_{n=1}^{\infty}\left(\frac{a_n - ib_n}{2}\right)e^{\frac{in\pi x}{l}} + \sum_{n=1}^{\infty}\left(\frac{a_n + ib_n}{2}\right)e^{-\frac{in\pi x}{l}} \qquad \left[\because \frac{1}{i} = -i\right]$$

$$= c_0 + \sum_{n=1}^{\infty} c_n e^{\frac{in\pi x}{l}} + \sum_{n=1}^{\infty} c_{-n}\, e^{-\frac{in\pi x}{l}} = \sum_{n=1}^{\infty} e^{\frac{in\pi x}{l}}$$

where $c_0 = \frac{a_0}{2},\ c_n = \frac{a_n - ib_n}{2},\ c_{-n} = \frac{a_n + ib_n}{2}$

Hence the *complex* or *exponential* form of the Fourier series is

$$\mathbf{f(x)} = \sum_{n=-\infty}^{\infty} \mathbf{c_n e^{\frac{in\pi x}{l}}} \qquad \ldots(2)$$

Now multiplying on both sides of (2) by $e^{-\frac{in\pi x}{l}}$ and integrating from $c$ to $c + 2l$ w.r.t. $x$, we get

$$\int_c^{c+2l} f(x) . e^{-\frac{in\pi x}{l}} dx = c_n \int_c^{c+2l} e^{\frac{in\pi x}{l}} e^{-\frac{in\pi x}{l}} dx$$

$$= c_n \int_c^{c+2l} dx = c_n [x]_c^{c+2l} = c_n (2l)$$

$$\therefore \qquad \mathbf{c_n = \frac{1}{2l} \int_c^{c+2l} f(x)\, e^{-\frac{in\pi x}{l}} dx.}$$

## ILLUSTRATIVE EXAMPLES

**Example 1.** *Find the complex form of Fourier series $f(x) = e^{ax}$ $(-\pi < x < \pi)$ in the form*

$$e^{ax} = \frac{\sinh a\pi}{\pi} \sum_{n=-\infty}^{\infty} (-1)^n \frac{a + in}{a^2 + n^2} e^{inx}$$

*and hence prove that* $\dfrac{\pi}{a \sinh a\pi} = \displaystyle\sum_{n=-\infty}^{\infty} \frac{(-1)^n}{n^2 + a^2}$.

**Sol.** The complex form of Fourier series of $f(x)$ in $c < x < c + 2l$ is given by

$$f(x) = \sum_{n=-\infty}^{\infty} c_n e^{\frac{in\pi x}{l}} \qquad \text{where } c_n = \frac{1}{2l} \int_c^{c+2l} f(x)\, e^{-\frac{in\pi x}{l}} dx$$

Here $2l = 2\pi \Rightarrow l = \pi \quad \therefore \quad f(x) = \displaystyle\sum_{n=-\infty}^{\infty} c_n e^{inx}$ ...(1)

Now

$$c_n = \frac{1}{2\pi} \int_{-\pi}^{\pi} f(x)\, e^{-\frac{in\pi x}{\pi}} dx$$

$$= \frac{1}{2\pi} \int_{-\pi}^{\pi} f(x)\, e^{-inx} dx = \frac{1}{2\pi} \int_{-\pi}^{\pi} e^{ax} . e^{-inx} dx \qquad [\because \ f(x) = e^{ax}]$$

$$= \frac{1}{2\pi} \int_{-\pi}^{\pi} e^{(a-in)x} dx = \frac{1}{2\pi} \left[ \frac{e^{(a-in)x}}{(a-in)} \right]_{-\pi}^{\pi} = \frac{1}{2\pi} \left[ \frac{e^{(a-in)\pi} - e^{-(a-in)\pi}}{a - in} \right]$$

$$= \frac{1}{2\pi} \left[ \frac{e^{a\pi} (\cos n\pi - i \sin n\pi) - e^{-a\pi} (\cos n\pi + i \sin n\pi)}{a - in} \right]$$

$$(e^{\pm in\pi} = \cos n\pi \pm i \sin n\pi)$$

$$= \frac{1}{2\pi(a-in)}(e^{a\pi} - e^{-a\pi})\cos n\pi = \frac{1}{2\pi(a-in)}(2\sinh a\pi)\cos n\pi$$

$$\left(\because \frac{e^{a\pi}-e^{-a\pi}}{2} = \sinh a\pi\right)$$

$$= \frac{(-1)^n \sinh a\pi}{\pi(a-in)} \qquad [\because \cos n\pi = (-1)^n]$$

or
$$c_n = \frac{(-1)^n (a+in)\sinh a\pi}{\pi(a^2+n^2)}$$

Substituting in (1), we get

$$f(x) = \sum_{n=-\infty}^{\infty} \frac{(-1)^n (a+in)\sinh a\pi}{\pi(a^2+n^2)} e^{inx}$$

*i.e.,*
$$e^{ax} = \frac{\sinh a\pi}{\pi} \sum_{n=-\infty}^{\infty} \frac{(-1)^n (a+in)}{a^2+n^2} e^{inx} \qquad ...(2)$$

Putting $x = 0$ in (2), we get $1 = \dfrac{\sinh a\pi}{\pi} \displaystyle\sum_{n=-\infty}^{\infty} \frac{(-1)^n (a+in)}{a^2+n^2}$

or
$$\frac{\pi}{\sinh a\pi} = \sum_{n=-\infty}^{\infty} (-1)^n \left\{\frac{a}{a^2+n^2} + i\frac{n}{a^2+n^2}\right\}$$

Equating the real part, we get

$$\frac{\pi}{\sinh a\pi} = \sum_{n=-\infty}^{\infty} (-1)^n \frac{a}{a^2+n^2} \quad \text{or} \quad \frac{\pi}{a\sinh a\pi} = \sum_{n=-\infty}^{\infty} \frac{(-1)^n}{a^2+n^2}$$

which proves the result.

**Example 2.** *Find the complex form of the Fourier series of*

*$f(x) = \cos ax$ in $-\pi < x < \pi$.*

**Sol.** The complex form of Fourier series in $-\pi$ to $\pi$ is given by

$$f(x) = \sum_{n=-\infty}^{\infty} C_n e^{inx} \qquad ...(1) \quad \text{where} \quad C_n = \frac{1}{2\pi}\int_{-\pi}^{\pi} f(x)\, e^{-inx}\, dx$$

$$C_n = \frac{1}{2\pi}\int_{-\pi}^{\pi} \cos ax \,.\, e^{-inx}\, dx = \frac{1}{2\pi}\left[\frac{e^{-inx}}{(-in)^2+a^2}\{-\text{in}\cos ax + a\sin ax\}\right]_{-\pi}^{\pi}$$

$$\left[\because \int e^{ax}\cos(bx+c) = \frac{e^{ax}}{a^2+b^2}\{a\cos(bx+c) + b\sin(bx+c)\}\right]$$

$$= \frac{1}{2\pi(a^2-n^2)}[e^{-inx}(-in\cos a\pi + a\sin a\pi) - e^{inx}(-in\cos a\pi - a\sin a\pi)]$$

$$= \frac{1}{2\pi(a^2 - n^2)} [\cos n\pi \{- in \cos a\pi + a \sin a\pi + in \cos a\pi + a \sin a\pi\}]$$

$$[\because e^{\pm inx} = \cos n\pi \pm i \sin n\pi = \cos n\pi = (-1)^n]$$

$$\therefore \qquad C_n = \frac{(-1)^n a \sin a\pi}{\pi(a^2 - n^2)}$$

Substituting in (1)

$$f(x) = \cos ax = \sum_{n=-\infty}^{\infty} \frac{(-1)^n a \sin a\pi}{\pi(a^2 - n^2)} e^{inx} = \frac{a \sin a\pi}{\pi} \sum_{n=-\infty}^{\infty} \frac{(-1)^n}{a^2 - n^2} e^{inx}.$$

## TEST YOUR KNOWLEDGE

1. Derive the complex form (or exponential form) of Fourier series for $f(x)$ in $-\pi < x < \pi$.
2. Find the complex form of Fourier series for $e^x$ in $-\pi < x < \pi$.
3. Find the complex form of Fourier series for $e^{-x}$ in $-1 < x < 1$.
4. Find the complex form of the Fourier series for the function $e^{\alpha x}$ in $-\pi < x < \pi$, given that $\alpha$ is a real constant. Deduce that

(*i*) When $\alpha$ is a constant other than an integer $\cos \alpha x = \dfrac{\sin \pi\alpha}{\pi} \displaystyle\sum_{n=-\infty}^{\infty} (-1)^n \frac{\alpha}{\alpha^2 - n^2} e^{inx}$ where $-\pi < x < \pi$ and

(*ii*) $\displaystyle\sum_{n=-\infty}^{\infty} \frac{(-1)^n}{n^2 + a^2} = \frac{\pi}{a \sinh a\pi}$.

### Answers

1. $f(x) = \displaystyle\sum_{n=-\infty}^{\infty} c_n e^{-inx}$ ; $c_n = \dfrac{1}{2\pi} \displaystyle\int_{-\pi}^{\pi} f(x)\, e^{-inx}\, dx$ **2.** $e^x = \dfrac{\sinh \pi}{\pi} \displaystyle\sum_{n=-\infty}^{\infty} (-1)^n \left(\frac{1 + in}{1 + n^2}\right) e^{inx}$

3. $e^{-x} = \displaystyle\sum_{n=-\infty}^{\infty} (-1)^n (\sinh 1) \left(\frac{1 - in\pi}{1 + n^2 \pi^2}\right) e^{in\pi x}$.

## 1.12. PRACTICAL HARMONIC ANALYSIS

When the function $f(x)$ is not given by an analytical expression, rather by its graph or a table of corresponding values at a number of equi-spaced points, we cannot evaluate the integrals for Fourier co-efficients. However, using the rules of approximate integration, we can find approximate values of the first few terms of the Fourier expansions.

Let the Fourier series for $y = f(x)$ in $(0, 2\pi)$ by

$$y = \frac{a_0}{2} + a_1 \cos x + a_2 \cos 2x + \ldots\ldots + b_1 \sin x + b_2 \sin 2x + \ldots\ldots$$

where $a_0 = \dfrac{1}{\pi} \displaystyle\int_0^{2\pi} y\, dx$, $a_n = \dfrac{1}{\pi} \displaystyle\int_0^{2\pi} y \cos nx\, dx$ ; $b_n = \dfrac{1}{\pi} \displaystyle\int_0^{2\pi} y \sin nx\, dx$.

Let the range $(0, 2\pi)$ be divided into $m$ equal parts by the points $x = x_0, x_1, x_2 ......, x_m = 2\pi$ so that each sub-interval is of the length $\frac{2\pi}{m}$. Let the ordinates at these points be denoted by $y_0, y_1, y_2, ......, y_m$.

Using the trapezoidal rule of approximate integration, we get

$$a_0 = \frac{1}{\pi}\int_0^{2\pi} y dx \approx \frac{1}{\pi} \cdot \frac{2\pi}{m} (y_0 + y_1 + y_2 + ...... + y_{m-1}) = 2 \times \frac{1}{m}\sum_{r=0}^{m-1} y_r$$

$$= 2 \text{ [mean value of } y \text{ in } (0, 2\pi)]$$

$$a_n = \frac{1}{\pi}\int_0^{2\pi} y \cos nx \, dx$$

$$\approx \frac{1}{\pi} \cdot \frac{2\pi}{m} (y_0 \cos nx_0 + y_1 \cos nx_1 + ...... + y_{m-1} \cos nx_{m-1})$$

$$= 2 \times \frac{1}{m}\sum_{r=0}^{m-1} y_r \cos nx_r = 2 \text{ [mean value of } y \cos nx \text{ in } (0, 2\pi)]$$

$$b_n = \frac{1}{\pi}\int_0^{2\pi} y \sin nx \, dx \approx \frac{1}{\pi} \cdot \frac{2\pi}{m} (y_0 \sin nx_0 + y_1 \sin nx_1 + ...... + y_{m-1} \sin nx_{m-1})$$

$$= 2 \times \frac{1}{m}\sum_{r=0}^{m-1} y_r \sin nx_r$$

$$= 2 \text{ [mean value of } y \sin nx \text{ in } (0, 2\pi)]$$

The process of finding the Fourier series for a function given by numerical values is known as *harmonic analysis*.

The term $(a_1 \cos x + b_1 \sin x)$ is called the *fundamental* or *first harmonic*, the term $(a_2 \cos 2x + b_2 \sin 2x)$ is called the *second harmonic* and so on.

*The number of ordinates used should not be less than twice the number of highest harmonic to be found.*

## ILLUSTRATIVE EXAMPLES

**Example 1.** *Analyse harmonically the data given below and express y in Fourier series upto the third harmonic :*

| $x$ : | 0 | $\frac{\pi}{3}$ | $\frac{2\pi}{3}$ | $\pi$ | $\frac{4\pi}{3}$ | $\frac{5\pi}{3}$ | $2\pi$ |
|---|---|---|---|---|---|---|---|
| $y$ : | 1.0 | 1.4 | 1.9 | 1.7 | 1.5 | 1.2 | 1.0 |

**Sol.** Since the last value of $y$ is a repetition of the first, only the first six values will be used. The length of the interval is $2\pi$.

Let $\quad y = \frac{a_0}{2} + (a_1 \cos x + b_1 \sin x) + (a_2 \cos 2x + b_2 \sin 2x) + (a_3 \cos 3x + b_3 \sin 3x)$

The values of $x$, $y$, $\sin x$, $\cos x$, $\sin 2x$, $\cos 2x$, $\sin 3x$, $\cos 3x$ are tabulated below :

| $x$ | $y$ | $\cos x$ | $\sin x$ | $\cos 2x$ | $\sin 2x$ | $\cos 3x$ | $\sin 3x$ |
|---|---|---|---|---|---|---|---|
| 0 | 1.0 | 1 | 0 | 1 | 0 | 1 | 0 |
| $\frac{\pi}{3}$ | 1.4 | 0.5 | 0.866 | – 0.5 | 0.866 | – 1 | 0 |
| $\frac{2\pi}{3}$ | 1.9 | – 0.5 | 0.866 | – 0.5 | – 0.866 | 1 | 0 |
| $\pi$ | 1.7 | – 1 | 0 | 1 | 0 | – 1 | 0 |
| $\frac{4\pi}{3}$ | 1.5 | – 0.5 | 0.866 | – 0.5 | 0.866 | 1 | 0 |
| $\frac{5\pi}{3}$ | 1.2 | 0.5 | – 0.866 | – 0.5 | – 0.866 | – 1 | 0 |

Using the values in the above table, we have

$$a_0 = \frac{2}{n} \Sigma y = \frac{2}{6}(8.7) = 2.9$$

$$a_1 = \frac{2}{n} \Sigma y \cos x = \frac{2}{6}[1(1.0 - 1.7) + 0.5\,(1.4 - 1.9 - 1.5 + 1.2)] = \frac{1}{3}(-1.1) \approx -0.37$$

$$b_1 = \frac{2}{n} \Sigma y \sin x = \frac{2}{6}[0.866\,(1.4 + 1.9 - 1.5 - 1.2)] = \frac{1}{3}[0.866\,(.6)] \approx 0.17$$

$$a_2 = \frac{2}{n} \Sigma y \cos 2x = \frac{2}{6}[1(1.0 + 1.7) - 0.5(1.4 + 1.9 - 1.5 + 1.2)] = \frac{1}{3}[2.7 - 3] = 0.1$$

$$b_2 = \frac{2}{n} \Sigma y \sin 2x = \frac{2}{6}[0.866\,(1.4 - 1.9 + 1.5 - 1.2)] = \frac{1}{3}[0.866\,(-2)] = -0.06$$

$$a_3 = \frac{2}{n} \Sigma y \cos 3x = \frac{2}{6}[1.0 - 1.4 + 1.9 - 1.7 + 1.5 - 1.2] = \frac{1}{3}(0.1) = 0.03$$

$$b_3 = \frac{2}{n} \Sigma y \sin 3x = 0$$

$$\therefore \quad y = 1.45 + (-0.37 \cos x + 0.17 \sin x) - (0.1 \cos 2x + 0.06 \sin 2x) + 0.03 \cos 3x.$$

**Example 2.** *The following values of y give the displacement in inches of a certain machine part for the rotation x of the flywheel. Expand y in the form of a Fourier series :*

| $x$ : | 0 | $\frac{\pi}{6}$ | $\frac{2\pi}{6}$ | $\frac{3\pi}{6}$ | $\frac{4\pi}{6}$ | $\frac{5\pi}{6}$ |
|---|---|---|---|---|---|---|
| $y$ : | 0 | 9.2 | 14.4 | 17.8 | 17.3 | 11.7 |

**Sol.** Here length of interval is $\pi$, *i.e.*, $l = \frac{\pi}{2}$

Let
$$y = \frac{a_0}{2} + \left(a_1 \cos \frac{\pi x}{\pi/2} + b_1 \sin \frac{\pi x}{\pi/2}\right) + \left(a_2 \cos \frac{2\pi x}{\pi/2} + b_2 \sin \frac{\pi x}{\pi/2}\right) + \ldots\ldots$$

$$= \frac{a_0}{2} + (a_1 \cos 2x + b_1 \sin 2x) + (a_2 \cos 4x + b_2 \sin 4x) + \ldots\ldots$$

The values of $x$, $y$, sin $2x$, cos $2x$, sin $4x$, cos $4x$ are tabulated below :

| $x$ | $y$ | $\cos 2x$ | $\sin 2x$ | $\cos 4x$ | $\sin 4x$ |
|---|---|---|---|---|---|
| 0 | 0 | 1 | 0 | 1 | 0 |
| $\frac{\pi}{6}$ | 9.2 | .5 | .87 | – .5 | .87 |
| $\frac{2\pi}{6}$ | 14.4 | – .5 | .87 | – .5 | – .87 |
| $\frac{3\pi}{6}$ | 17.8 | – 1 | 0 | 1 | 0 |
| $\frac{4\pi}{6}$ | 17.3 | – .5 | – .87 | – .5 | .87 |
| $\frac{5\pi}{6}$ | 11.7 | .5 | – .87 | – .5 | – 8.7 |

Using the values in the above table, we have

$$a_0 = \frac{2}{n} \Sigma y = \frac{2}{6}(70.4) = 23.46$$

$$a_1 = \frac{2}{n} \Sigma y \cos 2x = \frac{2}{6} [.5(9.2 - 14.4 - 17.3 + 11.7) - 17.8]$$

$$= \frac{1}{3}(-23.2) = -7.73$$

$$b_1 = \frac{2}{n} \Sigma y \sin 2x = \frac{2}{6} [.87(9.2 + 14.4 - 17.3 - 11.7)]$$

$$= \frac{1}{3} [.87(-5.4)] = -1.566$$

$$a_2 = \frac{2}{n} \Sigma y \cos 4x = \frac{2}{6} [-.5 (9.2 + 14.4 + 17.3 + 11.7) + 17.8]$$

$$= \frac{1}{3} [-26.3 + 17.8] = \frac{1}{3}(-8.5) = -2.83$$

$$b_2 = \frac{2}{n} \Sigma y \sin 4x = \frac{2}{6} [87 (9.2 - 14.4 + 17.3 - 11.7)] = \frac{1}{3} [.87 (4)] = .116$$

$$\therefore \quad y = 11.73 - (7.73 \cos 2x + 1.566 \sin 2x) + (-2.83 \cos 4x + .116 \sin 4x).$$

**Example 3.** *Obtain the constant term and the co-efficients of the first sine and cosine terms in the Fourier expansion of y as given in the following table :*

| $x$ : | 0 | 1 | 2 | 3 | 4 | 5 |
|---|---|---|---|---|---|---|
| $y$ : | 9 | 18 | 24 | 28 | 26 | 20 |

**Sol.** Let the Fourier series to represent $y$ be

$$y = \frac{a_0}{2} + \left(a_1 \cos \frac{\pi x}{3} + b_1 \sin \frac{\pi x}{3}\right) + \left(a_2 \cos \frac{2\pi x}{3} + b_2 \sin \frac{2\pi x}{3}\right) + \ldots\ldots$$

The values of $x$, $y$, $\sin\frac{\pi x}{3}$, $\cos\frac{\pi x}{3}$ are tabulated below :

| $x$ | $y$ | $\cos\frac{\pi x}{3}$ | $\sin\frac{\pi x}{3}$ |
|---|---|---|---|
| 0 | 9 | 1 | 0 |
| 1 | 18 | $\frac{1}{2}$ | $\frac{\sqrt{3}}{2}$ |
| 2 | 24 | $-\frac{1}{2}$ | $\frac{\sqrt{3}}{2}$ |
| 3 | 28 | $-1$ | 0 |
| 4 | 26 | $-\frac{1}{2}$ | $-\frac{\sqrt{3}}{2}$ |
| 5 | 20 | $\frac{1}{2}$ | $-\frac{\sqrt{3}}{2}$ |

Using the values in the above table, we have

$$a_0 = \frac{2}{n}\Sigma y = \frac{2}{6}(125) = 41.67$$

$$a_1 = \frac{2}{n}\Sigma y\cos\frac{\pi x}{3} = \frac{2}{6}\left[9 - 28 + \tfrac{1}{2}(18 - 24 - 26 + 20)\right] = \tfrac{1}{3}[-19 - 6] = -8.33$$

$$b_1 = \frac{2}{n}\Sigma y\sin\frac{\pi x}{3} = \frac{2}{6}\left[\frac{\sqrt{3}}{2}(18 + 24 - 26 - 20)\right] = \frac{\sqrt{3}}{6}(-4) = -\frac{2\sqrt{3}}{3} = -1.15.$$

**Example 4.** *The following table gives the variations of periodic current over a period :*

| *t (secs.) :* | *0* | *T/6* | *T/3* | *T/2* | *2T/3* | *5T/6* | *T* |
|---|---|---|---|---|---|---|---|
| *A (amp.) :* | *1.98* | *1.30* | *1.05* | *1.30* | *– 0.88* | *– 0.25* | *1.98* |

*Show, by numerical analysis, that there is a direct current part of 0.75 amp. in the variable current and obtain the amplitude of the first harmonic.*

**Sol.** Hence length of interval is T *i.e.*, $l = \frac{T}{2}$

Let
$$A = \frac{a_0}{2} + a_1\cos\frac{2\pi t}{T} + b_1\sin\frac{2\pi t}{T} + \ldots\ldots$$

where $\frac{a_0}{2}$ represents the direct current part and $\sqrt{a_1^2 + b_1^2}$ gives the amplitude of the first harmonic.

The values of $t$, A, $\sin \frac{2\pi t}{T}$, $\cos \frac{2\pi t}{T}$ are tabulated below :

| $t$ | A | $\cos \frac{2\pi t}{T}$ | $\sin \frac{2\pi t}{T}$ |
|---|---|---|---|
| 0 | 1.98 | 1 | 0 |
| T/6 | 1.30 | 0.5 | 0.866 |
| T/3 | 1.05 | – 0.5 | 0.866 |
| T/2 | 1.30 | – 1 | 0 |
| 2T/3 | – 0.88 | – 0.5 | – 0.866 |
| 5T/6 | – 0.25 | 0.5 | – 0.866 |

Using the values in the above table, we have

$$a_0 = \frac{2}{n} \Sigma A = \frac{2}{6} (4.5) = 1.50$$

$$a_1 = \frac{2}{n} \Sigma A \cos \frac{2\pi t}{T} = \frac{2}{6} [1.98 - 1.30 + 0.5 (1.30 - 1.05 + 0.88 - 0.25)]$$

$$= \frac{1}{3} [0.68 + 0.5 (.88)] = \frac{1}{3} (1.12) = 0.373$$

$$b_1 = \frac{2}{n} \Sigma A \sin \frac{2\pi t}{T} = \frac{2}{6} [0.866 (1.30 + 1.05 + 0.88 + 0.25)]$$

$$= \frac{1}{3} [0.866 \times 3.48] = 1.005$$

$$\therefore \quad A = 0.75 + 0.373 \cos \frac{2\pi t}{T} + 1.005 \sin \frac{2\pi t}{T} + \ldots\ldots$$

Direct current part $= \frac{a_0}{2} = 0.75$ amp.

The amplitude of the first harmonic $= \sqrt{a_1^2 + b_1^2} = \sqrt{(0.373)^2 + (1.005)^2} = 1.072$.

**Example 5.** *The turning moment T units of the crank shaft of a steam engine is given for a series of values of the crank-angle θ in degrees :*

| θ : | 0 | 30 | 60 | 90 | 120 | 150 | 180 |
|---|---|---|---|---|---|---|---|
| T : | 0 | 5224 | 8097 | 7850 | 5499 | 2626 | 0 |

*Find the first four terms in a series of sines to represent T. Also calculate T when θ = 75°.*

**Sol.** Let the half-range sine series to represent T be

$$T = b_1 \sin \theta + b_2 \sin 2\theta + b_3 \sin 3\theta + b_4 \sin 4\theta$$

The values of θ, T, sinθ, sin 2θ, sin 3θ, sin 4θ are tabulated below :

| θ | T | sin θ | sin 2θ | sin 3θ | sin 4θ |
|---|---|---|---|---|---|
| 0 | 0 | 0 | 0 | 0 | 0 |
| 30 | 5224 | 0.5 | 0.866 | 1 | 0.866 |
| 60 | 8097 | 0.866 | 0.866 | 0 | – 0.866 |
| 90 | 7850 | 1 | 0 | – 1 | 0 |
| 120 | 5499 | 0.866 | – 0.866 | 0 | 0.866 |
| 150 | 2626 | 0.5 | – 0.866 | 1 | – 0.866 |

Using the values in the above table, we have

$$b_1 = \frac{2}{n}\Sigma \text{T} \sin \theta$$

$$= \frac{2}{6}[0.5\,(5224 + 2626) + 0.866\,(8097 + 5499) + 7850]$$

$$= \frac{1}{3}(3925 + 11774 + 7850) = \frac{1}{3}(23549) = 7850$$

$$b_2 = \frac{2}{n}\Sigma \text{T} \sin 2\theta = \frac{2}{6}[0.866\,(5224 + 8097 - 5499 - 2626)]$$

$$= \frac{1}{3}[0.866 \times 5196] = 1500$$

$$b_3 = \frac{2}{n}\Sigma \text{T} \sin 3\theta = \frac{2}{6}[5224 - 7850 + 2626] = 0$$

$$b_4 = \frac{2}{n}\Sigma \text{T} \sin 4\theta = \frac{2}{6}[0.866\,(5224 - 8097 + 5499 - 2626)] = 0$$

$\therefore$ $\text{T} = 7850 \sin \theta + 1500 \sin 2\theta$

When $\theta = 75°$, $\text{T} = 7850 \sin 75° + 1500 \sin 150°$

$$= 7850 \times 0.9659 + 1500 \times 0.5 = 8332.$$

## TEST YOUR KNOWLEDGE

**1.** The following values of $y$ give the displacement of a certain machine part for the rotation $x$ of the flywheel

| $x$ : | 0° | 60° | 120° | 180° | 240° | 300° | 360° |
|---|---|---|---|---|---|---|---|
| $y$ : | 1.98 | 2.15 | 2.77 | – 0.22 | – 0.31 | 1.43 | 1.98 |

Express $y$ in Fourier series upto the third harmonic.

**2.** The displacement $y$ of a part of a mechanism is tabulated with corresponding angular movement $x°$ of the crank. Express $y$ as a Fourier series neglecting the harmonics above the third.

| $x°$ : | 0 | 30 | 60 | 90 | 120 | 150 | 180 | 210 | 240 | 270 | 300 | 330 |
|---|---|---|---|---|---|---|---|---|---|---|---|---|
| $y$ : | 1.80 | 1.10 | 0.30 | 0.16 | 0.50 | 1.30 | 2.16 | 1.25 | 1.30 | 1.52 | 1.76 | 2.00 |

**3.** Determine the first two harmonics of the Fourier series for the following values :

| $x°$ : | 30 | 60 | 90 | 120 | 150 | 180 | 210 | 240 | 270 | 300 | 330 | 360 |
|---|---|---|---|---|---|---|---|---|---|---|---|---|
| $y$ : | 2.34 | 3.01 | 3.68 | 4.15 | 3.69 | 2.20 | 0.83 | 0.51 | 0.88 | 1.09 | 1.19 | 1.64 |

**4.** In a machine the displacement $y$ of a given point is given for a certain angle $\theta$ as follows :

| $\theta°$ = | 0 | 30 | 60 | 90 | 120 | 150 | 180 | 210 | 240 | 270 | 300 | 330 |
|---|---|---|---|---|---|---|---|---|---|---|---|---|
| $y$ = | 7.9 | 8.0 | 7.2 | 5.6 | 3.6 | 1.7 | 0.5 | 0.2 | 0.9 | 2.5 | 4.7 | 6.8 |

Find the co-efficient of $\sin 2\theta$ in the Fourier series representing the above variation.

**5.** Obtain the first three co-efficients in the Fourier cosine series for $y$, where $y$ is given in the following table :

| $x$ : | 0 | 1 | 2 | 3 | 4 | 5 |
|---|---|---|---|---|---|---|
| $y$ : | 4 | 8 | 15 | 7 | 6 | 2 |

**6.** The turning moment T on the crank-shaft of a steam engine for the crank angle θ degrees is given as follows :

| θ : | 0 | 15 | 30 | 45 | 60 | 75 | 90 | 105 | 120 | 135 | 150 | 165 | 180 |
|---|---|---|---|---|---|---|---|---|---|---|---|---|---|
| $T$ : | 0 | 2.7 | 5.2 | 7.0 | 8.1 | 8.3 | 7.9 | 6.8 | 5.5 | 4.1 | 2.6 | 1.2 | 0 |

Expand T in a series of sines upto third harmonics.

## Answers

**1.** $y = 1.3 + (0.92 \cos x + 1.097 \sin x) - (0.42 \cos 2x + 0.681 \sin 2x) + 0.36 \cos 3x$

**2.** $y = 1.26 + (0.04 \cos x - 0.63 \sin x) + (0.53 \cos 2x - 0.23 \sin 2x) + (-0.1 \cos 3x + 0.085 \sin 3x)$

**3.** $y = 2.102 - 0.283 \cos x + 1.60 \sin x - 0.18 \cos 2x - 0.49 \sin 2x$

**4.** $-0.072$ **5.** $y = 7 - 2.8 \cos \theta - 1.5 \cos 2\theta + 2.7 \cos 3\theta$

**6.** $T = 7.8 \sin \theta + 1.5 \sin 2\theta - 0.03 \sin 3\theta$.

# 2
# Fourier Transform

## 2.1. INTEGRAL TRANSFORMS

The integral transform $\bar{f}(s)$ of a function $f(x)$ is defined by the equation

$$I\{f(x)\} = \bar{f}(s) = \int_a^b f(x)\, K(s, x)\, dx,$$

where $K(s, x)$ is a known function of $s$ and $x$, called the **kernel** of the transform ; $s$ is called the **parameter** of the transform and $f(x)$ is called the **inverse transform** of $\bar{f}(s)$.

Some of the well-known transforms are given below :

(*i*) **Laplace Transform.** $K(s, x) = e^{-sx}$

$$L\{f(x)\} = \bar{f}(s) = \int_0^\infty f(x)\, e^{-sx}\, dx$$

(*ii*) **Complex Fourier Transform**

$$F\{f(x)\} = \bar{f}(s) = \frac{1}{\sqrt{2\pi}} \int_{-\infty}^{\infty} f(x)\, e^{isx}\, dx$$

(*iii*) **Fourier Sine Transform**

$$F_s\{f(x)\} = \bar{f}(s) = \sqrt{\frac{2}{\pi}} \int_0^\infty f(x) \sin sx\, dx$$

(*iv*) **Fourier Cosine Transform**

$$F_c\{f(x)\} = \bar{f}(s) = \sqrt{\frac{2}{\pi}} \int_0^\infty f(x) \cos sx\, dx$$

(*v*) **Hankel Transform.** $K(s, x) = x\, J_n(sx)$

$$H_n\{f(x)\} = \bar{f}(s) = \int_0^\infty f(x)\, x J_n(sx)\, dx$$

where $J_n(sx)$ is the Bessel function of the first kind and order $n$.

(*vi*) **Mellin Transform.** $K(s, x) = x^{s-1}$

$$M\{f(x)\} = \bar{f}(s) = \int_0^\infty f(x)\, x^{s-1}\, dx$$

We have already discussed Laplace transform and its application to the solution of ordinary differential equations. In the present chapter, we shall discuss other transforms and their application to the solution of partial differential equations.

The effect of applying an integral transform to a partial differential equation is to reduce the number of independent variables by one. The choice of a particular transform is decided by the nature of the boundary conditions and the facility with which the transform $\bar{f}(s)$ can be inverted to give $f(x)$.

## 2.2. FOURIER INTEGRAL THEOREM

Consider a function $f(x)$ satisfying Dirichlet's conditions in every interval $(-c, c)$, however large. Then

$$f(x) = \frac{a_0}{2} + \sum_{n=1}^{\infty} \left( a_n \cos \frac{n\pi x}{c} + b_n \sin \frac{n\pi x}{x} \right) \quad ...(1)$$

where, $a_0 = \frac{1}{c} \int_{-c}^{c} f(t)\, dt, a_n = \frac{1}{c} \int_{-c}^{c} f(t) \cos \frac{n\pi t}{c}\, dt$ and $b_n = \frac{1}{c} \int_{-c}^{c} f(t) \sin \frac{n\pi t}{c}\, dt$

Substituting the values of $a_0$, $a_n$ and $b_n$ in (1), we get

$$f(x) = \frac{1}{2c} \int_{-c}^{c} f(t)\, dt + \frac{1}{c} \sum_{n=1}^{\infty} \int_{-c}^{c} \left[ \cos \frac{n\pi x}{c} \cos \frac{n\pi t}{c} + \sin \frac{n\pi x}{c} \sin \frac{n\pi t}{c} \right] f(t)\, dt$$

$$= \frac{1}{2c} \int_{-c}^{c} f(t)\, dt + \frac{1}{c} \sum_{n=1}^{\infty} \int_{-c}^{c} \cos \frac{n\pi(t-x)}{c} \,.\, f(t)\, dt \quad ...(2)$$

If we assume that the integral $\int_{-\infty}^{\infty} |f(x)|\, dx$ converges, then

$$\operatorname*{Lt}_{c \to \infty} \left[ \frac{1}{2c} \int_{-c}^{c} f(t)\, dt \right] = 0$$

Putting $\frac{\pi}{c} = \Delta\lambda$, the second term in (2) becomes

$$\frac{1}{\pi} \sum_{n=1}^{\infty} \Delta\lambda \int_{-c}^{c} \cos \{n\Delta\lambda(t-x)\} f(t)\, dt$$

This is of the form $\sum_{n=1}^{\infty} F(n\Delta\lambda)\, \Delta\lambda$ whose limit as $\Delta\lambda \to 0$, is $\int_0^{\infty} F(\lambda)\, d\lambda$.

Hence as $c \to \infty$, (2) reduces to

$$f(x) = \frac{1}{\pi} \int_0^{\infty} \int_{-\infty}^{\infty} f(t) \cos \lambda(t-x)\, dt\, d\lambda \quad ...(3)$$

which is known as **Fourier integral** of $f(x)$.

Equation (3) is true at a point of continuity. At a point of discontinuity, the value of the integral on the right is

$$\frac{1}{2} [f(x+0) + f(x-0)].$$

## 2.3. FOURIER SINE AND COSINE INTEGRALS

We know that $\cos \lambda(t-x) = \cos \lambda t \cos \lambda x + \sin \lambda t \sin \lambda x$

∴ Fourier integral of $f(x)$ can be written as

$$f(x) = \frac{1}{\pi} \int_0^{\infty} \int_{-\infty}^{\infty} f(t) \{\cos \lambda t \cos \lambda x + \sin \lambda t \sin \lambda x\}\, dt\, d\lambda$$

$$= \frac{1}{\pi}\int_0^\infty \cos \lambda x \int_{-\infty}^\infty f(t) \cos \lambda t \, dt \, d\lambda + \frac{1}{\pi}\int_0^\infty \sin \lambda x \int_{-\infty}^\infty f(t) \sin \lambda t \, dt \, d\lambda \quad ...(4)$$

**When f(x) is an odd function,** $f(t) \cos \lambda t$ is odd while $f(t) \sin \lambda t$ is even. Thus the first integral in (4) vanishes and we get

$$f(x) = \frac{2}{\pi}\int_0^\infty \sin \lambda x \int_0^\infty f(t) \sin \lambda t \, dt \, d\lambda \quad ...(5)$$

This is called **Fourier sine integral.**

**When f(x) is an even function,** $f(t) \cos \lambda t$ is even while $f(t) \sin \lambda t$ is odd. Thus the second integral in (4) vanishes and we get

$$f(x) = \frac{2}{\pi}\int_0^\infty \cos \lambda x \int_0^\infty f(t) \cos \lambda t \, dt \, d\lambda \quad ...(6)$$

This is called **Fourier cosine integral.**

## 2.4. COMPLEX FORM OF FOURIER INTEGRAL

Since $\cos \lambda(t - x)$ is an even function of $\lambda$, we have from (3),

$$f(x) = \frac{1}{2\pi}\int_{-\infty}^\infty \int_{-\infty}^\infty f(t) \cos \lambda(t - x) \, dt \, d\lambda \quad ...(7)$$

$$\left[\because \; 2\int_0^a f(x)\,dx = \int_{-a}^a f(x)\,dx, \text{ if } f(x) \text{ is even}\right]$$

Also $\sin \lambda(t - x)$ is an odd function of $\lambda$, so that

$$0 = \frac{1}{2\pi}\int_{-\infty}^\infty \int_{-\infty}^\infty f(t) \sin \lambda(t - x) \, dt \, d\lambda \quad ...(8)$$

$$\left[\because \; \int_{-a}^a f(x)\,dx = 0, \text{ if } f(x) \text{ is odd}\right]$$

Multiplying (8) by $i$ and adding to (7), we get

$$f(x) = \frac{1}{2\pi}\int_{-\infty}^\infty \int_{-\infty}^\infty f(t) \, \{\cos \lambda(t - x) + i \sin \lambda(t - x)\} \, dt \, d\lambda$$

$$= \frac{1}{2\pi}\int_{-\infty}^\infty \int_{-\infty}^\infty f(t) \, e^{i\lambda(t-x)} \, dt \, d\lambda$$

$$= \frac{1}{2\pi}\int_{-\infty}^\infty e^{-i\lambda x} \int_{-\infty}^\infty f(t) \, e^{i\lambda t} \, dt \, d\lambda$$

which is known as the **complex form of Fourier integral.**

**Example.** *Express the function* $f(x) = \begin{cases} 1 & \text{for } |x| \le 1, \\ 0 & \text{for } |x| > 1, \end{cases}$

*as a Fourier integral. Hence evaluate* $\displaystyle\int_0^\infty \frac{\sin \lambda \cos \lambda x}{\lambda} \, d\lambda$.

**Sol.** The Fourier integral for $f(x)$ is

$$\frac{1}{\pi}\int_0^\infty \int_{-\infty}^\infty f(t)\cos\lambda(t-x)\,dt\,d\lambda$$

$$= \frac{1}{\pi}\int_0^\infty \int_{-1}^{1} \cos\lambda(t-x)\,dt\,d\lambda$$

[$\because$ $f(t) = 0$ when $-\infty < t < -1$, $f(t) = 1$ when $-1 < t < 1$ and $f(t) = 0$ when $1 < t < \infty$]

$$= \frac{1}{\pi}\int_0^\infty \left[\frac{\sin\lambda(t-x)}{\lambda}\right]_{-1}^{1} d\lambda = \frac{1}{\pi}\int_0^\infty \frac{\sin\lambda(1-x)-\sin\lambda(-1-x)}{\lambda}\,d\lambda$$

$$= \frac{1}{\pi}\int_0^\infty \frac{\sin\lambda(1+x)+\sin\lambda(1-x)}{\lambda}\,d\lambda \quad = \frac{2}{\pi}\int_0^\infty \frac{\sin\lambda\cos\lambda x}{\lambda}\,d\lambda$$

$$\therefore \quad \int_0^\infty \frac{\sin\lambda\cos\lambda x}{\lambda}\,d\lambda = \frac{1}{2}\pi f(x) = \begin{cases} \frac{1}{2}\pi & \text{for } |x| < 1, \\ 0 & \text{for } |x| > 1 \end{cases}$$

At $|x| = 1$, *i.e.*, $x = \pm 1$, $f(x)$ is discontinuous and the integral has the value $\frac{1}{2}\left(\frac{\pi}{2}+0\right) = \frac{\pi}{4}$.

**Note.** Putting $x = 0$, we get $\int_0^\infty \frac{\sin\lambda}{\lambda}\,d\lambda = \frac{\pi}{2}$ or $\int_0^\infty \frac{\sin x}{x}\,dx = \frac{\pi}{2}$.

## 2.5. INVERSION FORMULAE FOR FOURIER TRANSFORMS

(1) *Fourier sine transform and its inversion formula*

Fourier sine integral is $\quad f(x) = \frac{2}{\pi}\int_0^\infty \sin\lambda x \int_0^\infty f(t)\sin\lambda t\,dt\,d\lambda$

Replacing $\lambda$ by $s$, we get $\quad f(x) = \frac{2}{\pi}\int_0^\infty \sin sx \int_0^\infty f(t)\sin st\,dt\,ds$

Denoting the value of the inner integral by $\sqrt{\frac{\pi}{2}}\ F_s\{f(x)\}$, we have

$$f(x) = \sqrt{\frac{2}{\pi}}\int_0^\infty F_s\{f(x)\}\sin sx\,ds \qquad ...(1)$$

where

$$F_s\{f(x)\} = \bar{f}(s) = \sqrt{\frac{2}{\pi}}\int_0^\infty f(t)\sin st\,dt \qquad ...(2)$$

Equation (2) is defined as Fourier sine transform of the function $f(x)$. Equation (1) which determines the function $f(x)$ is known as the inversion formula for the Fourier sine transform.

(2) *Fourier cosine transform and its inversion formula*

Fourier cosine integral is $f(x) = \frac{2}{\pi}\int_0^\infty \cos\lambda x \int_0^\infty f(t)\cos\lambda t\,dt\,d\lambda$

Replacing $\lambda$ by $s$, we get $\quad f(x) = \frac{2}{\pi}\int_0^\infty \cos sx \int_0^\infty f(t)\cos st\,dt\,ds$

Denoting the value of the inner integral by $\sqrt{\frac{\pi}{2}}\ F_c\ \{f(x)\}$, we have

$$f(x) = \sqrt{\frac{2}{\pi}} \int_0^{\infty} F_c\ \{f(x)\} \cos sx\ ds \qquad ...(3)$$

where
$$F_c\ \{f(x)\} = \bar{f}(s) = \sqrt{\frac{2}{\pi}} \int_0^{\infty} f(t) \cos st\ dt \qquad ...(4)$$

Equation (4) is defined as Fourier cosine transform of the function $f(x)$. Equation (3) which determines the function $f(x)$ is known as the inversion formula for the Fourier cosine transform.

(3) *Complex Fourier transform and its inversion formula*

Complex form of Fourier integral is $\quad f(x) = \dfrac{1}{2\pi} \displaystyle\int_{-\infty}^{\infty} e^{-i\lambda x} \int_{-\infty}^{\infty} f(t)\, e^{i\lambda t}\ dt\ d\lambda$

Replacing $\lambda$ by $s$, we get $\quad f(x) = \dfrac{1}{2\pi} \displaystyle\int_{-\infty}^{\infty} e^{-isx} \int_{-\infty}^{\infty} f(t)\, e^{ist}\, dt\ ds$

Denoting the value of the inner integral by $\sqrt{2\pi}\ F\{f(x)\}$, we have

$$f(x) = \frac{1}{\sqrt{2\pi}} \int_{-\infty}^{\infty} F\{f(x)\}\ e^{-isx}\ ds \qquad ...(5)$$

where
$$F\{f(x)\} = \bar{f}(s) = \frac{1}{\sqrt{2\pi}} \int_{-\infty}^{\infty} f(t)\ e^{ist}\ dt \qquad ...(6)$$

Equation (6) is defined as complex Fourier transform of the function $f(x)$. Equation (5) which determines the function $f(x)$ is known as the inversion formula for the complex Fourier transform.

## ILLUSTRATIVE EXAMPLES

**Example 1.** *Using Fourier sine integral, show that*

$$\int_0^{\infty} \frac{1 - \cos \pi\lambda}{\lambda} \sin x\lambda\ d\lambda = \begin{cases} \frac{1}{2}\pi, & \text{when } 0 < x < \pi \\ 0, & \text{when } x > \pi \end{cases}$$

**Sol.** Let
$$f(x) = \begin{cases} \frac{1}{2}\pi, & \text{when } 0 < x < \pi \\ 0, & \text{when } x > \pi \end{cases}$$

Using Fourier sine integral, we have

$$f(x) = \frac{2}{\pi} \int_0^{\infty} \sin \lambda x \int_0^{\infty} f(t) \sin \lambda t\ dt\ d\lambda$$

$$= \frac{2}{\pi} \int_0^{\infty} \sin \lambda x \left[ \int_0^{\pi} f(t) \sin \lambda t\ dt + \int_{\pi}^{\infty} f(t) \sin \lambda t\ dt \right] d\lambda$$

$$= \frac{2}{\pi} \int_0^{\infty} \sin \lambda x \int_0^{\pi} \frac{1}{2} \pi \sin \lambda t\ dt\ d\lambda \qquad \text{[on substituting for } f(t)]$$

$$= \int_0^\infty \sin \lambda x \left[ -\frac{\cos \lambda t}{\lambda} \right]_0^\pi d\lambda = \int_0^\infty \frac{1 - \cos \pi\lambda}{\lambda} \sin x\lambda \, d\lambda$$

$$\therefore \quad \int_0^\infty \frac{1 - \cos \pi\lambda}{\lambda} . \sin x\lambda \, d\lambda = f(x) = \begin{cases} \frac{1}{2}\pi, & \text{when } 0 < x < \pi \\ 0, & \text{when } x > \pi \end{cases}.$$

**Example 2.** *Find the Fourier sine transform of* $e^{-|x|}$. *Hence evaluate* $\int_0^\infty \frac{x \sin mx}{1 + x^2} dx$.

**Sol.** In the interval $(0, \infty)$, $x$ is positive so that $e^{-|x|} = e^{-x}$. Fourier sine transform of $f(x) = e^{-x}$ is given by

$$F_s \{f(x)\} = \sqrt{\frac{2}{\pi}} \int_0^\infty f(x) \sin sx \, dx = \sqrt{\frac{2}{\pi}} \int_0^\infty e^{-x} \sin sx \, dx$$

$$= \sqrt{\frac{2}{\pi}} \left[ \frac{e^{-x}}{1 + s^2} (-\sin sx - s \cos sx) \right]_0^\infty = \sqrt{\frac{2}{\pi}} \left( \frac{s}{1 + s^2} \right)$$

Using inversion formula for Fourier sine transform, we get

$$f(x) = \sqrt{\frac{2}{\pi}} \int_0^\infty F_s \{f(x)\} \sin sx \, ds \quad \text{or} \quad e^{-x} = \frac{2}{\pi} \int_0^\infty \frac{s}{1 + s^2} \sin sx \, ds$$

Replacing $x$ by $m$, we have $\quad e^{-m} = \frac{2}{\pi} \int_0^\infty \frac{s}{1 + s^2} \sin ms \, ds = \frac{2}{\pi} \int_0^\infty \frac{x \sin mx}{1 + x^2} dx$

Hence $\quad \int_0^\infty \frac{x \sin mx}{1 + x^2} dx = \frac{\pi}{2} e^{-m}.$

**Example 3.** *Find the Fourier cosine transform of* $e^{-x^2}$. (M.G.U. Dec., 2007)

**Sol.** Fourier cosine transform of $e^{-x^2}$ is given by

$$F_c\{e^{-x^2}\} = \sqrt{\frac{2}{\pi}} \int_0^\infty e^{-x^2} \cos sx \, dx = I \text{ (say)} \quad \ldots(1)$$

Differentiating w.r.t. $s$, we have

$$\frac{dI}{ds} = -\sqrt{\frac{2}{\pi}} \int_0^\infty x e^{-x^2} \sin sx \, dx = \frac{1}{2} \sqrt{\frac{2}{\pi}} \int_0^\infty (\sin sx)(-2x \, e^{-x^2}) \, dx$$

$$= \frac{1}{2} \sqrt{\frac{2}{\pi}} \left[ \left\{ \sin sx \, e^{-x^2} \right\}_0^\infty - s \int_0^\infty \cos sx \, e^{-x^2} \, dx \right] \quad \text{(Integrating by parts)}$$

$$= -\frac{s}{2} \sqrt{\frac{2}{\pi}} \int_0^\infty e^{-x^2} \cos sx \, dx = -\frac{s}{2} I$$

or $\quad \frac{dI}{I} = -\frac{s}{2} ds$

Integrating, we have

$$\log I = -\frac{s^2}{4} + \log A \quad \text{or} \quad I = A \, e^{-\frac{s^2}{4}} \quad \ldots(2)$$

Now when $s = 0$, from (1), $\quad \mathrm{I} = \sqrt{\dfrac{2}{\pi}} \displaystyle\int_0^\infty e^{-x^2}\,dx = \sqrt{\dfrac{2}{\pi}} \cdot \dfrac{\sqrt{\pi}}{2} = \dfrac{1}{\sqrt{2}}$

$\therefore$ From (2), $\qquad \dfrac{1}{\sqrt{2}} = \mathrm{A}$

Hence $\qquad \mathrm{I} = \mathrm{F}_c\{e^{-x^2}\} = \dfrac{1}{\sqrt{2}}\, e^{-\frac{s^2}{4}}.$

**Example 4.** *Find the Fourier transform of* $f(x) = \begin{cases} 1 - x^2, & \text{if } |x| < 1 \\ 0, & \text{if } |x| > 1 \end{cases}$

*and use it to evaluate* $\displaystyle\int_0^\infty \left(\frac{x\cos x - \sin x}{x^3}\right) \cos\frac{x}{2}\,dx.$ (M.G.U. May 2010)

**Sol.** Fourier transform of $f(x)$ is given by

$$\mathrm{F}\{f(x)\} = \frac{1}{\sqrt{2\pi}} \int_{-\infty}^{\infty} f(x)\, e^{isx}\,dx = \frac{1}{\sqrt{2\pi}} \int_{-1}^{1} (1 - x^2)\, e^{isx}\,dx$$

$$= \frac{1}{\sqrt{2\pi}} \left[(1 - x^2) \cdot \frac{e^{isx}}{is} - (-2x)\frac{e^{isx}}{(is)^2} + (-2)\frac{e^{isx}}{(is)^3}\right]_{-1}^{1}$$

$$= \frac{1}{\sqrt{2\pi}} \left[-\frac{2}{s^2}(e^{is} + e^{-is}) + \frac{2}{is^3}(e^{is} - e^{-is})\right]$$

$$= \frac{1}{\sqrt{2\pi}} \left[-\frac{4}{s^2}\left(\frac{e^{is} + e^{-is}}{2}\right) + \frac{4}{s^3}\left(\frac{e^{is} - e^{-is}}{2i}\right)\right]$$

$$= \frac{4}{\sqrt{2\pi}} \left[-\frac{\cos s}{s^2} + \frac{\sin s}{s^3}\right] = -2\sqrt{\frac{2}{\pi}} \left(\frac{s\cos s - \sin s}{s^3}\right)$$

By inversion formula for Fourier transform, we have

$$f(x) = \frac{1}{\sqrt{2\pi}} \int_{-\infty}^{\infty} \mathrm{F}\{f(x)\}\, e^{-isx}\,ds = -\frac{2}{\pi} \int_{-\infty}^{\infty} \left(\frac{s\cos s - \sin s}{s^3}\right) (\cos sx - i\sin sx)\,ds$$

$$= -\frac{2}{\pi} \int_{-\infty}^{\infty} \left(\frac{s\cos s - \sin s}{s^3}\right) \cos sx\,ds + \frac{2i}{\pi} \int_{-\infty}^{\infty} \left(\frac{s\cos s - \sin s}{s^3}\right) \sin sx\,ds$$

$$= -\frac{2}{\pi} \int_{-\infty}^{\infty} \left(\frac{s\cos s - \sin s}{s^3}\right) \cos sx\,ds$$

(since the integrand in the second integral on R.H.S is odd)

$$= -\frac{4}{\pi} \int_0^{\infty} \left(\frac{s\cos s - \sin s}{s^3}\right) \cos sx\,ds$$

or $$\int_0^{\infty} \left(\frac{s\cos s - \sin s}{s^3}\right) \cos sx\,ds = -\frac{\pi}{4} f(x) = \begin{cases} -\dfrac{\pi}{4}(1 - x^2), & \text{if } |x| < 1 \\ 0, & \text{if } |x| > 1 \end{cases}$$

Taking $x = \frac{1}{2}$, we have $\int_0^{\infty} \left( \frac{s \cos s - \sin s}{s^3} \right) \cos \frac{s}{2} \, ds = -\frac{3\pi}{16}$

Hence $$\int_0^{\infty} \left( \frac{x \cos x - \sin x}{x^3} \right) \cos \frac{x}{2} \, dx = -\frac{3\pi}{16}.$$

**Example 5.** *Solve the integral equation* $\int_0^{\infty} F(x) \cos px \, dx = \begin{cases} 1 - p, & 0 \le p \le 1 \\ 0, & p > 1 \end{cases}$

*Hence deduce that* $\int_0^{\infty} \frac{\sin^2 t}{t^2} dt = \frac{\pi}{2}$.

**Sol.** Let $$\int_0^{\infty} F(x) \cos px \, dx = f(p), \quad \text{then } f(p) = \begin{cases} 1 - p, & 0 \le p \le 1 \\ 0, & p > 1 \end{cases}$$

$$\therefore \quad \sqrt{\frac{2}{\pi}} \int_0^{\infty} F(x) \cos px \, dx = \sqrt{\frac{2}{\pi}} f(p) = \bar{f}(p)$$

By inversion formula for Fourier cosine transform, we have

$$F(x) = \sqrt{\frac{2}{\pi}} \int_0^{\infty} \bar{f}(p) \cos px \, dp = \frac{2}{\pi} \int_0^{\infty} f(p) \cos px \, dp$$

$$= \frac{2}{\pi} \left[ \int_0^1 (1 - p) \cos px \, dp + \int_1^{\infty} 0 \,.\, \cos px \, dp \right]$$

$$= \frac{2}{\pi} \left[ (1 - p) \,.\, \frac{\sin px}{x} - (-1) \,.\, \frac{-\cos px}{x^2} \right]_0^1 = \frac{2}{\pi} \left[ -\frac{\cos x}{x^2} + \frac{1}{x^2} \right] = \frac{2(1 - \cos x)}{\pi x^2}.$$

**Deduction.** Since $\int_0^{\infty} F(x) \cos px \, dx = \begin{cases} 1 - p, & 0 \le p \le 1 \\ 0, & p > 1 \end{cases}$ where $F(x) = \frac{2(1 - \cos x)}{\pi x^2}$

$$\therefore \quad \frac{2}{\pi} \int_0^{\infty} \frac{1 - \cos x}{x^2} \,.\, \cos px \, dx = \begin{cases} 1 - p, & 0 \le p \le 1 \\ 0, & p > 1 \end{cases}$$

When $p = 0$, we have $\frac{2}{\pi} \int_0^{\infty} \frac{1 - \cos x}{x^2} dx = 1$ or $\int_0^{\infty} \frac{2 \sin^2 \frac{x}{2}}{x^2} dx = \frac{\pi}{2}$

Putting $x = 2t$ so that $dx = 2dt$, we get $\int_0^{\infty} \frac{\sin^2 t}{t^2} dt = \frac{\pi}{2}$.

**Example 6.** *Find the Fourier sine integral for* $f(x) = e^{-\beta x}$. *Hence show that* $\int_0^{\infty} \frac{\lambda \sin \lambda x}{\beta^2 + \lambda^2} d\lambda = e^{-\beta x}$. (M.G.U. May 2009 ; June 2006)

**Sol.** The Fourier sine Integral is

$$f(x) = \frac{2}{\pi} \int_0^{\infty} \sin \lambda x \int_0^{\infty} e^{-\beta t} \sin \lambda t \, dt \, d\lambda = e^{-\beta x}.$$

But $\int_0^\infty e^{-\beta t} \sin \lambda t \, dt = \frac{\lambda}{\beta^2 + \lambda^2}$

Hence we get $\frac{2}{\pi}\int_0^\infty \sin \lambda x \int_0^\infty e^{-\beta t} \sin \lambda t \, dt \, d\lambda$

$$= \frac{2}{\pi}\int_0^\infty (\sin \lambda x).\frac{\lambda}{\beta^2 + \lambda^2} \, d\lambda$$

$$= \frac{2}{\pi}\int_0^\infty \frac{\lambda \sin \lambda x}{\beta^2 + \lambda^2} \, d\lambda = e^{-\beta x}.$$

*i.e.,*
$$\int_0^\infty \frac{\lambda \sin \lambda x}{\beta^2 + \lambda^2} \, d\lambda = \frac{\pi}{2} e^{-\beta x}.$$

**Example 7.** *Find the Fourier Cosine transform of* $f(x) = \begin{cases} x, & 0 < x < \frac{1}{2} \\ 1 - x, & \frac{1}{2} < x < 1. \\ 0, & x > 1 \end{cases}$

(M.G.U. June 2006)

**Sol.** The cosine transform of $f(x)$ is $\sqrt{\frac{2}{\pi}} \int_0^\infty f(x) \cos sx \, dx.$

In the present case, cosine transform is $\sqrt{\frac{2}{\pi}} \int_0^{\frac{1}{2}} x \cos sx \, dx + \sqrt{\frac{2}{\pi}} \int_{\frac{1}{2}}^1 (1 - x) \cos sx \, dx$

$$= \sqrt{\frac{2}{\pi}} \left[ x \frac{\sin sx}{s} + \frac{\cos sx}{s^2} \right]_0^{\frac{1}{2}} + \sqrt{\frac{2}{\pi}} \left[ (1 - x) \frac{\sin sx}{s} - \frac{\cos sx}{s^2} \right]_{\frac{1}{2}}^1$$

$$= \sqrt{\frac{2}{\pi}} \left[ \frac{2 \cos \left( \frac{s}{2} \right) - \cos s - 1}{s^2} \right].$$

**Example 8.** *Find the Fourier cosine transform of* $f(x) = e^{-|x|}$ *and hence evaluate* $\int_0^\infty \frac{\cos t}{1 + t^2} \, dt.$

**Sol.** In the interval $(0, \infty)$, $x$ is positive, and $e^{-|x|} = e^{-x}$.

The Fourier cosine transform of

$$e^{-|x|} \text{ is } F_c \{e^{-|x|}\} = \sqrt{\frac{2}{\pi}} \int_0^\infty e^{-x} \cos sx \, ds = \sqrt{\frac{2}{\pi}} \frac{1}{1 + s^2}.$$

Using the inverse formula, we get

$$e^{-x} = \sqrt{\frac{2}{\pi}} \int_0^\infty F_c \{e^{-|x|}\} \cos sx \, ds$$

$$= \sqrt{\frac{2}{\pi}} \int_0^\infty \sqrt{\frac{2}{\pi}} \frac{1}{1+s^2} \cos sx \, ds$$

$$= \frac{2}{\pi} \int_0^\infty \frac{\cos sx}{1+s^2} \, ds$$

When $x = 1$

$$\int_0^\infty \frac{\cos s}{1+s^2} \, ds = \frac{\pi}{2} e^{-1}.$$

Hence the result.

## TEST YOUR KNOWLEDGE

**1.** Find the Fourier integral representation of the function $f(x) = \begin{cases} 0, & x < 0 \\ \frac{1}{2}, & x = 0 \\ e^{-x}, & x > 0 \end{cases}$ *(M.G.U. Nov. 2009)*

**2.** Using Fourier integrals, show that

(*i*) $\displaystyle\int_0^\infty \frac{\sin \pi\lambda \sin x\lambda}{1-\lambda^2} \, d\lambda = \begin{cases} \frac{1}{2}\pi \sin x, & \text{when } 0 \le x \le \pi \\ 0, & \text{when } x > \pi \end{cases}$ *(M.G.U. Dec. 2007)*

(*ii*) $\displaystyle\int_0^\infty \frac{\cos x\lambda}{1+\lambda^2} \, d\lambda = \frac{\pi}{2} e^{-x}, x \ge 0$ (*iii*) $\displaystyle\int_0^\infty \frac{\lambda \sin \lambda x}{k^2+\lambda^2} \, d\lambda = \frac{\pi}{2} e^{-kx} ; x > 0, k > 0.$

*(M.G.U. Dec. 2007)*

**3.** Find the Fourier sine transform of $\dfrac{e^{-ax}}{x}$. *(M.G.U. Nov. 2009)*

**4.** Find the Fourier cosine transform of the function $f(x)$, if $f(x) = \begin{cases} \cos x, & 0 < x < a \\ 0, & x > a \end{cases}$

**5.** Find the Fourier sine and cosine transforms of

(*i*) $2e^{-5x} + 5e^{-2x}$ (*ii*) $f(x) = \begin{cases} 1, & \text{for } 0 \le x < a \\ 0, & \text{for } x > a \end{cases}$

(*iii*) $f(x) = \begin{cases} x, & \text{for } 0 < x < 1 \\ 2-x, & \text{for } 1 < x < 2 \\ 0, & \text{for } x > 2 \end{cases}$

**6.** Show that the Fourier transform of $f(x) = e^{-x^2/2}$ is $e^{-s^2/2}$.

**7.** Find the Fourier transform of

(*i*) $f(x) = \begin{cases} 1, & |x| < a \\ 0, & |x| > a \end{cases}$ (*ii*) $f(x) = \begin{cases} x, & |x| < a \\ 0, & |x| > a \end{cases}$ *(M.G.U. June 2006)*

**8.** Solve the integral equation $\displaystyle\int_0^\infty f(x) \cos \lambda x \, dx = e^{-\lambda}$. *(M.G.U. June 2006 ; Nov 2009)*

**9.** Solve for F($x$) the integral equation $\int_0^\infty F(x) \sin tx \, dx = \begin{cases} 1, & 0 \le t < 1 \\ 2, & 1 \le t < 2 \\ 0, & t \ge 2 \end{cases}$

**10.** Find the Fourier sine and cosine transform of $f(x) = e^{-ax}$. *(M.G.U. Jan. 2007 ; 2009)*

**11.** Find the Fourier cosine transform of $f(x) = \dfrac{1}{1+x^2}$ and deduce the sine transform of $\dfrac{x}{1+x^2}$. *(M.G.U. May 2010)*

## Answers

**1.** $f(x) = \dfrac{1}{\pi} \displaystyle\int_0^\infty \dfrac{\lambda \sin \lambda x + \cos \lambda x}{1+\lambda^2} \, d\lambda$

**3.** $\sqrt{\dfrac{2}{\pi}} \tan^{-1}\left(\dfrac{s}{a}\right)$

**4.** $\dfrac{1}{\sqrt{2\pi}} \left[ \dfrac{\sin(1+s)a}{1+s} + \dfrac{\sin(1-p)a}{1-p} \right]$

**5.** (*i*) $s\sqrt{\dfrac{2}{\pi}} \left( \dfrac{2}{s^2+25} + \dfrac{5}{s^2+4} \right)$ ; $10\sqrt{\dfrac{2}{\pi}} \left( \dfrac{1}{s^2+25} + \dfrac{1}{s^2+4} \right)$

(*ii*) $\sqrt{\dfrac{2}{\pi}} \left( \dfrac{1-\cos as}{s} \right)$ ; $\sqrt{\dfrac{2}{\pi}} \cdot \dfrac{\sin as}{s}$

(*iii*) $\dfrac{2}{s^2}\sqrt{\dfrac{2}{\pi}} \sin s(1-\cos s)$ ; $\dfrac{2}{s^2}\sqrt{\dfrac{2}{\pi}} \cos s(1-\cos s)$

**7.** (*i*) $\sqrt{\dfrac{2}{\pi}} \cdot \dfrac{\sin as}{s}$

(*ii*) $i\sqrt{\dfrac{2}{\pi}} \left( \dfrac{as \cos as - \sin as}{s^2} \right)$

**8.** $f(x) = \dfrac{2}{\pi(1+x^2)}$

**9.** $F(x) = \dfrac{2}{\pi x}(1 + \cos x - 2\cos 2x)$

**10.** $F_s(e^{-ax}) = \sqrt{\dfrac{2}{\pi}} \dfrac{s}{a^2+s^2}$ ; $F_c(e^{-ax}) = \sqrt{\dfrac{2}{\pi}} \dfrac{s}{a^2+s^2}$

**11.** $\sqrt{\dfrac{\pi}{2}} e^{-s}$, $\sqrt{\dfrac{\pi}{2}} e^{-s}$.

## 2.6. FOURIER TRANSFORMS OF THE DERIVATIVES OF A FUNCTION

Let $\overline{u}(s, t)$ be the Fourier transform of the function $u(x, t)$.

Then
$$\overline{u}(s, t) = \frac{1}{\sqrt{2\pi}} \int_{-\infty}^{\infty} u(x, t)\, e^{isx} \, dx$$

Suppose $u$ and $\dfrac{\partial u}{\partial x}$ both vanish as $x \to \pm\infty$. Then the Fourier transform of $\dfrac{\partial^2 u}{\partial x^2}$ is given by

$$F\left\{\frac{\partial^2 u}{\partial x^2}\right\} = \frac{1}{\sqrt{2\pi}} \int_{-\infty}^{\infty} \frac{\partial^2 u}{\partial x^2} e^{isx} \, dx$$

$$= \frac{1}{\sqrt{2\pi}} \left[ \left\{ e^{isx} \frac{\partial u}{\partial x} - ise^{isx} . u \right\}_{-\infty}^{\infty} + \int_{-\infty}^{\infty} (is)^2 e^{isx} . u \, dx \right]$$

$$= -\frac{s^2}{\sqrt{2\pi}} \int_{-\infty}^{\infty} ue^{isx} \, dx = -s^2 \, \overline{u}$$

If $\bar{u}_s$ $(s, t)$ and $\bar{u}_c$ $(s, t)$ be the Fourier sine and cosine transforms of $u(x, t)$, then

$$\bar{u}_s(s,t) = \sqrt{\frac{2}{\pi}} \int_0^\infty u \sin sx \, dx \quad \text{and} \quad \bar{u}(s,t) = \sqrt{\frac{2}{\pi}} \int_0^\infty u \cos sx \, dx$$

The Fourier sine transform of $\frac{\partial^2 u}{\partial x^2}$ is given by

$$F_s \left\{ \frac{\partial^2 u}{\partial x^2} \right\} = \sqrt{\frac{2}{\pi}} \int_0^\infty \frac{\partial^2 u}{\partial x^2} \sin sx \, dx$$

$$= \sqrt{\frac{2}{\pi}} \left[ \left\{ \sin sx \frac{\partial u}{\partial x} - s \cos sx \, . \, u \right\}_0^\infty - \int_0^\infty s^2 \sin sx \, . \, u \, dx \right]$$

$$= \sqrt{\frac{2}{\pi}} \left[ s \, \{u\}_{x=0} - s^2 \int_0^\infty u \sin sx \, dx \right] = \sqrt{\frac{2}{\pi}} \, [s \, \{u\}_{x=0} - s^2 \, \bar{u}_s]$$

Similarly, we have

$$F_c \left\{ \frac{\partial^2 u}{\partial x^2} \right\} = \sqrt{\frac{2}{\pi}} \left[ - \left\{ \frac{\partial u}{\partial x} \right\}_{x=0} - s^2 \, \bar{u}_c \right].$$

## 2.7. APPLICATION OF FOURIER TRANSFORMS TO BOUNDARY VALUE PROBLEMS

This is illustrated through the following examples.

## ILLUSTRATIVE EXAMPLES

**Example 1.** *Solve the equation* $\frac{\partial u}{\partial t} = \frac{\partial^2 u}{\partial x^2}$, $x > 0, t > 0$ *subject to the conditions*

*(i)* $u = 0$, *when* $x = 0, t > 0$ *(ii)* $u = \begin{cases} 1, & 0 < x < 1 \\ 0, & x \geq 1 \end{cases}$ *when* $t = 0$

*and (iii)* $u(x, t)$ *is bounded.*

**Sol.** Since $(u)_{x=0}$ is given, taking Fourier sine transform of both sides of the given equation, we have

$$\sqrt{\frac{2}{\pi}} \int_0^\infty \frac{\partial u}{\partial t} \sin sx \, dx = \sqrt{\frac{2}{\pi}} \int_0^\infty \frac{\partial^2 u}{\partial x^2} \sin sx \, dx$$

or
$$\sqrt{\frac{2}{\pi}} \frac{\partial}{\partial t} \int_0^\infty u \sin sx \, dx = \sqrt{\frac{2}{\pi}} \, [s(u)_{x=0} - s^2 \, \bar{u}_s]$$

or
$$\frac{d\bar{u}_s}{dt} + s^2 \, \bar{u}_s = \sqrt{\frac{2}{\pi}} \, s(u)_{x=0}$$

or $$\frac{d\overline{u}_s}{dt} + s^2\,\overline{u}_s = 0 \quad \text{since } u = 0,\ t > 0 \text{ when } x = 0,\ t > 0$$

Its solution is $\overline{u}_s = Ae^{-s^2 t}$, where A is a constant ...(1)

Now, when $t = 0$, Fourier sine transform of $u(x, t)$

i.e., $$\overline{u}_s(s, 0) = \sqrt{\frac{2}{\pi}}\int_0^{\infty} u(x, 0)\sin sx\,dx = \sqrt{\frac{2}{\pi}}\int_0^{1} 1.\sin sx\,dx + \sqrt{\frac{2}{\pi}}\int_1^{\infty} 0.\sin sx\,dx$$

$$= \sqrt{\frac{2}{\pi}}\left[-\frac{\cos sx}{s}\right]_0^1 = \sqrt{\frac{2}{\pi}}\left(\frac{1-\cos s}{s}\right)$$

$\therefore$ From (1), $A = \overline{u}_s(s, 0) = \sqrt{\frac{2}{\pi}}\left(\frac{1-\cos s}{s}\right)$ so that $\overline{u}_s = \sqrt{\frac{2}{\pi}}\left(\frac{1-\cos s}{s}\right)e^{-s^2 t}$

Applying the inverse Fourier sine transform, we have

$$u(x, t) = \frac{2}{\pi}\int_0^{\infty}\frac{1-\cos s}{s}\,e^{-s^2 t}\sin sx\,ds \quad \text{which is the required solution.}$$

**Example 2.** *If the initial temperature of an infinite bar is given by*

$$\theta(x) = \begin{cases}\theta_0 & \text{for } |x| < a\\ 0 & \text{for } |x| > a,\end{cases}$$

*determine the temperature at any instant x and at any instant t.*

**Sol.** To determine the temperature $\theta(x, t)$, we have to solve the heat-flow equation

$$\frac{\partial\theta}{\partial t} = c^2\frac{\partial^2\theta}{\partial t^2}, \qquad t > 0 \qquad ...(1)$$

subject to the initial condition $\theta(x, 0) = \begin{cases}\theta_0 & \text{for } |x| < a\\ 0 & \text{for } |x| > a\end{cases}$ ...(2)

Taking Fourier transform of (1), we get

$$\frac{1}{\sqrt{2\pi}}\int_{-\infty}^{\infty}\frac{\partial\theta}{\partial t}e^{isx}\,dx = \frac{c^2}{\sqrt{2\pi}}\int_{-\infty}^{\infty}\frac{\partial^2\theta}{\partial t^2}e^{isx}\,dx$$

or $$\frac{1}{\sqrt{2\pi}}\frac{d}{dt}\int_{-\infty}^{\infty}\theta\,e^{isx}\,dx = -c^2 s^2\overline{\theta}$$

or $$\frac{d\overline{\theta}}{dt} = -c^2 s^2\overline{\theta} \qquad ...(3)$$

Now taking the Fourier transform of (2), we get

$$\overline{\theta}(s, 0) = \frac{1}{\sqrt{2\pi}}\int_{-\infty}^{\infty}\theta(x, 0)\,e^{isx}\,dx = \frac{1}{\sqrt{2\pi}}\int_{-a}^{a}\theta_0\,e^{isx}\,dx = \frac{\theta_0}{\sqrt{2\pi}}\left[\frac{e^{isx}}{is}\right]_{-a}^{a}$$

$$= \frac{\theta_0}{\sqrt{2\pi}} \left[ \frac{e^{isa} - e^{-isa}}{is} \right] = \frac{2\theta_0}{s\sqrt{2\pi}} \left[ \frac{e^{isa} - e^{-isa}}{2i} \right]$$

$$= \frac{2\theta_0 \sin sa}{s\sqrt{2\pi}}$$

From (3), $$\frac{d\bar{\theta}}{\bar{\theta}} = -c^2s^2\,dt \qquad \ldots(4)$$

Integrating $\log\bar{\theta} = -c^2s^2t + \log A$ or $\bar{\theta} = Ae^{-c^2s^2t}$

Since $\bar{\theta} = \dfrac{2\theta_0 \sin sa}{s\sqrt{2\pi}}$ when $t = 0$, from (4), we get $A = \dfrac{2\theta_0 \sin sa}{s\sqrt{2\pi}}$

$$\therefore \qquad \bar{\theta} = \frac{2\theta_0 \sin sa}{s\sqrt{2\pi}} e^{-c^2s^2t}$$

Taking its inverse Fourier transform, we get

$$\theta(x, t) = \frac{1}{2\pi} \int_{-\infty}^{\infty} \frac{2\theta_0 \sin as}{s} . e^{-c^2s^2t} . e^{-sx}\, ds$$

$$= \frac{\theta_0}{\pi} \int_{-\infty}^{\infty} \frac{\sin as}{s} . e^{-c^2s^2t} (\cos xs - i \sin xs)\, ds$$

$$= \frac{\theta_0}{\pi} \left[ \int_{-\infty}^{\infty} \frac{\sin as}{s} . e^{-c^2s^2t} \cos xs\, ds - i \int_{-\infty}^{\infty} \frac{\sin as}{s} . e^{-c^2s^2t} \sin xs\, ds \right]$$

$$= \frac{\theta_0}{\pi} \int_{-\infty}^{\infty} \frac{\sin as}{s} . e^{-c^2s^2t} \cos xs\, ds$$

(The second integral vanishes since its integrand is an odd function)

$$= \frac{2\theta_0}{\pi} \int_0^{\infty} \frac{\sin as}{s} . e^{-c^2s^2t} \cos xs\, ds = \frac{\theta_0}{\pi} \int_0^{\infty} \frac{e^{-c^2s^2t}}{s} . 2 \sin as \cos xs\, ds$$

$$= \frac{\theta_0}{\pi} \int_0^{\infty} e^{-c^2s^2t} \left( \frac{\sin (a + x)\, s + \sin (a - x)\, s}{s} \right) ds$$

$$= \frac{\theta_0}{\pi} \int_0^{\infty} e^{-v^2} \left\{ \sin \frac{(a + x)v}{c\sqrt{t}} + \sin \frac{(1 - x)v}{c\sqrt{t}} \right\} \frac{dv}{v} \qquad \text{where } v^2 = c^2s^2t$$

$$= \frac{\theta_0}{2} \left\{ erf\left( \frac{a + x}{2c\sqrt{t}} \right) + erf\left( \frac{a - x}{2c\sqrt{t}} \right) \right\}.$$

## 2.8. CONVOLUTION THEOREM

**Definition.** Let $f(x)$ and $g(x)$ be two functions defined over the set of real numbers. The convolution of $f$ and $g$, denoted by $f * g$, is defined as

$$(f * g)(x) = \int_{-\infty}^{\infty} f(u)\, g(x-u)\, du$$

$$= \int_{-\infty}^{\infty} f(x-u)\, g(u)\, du.$$

**Convolution theorem :**

The Fourier transform of the convolution of $f$ and $g$ is the product of the Fourier transform of $f$ and the Fourier transform of $g$.

*i.e.,* $\quad F\{(f * g)(x)\} = F\{f(x)\} \,.\, F\{g(x)\}.$

## 2.9. PARSEVALS' IDENTITY

*If $\bar{f}(s)$ and $\bar{g}(s)$ are the Fourier transform of $f(x)$ and $g(x)$ respectively. Then*

$$\int_{-\infty}^{\infty} \bar{f}(s)\, \overset{c}{\bar{g}}(s)\, ds = \int_{-\infty}^{\infty} f(x)\, \overset{c}{\bar{g}}(x)\, dx.$$

**Proof.** We have

$$\overset{c}{\bar{g}}(x) = \frac{1}{\sqrt{2\pi}} \int_{-\infty}^{\infty} \overset{c}{\bar{g}}(s)\, e^{isx}\, ds$$

$$\int_{-\infty}^{\infty} f(x)\, \overset{c}{\bar{g}}(x)\, dx = \int_{-\infty}^{\infty} f(x) \left( \frac{1}{\sqrt{2\pi}} \int_{-\infty}^{\infty} \overset{c}{\bar{g}}(s)\, e^{isx}\, ds \right) dx$$

$$= \int_{-\infty}^{\infty} \overset{c}{\bar{g}}(s) \left( \frac{1}{\sqrt{2\pi}} \int_{-\infty}^{\infty} f(x)\, e^{isx}\, dx \right) ds$$

$$= \int_{-\infty}^{\infty} \overset{c}{\bar{g}}(s)\, \bar{f}(s)\, ds \quad \text{(On interchanging the order of integration)}$$

Hence the result.

## TEST YOUR KNOWLEDGE

1. Express $f(x) = \begin{cases} 1, & 0 \le x \le \pi \\ 0, & x > \pi \end{cases}$ as a Fourier sine integral and hence evaluate

$$\int_0^{\infty} \frac{1 - \cos \lambda\pi}{\lambda} \sin \lambda x\, d\lambda.$$

*(M.G.U. May 2009)*

2. Find the Fourier transforms of $f(x) = \begin{cases} 1, & |x| < a \\ 0, & |x| > a \end{cases}$ and hence evaluate $\int_0^{\infty} \frac{\sin ax}{x}\, dx$.

**3.** Solve the integral equation

$$\int_0^\infty f(x) \cos sx \, dx = \begin{cases} 1 - s, & 0 \le s \le 1 \\ 0, & s > 1 \end{cases}$$

and hence evaluate $\int_0^\infty \frac{\sin^2 t}{t^2} dt$.

## Answers

**1.** $\int_0^\infty \frac{1 - \cos \lambda\pi}{\lambda} \sin \lambda x \, d\lambda = \begin{cases} \frac{\pi}{2}, & 0 \le x < \pi \\ 0, & x > \pi \end{cases}$. At $x = \pi$, the value of the integral is $\frac{\pi}{4}$.

**2.** $F(s) = \frac{2 \sin as}{s}$

**3.** $f(x) = \frac{2}{\pi x^2} (1 - \cos x)$, $\int_0^\infty \frac{\sin^2 t}{t^2} dt = \frac{\pi}{2}$.

# 3

# Partial Differential Equations

## 3.1. INTRODUCTION

A differential equation which involves partial derivatives is called a *partial differential equation*.

For example,

$$x\frac{\partial z}{\partial x} + y\frac{\partial z}{\partial y} = z \qquad ...(1)$$

$$\frac{\partial^2 z}{\partial x^2} + \frac{\partial^2 z}{\partial y^2} = 0 \qquad ...(2)$$

$$\frac{\partial^2 u}{\partial x \partial y} = \left(\frac{\partial u}{\partial z}\right)^3 \qquad ...(3)$$

are partial differential equations.

The *order* of a partial differential equation is the order of the highest partial derivative in the equation. The *degree* of a partial differential equation is the degree of the highest order partial derivative occurring in the equation.

Thus, equation (1) is of first order, equations (2) and (3) are of second order. The degree of all the above equations is one.

If $z$ is a function of two independent variables $x$ and $y$, then we shall use the following notation for the partial derivatives of $z$ :

$$\frac{\partial z}{\partial x} = p, \frac{\partial z}{\partial y} = q, \frac{\partial^2 z}{\partial x^2} = r, \frac{\partial^2 z}{\partial x \partial y} = s, \frac{\partial^2 z}{\partial y^2} = t.$$

## 3.2. FORMATION OF PARTIAL DIFFERENTIAL EQUATIONS

Partial differential equations can be formed either by the elimination of arbitrary constants or by the elimination of arbitrary functions. If the number of arbitrary constants to be eliminated is equal to the number of independent variables, the partial differential equations that arise are of the first order. If the number of arbitrary constants to be eliminated is more than the number of independent variables, the partial differential equations obtained are of second or higher order. If the partial differential equation is obtained by elimination of arbitrary functions, then the order of the partial differential equation is, in general, equal to the number of arbitrary functions eliminated.

The following examples illustrate the method.

## ILLUSTRATIVE EXAMPLES

**Example 1.** *Form partial differential equations from the following equations by eliminating the arbitrary constants :*

(*i*) $z = ax + by + ab$ (*ii*) $z = ax + a^2y^2 + b$.

**Sol.** (*i*) Differentiating $z$ partially w.r.t. $x$ and $y$

$$p = \frac{\partial z}{\partial x} = a, q = \frac{\partial z}{\partial y} = b$$

Substituting for $a$ and $b$ in the given equation, we get

$$z = px + qy + pq$$

which is a partial differential equation of the first order.

(*ii*) Differentiating $z$ partially w.r.t. $x$ and $y$

$$p = \frac{\partial z}{\partial x} = a, q = \frac{\partial z}{\partial y} = 2a^2y$$

Eliminating $a$ between these results, we get $q = 2p^2y$

which is a partial differential equation of the first order.

**Example 2.** *Form partial differential equations from the following equations by eliminating the arbitrary constants :*

(*i*) $z = (x^2 + a)(y^2 + b)$ (*ii*) $2z = \frac{x^2}{a^2} + \frac{y^2}{b^2}$ (*iii*) $\frac{x^2}{a^2} + \frac{y^2}{b^2} + \frac{z^2}{c^2} = 1$.

**Sol.** (*i*) Differentiating $z$ partially w.r.t. $x$ and $y$

$$p = \frac{\partial z}{\partial x} = 2x(y^2 + b) \quad ...(1)$$

$$q = \frac{\partial z}{\partial y} = 2y(x^2 + a) \quad ...(2)$$

Multiplying (1) and (2), we get

$$pq = 4xy(x^2 + a)(y^2 + b) \quad \text{or} \quad pq = 4xyz$$

which is a partial differential equation of the first order.

(*ii*) Here $2z = \frac{x^2}{a^2} + \frac{y^2}{b^2}$

Differentiating partially w.r.t. $x$ and $y$

$$2\frac{\partial z}{\partial x} = \frac{2x}{a^2} \text{ or } \frac{1}{a^2} = \frac{p}{x} \quad \text{and} \quad 2\frac{\partial z}{\partial y} = \frac{2y}{b^2} \text{ or } \frac{1}{b^2} = \frac{q}{y}$$

Substituting for $\frac{1}{a^2}$ and $\frac{1}{b^2}$ in the given equation, we get

$$2z = px + qy$$

which is a partial differential equation of the first order.

(*iii*) Here the number of arbitrary constants ($a$, $b$, $c$) is greater than the number of independent variables ($x$, $y$).

Differentiating partially w.r.t. $x$ and $y$, we have

$$\frac{2x}{a^2} + \frac{2z}{c^2} \cdot \frac{\partial z}{\partial x} = 0 \quad \text{or} \quad c^2x + a^2z\frac{\partial z}{\partial x} = 0 \quad ...(1)$$

and $$\frac{2y}{b^2} + \frac{2z}{c^2} \cdot \frac{\partial z}{\partial y} = 0 \quad \text{or} \quad c^2 y + b^2 z \frac{\partial z}{\partial y} = 0 \qquad \ldots(2)$$

Again differentiating (1) partially w.r.t. $x$, we have

$$c^2 + a^2 \left(\frac{\partial z}{\partial x}\right)^2 + a^2 z \frac{\partial^2 z}{\partial x^2} = 0 \quad \text{or} \quad \frac{c^2}{a^2} + \left(\frac{\partial z}{\partial x}\right)^2 + z \frac{\partial^2 z}{\partial x^2} = 0$$

Substituting $\frac{c^2}{a^2} = -\frac{z}{x}\frac{\partial z}{\partial x}$ from (1), we have

$$-\frac{z}{x}\frac{\partial z}{\partial x} + \left(\frac{\partial z}{\partial x}\right)^2 + z\frac{\partial^2 z}{\partial x^2} = 0 \quad \text{or} \quad xz\frac{\partial^2 z}{\partial x^2} + x\left(\frac{\partial z}{\partial x}\right)^2 - z\frac{\partial z}{\partial x} = 0$$

which is a partial differential equation of the second order.

**Note.** Instead of differentiating (1) partially w.r.t. $x$, if we differentiate (2) partially w.r.t. $y$ and substitute for $\frac{c^2}{b^2}$ from (2), we shall get $yz\frac{\partial^2 z}{\partial y^2} + y\left(\frac{\partial z}{\partial y}\right)^2 - z\frac{\partial z}{\partial y} = 0.$

**Example 3.** *Form the partial differential equation by eliminating the function f from the relation*

$$z = y^2 + 2f\left(\frac{1}{x} + \log y\right).$$

**Sol.** Differentiating $z$ partially w.r.t. $x$ and $y$

$$p = \frac{\partial z}{\partial x} = 2f'\left(\frac{1}{x} + \log y\right).\left(-\frac{1}{x^2}\right)$$

or $$-px^2 = 2f'\left(\frac{1}{x} + \log y\right) \qquad \ldots(1)$$

and $$q = \frac{\partial z}{\partial y} = 2y + 2f'\left(\frac{1}{x} + \log y\right)\left(\frac{1}{y}\right)$$

or $$qy - 2y^2 = 2f'\left(\frac{1}{x} + \log y\right) \qquad \ldots(2)$$

From (1) and (2), we have $-px^2 = qy - 2y^2$ or $x^2 p + yq = 2y^2$

which is a partial differential equation of the first order.

**Example 4.** *Form the partial differential equation by eliminating the arbitrary functions from*

(*i*) $z = f(x + it) + g(x - it)$, *where* $i = \sqrt{-1}$

(*ii*) $z = xf_1(x + t) + f_2(x + t)$

(*iii*) $f(x + y + z, x^2 + y^2 + z^2) = 0.$

**Sol.** (*i*) Given $z = f(x + it) + g(x - it)$

Differentiating $z$ twice partially w.r.t. $x$ and $t$, we have

$$\frac{\partial z}{\partial x} = f'(x + it) + g'(x - it)$$

$$\frac{\partial^2 z}{\partial x^2} = f''(x + it) + g''(x - it) \qquad \ldots(1)$$

$$\frac{\partial z}{\partial t} = if'(x+it) - ig'(x-it)$$

$$\frac{\partial^2 z}{\partial t^2} = i^2 f''(x+it) + i^2 g''(x-it)$$

or
$$\frac{\partial^2 z}{\partial t^2} = -f''(x+it) - g''(x-it) \quad ...(2)$$

Adding (1) and (2), we have $\frac{\partial^2 z}{\partial x^2} + \frac{\partial^2 z}{\partial t^2} = 0$

which is a partial differential equation of the second order.

(*ii*) Given $z = xf_1(x+t) + f_2(x+t)$

$$\therefore \quad \frac{\partial z}{\partial x} = f_1(x+t) + xf_1'(x+t) + f_2'(x+t)$$

$$\frac{\partial^2 z}{\partial x^2} = f_1'(x+t) + f_1'(x+t) + xf_1''(x+t) + f_2''(x+t)$$

or
$$\frac{\partial^2 z}{\partial x^2} = 2f_1'(x+t) + xf_1''(x+t) + f_2''(x+t) \quad ...(1)$$

$$\frac{\partial z}{\partial t} = xf_1'(x+t) + f_2'(x+t)$$

$$\frac{\partial^2 z}{\partial t^2} = xf_1''(x+t) + f_2''(x+t) \quad ...(2)$$

Subtracting (2) from (1) $\frac{\partial^2 z}{\partial x^2} - \frac{\partial^2 z}{\partial t^2} = 2f_1'(x+t)$ ...(3)

Also
$$\frac{\partial^2 z}{\partial x \partial t} = f_1'(x+t) + xf_1''(x+t) + f_2''(x+t)$$

$$= \frac{1}{2}\left[\frac{\partial^2 z}{\partial x^2} - \frac{\partial^2 z}{\partial t^2}\right] + \frac{\partial^2 z}{\partial t^2} \quad \text{[Using (2) and (3)]}$$

or
$$\frac{\partial^2 z}{\partial x^2} - 2\frac{\partial^2 z}{\partial x \partial t} + \frac{\partial^2 z}{\partial t^2} = 0$$

which is a partial differential equation of the second order.

(*iii*) Let $x + y + z = u$, $x^2 + y^2 + z^2 = v$, then $f(u, v) = 0$

Differentiating partially w.r.t. $x$ and $y$, we have

$$\frac{\partial f}{\partial u}\left(\frac{\partial u}{\partial x} + \frac{\partial u}{\partial z}p\right) + \frac{\partial f}{\partial v}\left(\frac{\partial v}{\partial x} + \frac{\partial v}{\partial z}p\right) = 0$$

or
$$\frac{\partial f}{\partial u}(1+p) + \frac{\partial f}{\partial v}(2x + 2zp) = 0 \quad ...(1)$$

and
$$\frac{\partial f}{\partial u}\left(\frac{\partial u}{\partial y} + \frac{\partial u}{\partial z}q\right) + \frac{\partial f}{\partial v}\left(\frac{\partial v}{\partial y} + \frac{\partial v}{\partial z}q\right) = 0$$

or
$$\frac{\partial f}{\partial u}(1+q) + \frac{\partial f}{\partial v}(2y + 2zq) = 0 \quad ...(2)$$

Eliminating $\frac{\partial f}{\partial u}$ and $\frac{\partial f}{\partial v}$ from (1) and (2), we get

$$(1 + p)(2y + 2zq) = (1 + q)(2x + 2zp)$$

or
$$(y - z)p + (z - x)q = x - y$$

which is a partial differential equation of the first order.

## TEST YOUR KNOWLEDGE

*Form the partial differential equations by eliminating the arbitrary constants from the following :*

1. $z = ax + by + a^2 + b^2$
2. $(x - a)^2 + (y - b)^2 + z^2 = 1$
3. $z = xy + y\sqrt{x^2 - a^2} + b$
4. $z = ax^2 + bxy + cy^2$
5. $z = axe^y + \frac{1}{2}a^2e^{2y} + b$.
6. Find the differential equation of all planes which are at a constant distance '$a$' from the origin.
7. (*a*) Find the differential equation of all spheres whose centres lie on the $z$-axis.
   (*b*) Find the differential equation of all spheres of radius 3 units having their centres in the $xy$-plane.

*Form partial differential equations by eliminating the arbitrary functions from the following :*

8. $z = f(x^2 - y^2)$
9. $z = f(y/x)$
10. $xyz = \phi(x + y + z)$
11. $z = f_1(x)\, f_2(y)$
12. $z = yf(x) + xg(y)$
13. $z = f(x + ay) + g(x - ay)$
14. $z = f(x + 4t) + g(x - 4t)$
15. $z = f_1(y + 2x) + f_2(y - 3x)$
16. $f(xy + z^2, x + y + z) = 0$
17. $f(x^2 + y^2, z - xy) = 0$
18. Form the partial differential equation for $x^2 + y^2 + (z - c)^2 = a^2$.
19. Form a partial differential equation from $z = (x - a)^2 + (y - b)^2$. (*M.G.U. May 2010*)
20. If $z = f(u, v)$, $u = x^2 - y^2$, $v = 2xy$ show that $xp - yq = 2(x^2 + y^2)\frac{\partial z}{\partial u}$. (*M.G.U. May 2008*)
21. If $u = \frac{1}{\sqrt{x^2 + y^2 + z^2}}$, show that $\frac{\partial^2 u}{\partial x^2} + \frac{\partial^2 u}{\partial y^2} + \frac{\partial^2 u}{\partial z^2} = 0$. (*M.G.U. May 2008*)

### Answers

1. $z = px + qy + p^2 + q^2$
2. $z^2(p^2 + q^2 + 1) = 1$
3. $px + qy = pq$
4. $x^2r + 2xys + y^2t = 2z$
5. $q = px + p^2$
6. $z = px + qy \pm a\sqrt{1 + p^2 + q^2}$
7. (*a*) $py - qx = 0$ (*b*) $z^2(p^2 + q^2 + 1) = 9$
8. $py + qx = 0$
9. $px + qy = 0$
10. $x(y - z)p + y(z - x)q = z(x - y)$
11. $z\frac{\partial^2 z}{\partial x \partial y} - \frac{\partial z}{\partial x} \cdot \frac{\partial z}{\partial y} = 0$
12. $xy\frac{\partial^2 z}{\partial x \partial y} = x\frac{\partial z}{\partial x} + y\frac{\partial z}{\partial y} - z$
13. $\frac{\partial^2 z}{\partial y^2} = a^2\frac{\partial^2 z}{\partial x^2}$
14. $16\frac{\partial^2 z}{\partial x^2} - \frac{\partial^2 z}{\partial t^2} = 0$
15. $\frac{\partial^2 z}{\partial x^2} + \frac{\partial^2 z}{\partial x \partial y} - 6\frac{\partial^2 z}{\partial y^2} = 0$
16. $p(x - 2z) + q(2z - y) = y - x$
17. $py - qx = y^2 - x^2$
18. $yp - xq = 0$
19. $4z = p^2 + q^2$.

### 3.3. DEFINITIONS

The solution
$$f(x, y, z, a, b) = 0 \quad ...(1)$$
of a first order partial differential equation, which contains two arbitrary constants is called a *complete solution* or *complete integral*.

If in this solution, we put $b = \phi(a)$ and find the envelope of the family of surfaces $f(x, y, z, a, \phi(a)) = 0$, we get a solution involving an arbitrary function $\phi$. This is called the *general solution* or *general integral*.

A solution obtained from the complete integral by giving particular values to the arbitrary constant is called a *particular solution* or *particular integral*.

A solution of a partial differential equation in a region R is a function of the independent variables whose partial derivatives satisfy the partial differential equation at every point in R. As such, a partial differential equation may have a large number of entirely different solutions. For example, $u = x^2 - y^2$, $u = \log(x^2 + y^2)$, $u = \sin kx \cosh ky$ are solutions of the Laplace equation $\frac{\partial^2 u}{\partial x^2} + \frac{\partial^2 u}{\partial y^2} = 0$. The unique solution of a partial differential equation corresponding to a physical problem must satisfy certain other conditions at the boundary of the region R. These are known as the *boundary conditions*.

If these conditions are given for the time $t = 0$, they are known as the *initial conditions*.

## ILLUSTRATIVE EXAMPLES

**Example 1.** *Show that if $u_1$ and $u_2$ are two solutions of the equation*

$$\frac{\partial^2 u}{\partial x^2} + \frac{\partial^2 u}{\partial y^2} + \frac{\partial^2 u}{\partial z^2} = A\frac{\partial^2 u}{\partial t^2} + B\frac{\partial u}{\partial t}, \quad \textit{then } c_1u_1 + c_2u_2 \textit{ is also a solution.}$$

**Sol.** Since $u_1$ and $u_2$ are solutions of the given equation, we have

$$\frac{\partial^2 u_1}{\partial x^2} + \frac{\partial^2 u_1}{\partial y^2} + \frac{\partial^2 u_1}{\partial z^2} = A\frac{\partial^2 u_1}{\partial t^2} + B\frac{\partial u_1}{\partial t} \quad \text{...(1)}$$

and

$$\frac{\partial^2 u_2}{\partial x^2} + \frac{\partial^2 u_2}{\partial y^2} + \frac{\partial^2 u_2}{\partial z^2} = A\frac{\partial^2 u_2}{\partial t^2} + B\frac{\partial u_2}{\partial t} \quad \text{...(2)}$$

Now $\frac{\partial^2}{\partial x^2}(c_1u_1 + c_2u_2) + \frac{\partial^2}{\partial y^2}(c_1u_1 + c_2u_2) + \frac{\partial^2}{\partial z^2}(c_1u_1 + c_2u_2)$

$$= c_1\left(\frac{\partial^2 u_1}{\partial x^2} + \frac{\partial^2 u_1}{\partial y^2} + \frac{\partial^2 u_1}{\partial z^2}\right) + c_2\left(\frac{\partial^2 u_2}{\partial x^2} + \frac{\partial^2 u_2}{\partial y^2} + \frac{\partial^2 u_2}{\partial z^2}\right)$$

$$= c_1\left(A\frac{\partial^2 u_1}{\partial t^2} + B\frac{\partial u_1}{\partial t}\right) + c_2\left(A\frac{\partial^2 u_2}{\partial t^2} + B\frac{\partial u_2}{\partial t}\right) \quad \text{[Using (1) and (2)]}$$

$$= A\frac{\partial^2}{\partial t^2}(c_1u_1 + c_2u_2) + B\frac{\partial}{\partial t}(c_1u_1 + c_2u_2)$$

$\Rightarrow$ $c_1u_1 + c_2u_2$ is also a solution of the given equation.

**Generalisation.** If $u_1, u_2, u_3, \ldots\ldots, u_n$ are $n$ independent solutions, then $c_1u_1 + c_2u_2 + c_3u_3 + \ldots\ldots + c_nu_n$ is also a solution.

**Example 2.** *Verify that $e^{-n^2t} \sin nx$ is a solution of the heat equation $\frac{\partial u}{\partial t} = \frac{\partial^2 u}{\partial x^2}$.*

*Hence show that $\sum_{n=1}^{N} c_n e^{-n^2t} \sin nx$, where $c_1, c_2, \ldots\ldots, c_N$ are arbitrary constants, is a solution of this equation satisfying the boundary conditions $u(0, t) = 0$ and $u(\pi, t) = 0$.*

**Sol.** Let $u = e^{-n^2 t} \sin nx$

then $\dfrac{\partial u}{\partial t} = - n^2 e^{-n^2 t} \sin nx$

$$\frac{\partial u}{\partial x} = n e^{-n^2 t} \cos nx$$

$$\frac{\partial^2 u}{\partial x^2} = - n^2 e^{-n^2 t} \sin nx$$

so that $\dfrac{\partial u}{\partial t} = \dfrac{\partial^2 u}{\partial x^2}$

$\therefore$ $u = e^{-n^2 t} \sin nx$ is a solution of the given equation.

For $n = 1, 2, \ldots\ldots, \mathrm{N}$, we get N different solutions. Their linear combination

$$u = c_1 e^{-1^2 t} \sin 1x + c_2 e^{-2^2 t} \sin 2x + \ldots\ldots + c_{\mathrm{N}} e^{-\mathrm{N}^2 t} \sin \mathrm{N}x$$

or $u(x, t) = \displaystyle\sum_{n=1}^{\mathrm{N}} c_n e^{-n^2 t} \sin nx$ is also a solution.

Clearly, $u(0, t) = 0$ and $u(\pi, t) = 0$, since $\sin n\pi = 0$, where $n$ is an integer.

## TEST YOUR KNOWLEDGE

1. Verify that $z = f(x^2 + y^2)$ is a solution of $y \dfrac{\partial z}{\partial x} - x \dfrac{\partial z}{\partial y} = 0$.

2. Verify that $u = \cos kx \sinh ky$ is a solution of the Laplace equation $\dfrac{\partial^2 u}{\partial x^2} + \dfrac{\partial^2 u}{\partial y^2} = 0$.

3. Verify that $e^{-k^2 t} \sin\left(\dfrac{kx}{c}\right)$ is a solution of the heat equation $\dfrac{\partial u}{\partial t} = c^2 \dfrac{\partial^2 u}{\partial x^2}$.

   Hence show that $\displaystyle\sum_{k=1}^{n} \mathrm{A}_k e^{-k^2 t} \sin\left(\frac{kx}{c}\right)$, where $\mathrm{A}_1, \mathrm{A}_2, \ldots\ldots$ are arbitrary constants, is also a solution satisfying the boundary conditions $u(0, t) = u(c\pi, t) = 0$.

## 3.4. EQUATIONS SOLVABLE BY DIRECT INTEGRATION

Those equations which contain **only one** partial derivative can be solved by direct integration. However, in place of the constants of integration, we must use arbitrary functions of the variable kept constant.

## ILLUSTRATIVE EXAMPLES

**Example 1.** *Solve* $\dfrac{\partial^2 z}{\partial x \partial y} = \sin x \sin y$, *given that* $\dfrac{\partial z}{\partial y} = -2 \sin y$ *when* $x = 0$ *and* $z = 0$ *when* $y$ *is an odd multiple of* $\dfrac{\pi}{2}$.

**Sol.** Given $\dfrac{\partial^2 z}{\partial x \partial y} = \sin x \sin y$

Integrating w.r.t. $x$, keeping $y$ as constant, we have

$$\frac{\partial z}{\partial y} = -\cos x \sin y + f(y) \quad ...(1)$$

When $x = 0$, $\dfrac{\partial z}{\partial y} = -2 \sin y$ | given

$\therefore$ $-2 \sin y = -\sin y + f(y)$ or $f(y) = -\sin y$

$\therefore$ From (1), $\dfrac{\partial z}{\partial y} = -\cos x \sin y - \sin y$

Integrating w.r.t. $y$, keeping $x$ as constant, we have

$$z = \cos x \cos y + \cos y + \phi(x) \quad ...(2)$$

When $y$ is an odd multiple of $\dfrac{\pi}{2}$, $z = 0$ | given

$\therefore$ $0 = 0 + 0 + \phi(x)$, since $\cos (2n + 1) \dfrac{\pi}{2} = 0$ or $\phi(x) = 0$

$\therefore$ From (2), $z = (1 + \cos x) \cos y$ which is the required particular solution.

**Example 2.** *Solve* $\dfrac{\partial^2 z}{\partial x^2} + z = 0$, *given that when* $x = 0$, $z = e^y$ *and* $\dfrac{\partial z}{\partial x} = 1$.

**Sol.** If $z$ were a function of **x alone**, the solution would have been $z = c_1 \cos x + c_2 \sin x$, where $c_1$ and $c_2$ are arbitrary constants.

But here $z$ is a function of $x$ and $y$, therefore, $c_1$ and $c_2$ are arbitrary functions of $y$, the independent variable kept constant.

$\therefore$ The solution of the given equation is

$$z = f(y) \cos x + \phi(y) \sin x \quad \text{and} \quad \frac{\partial z}{\partial x} = -f(y) \sin x + \phi(y) \cos x$$

When $x = 0$, $z = e^y$ $\therefore$ $e^y = f(y)$

When $x = 0$, $\dfrac{\partial z}{\partial x} = 1$ $\therefore$ $1 = \phi(y)$

$\therefore$ The required particular solution is $z = e^y \cos x + \sin x$.

## TEST YOUR KNOWLEDGE

*Solve the following equations :*

**1.** $\dfrac{\partial^2 z}{\partial x^2} = xy$

**2.** $\dfrac{\partial^2 z}{\partial x \partial y} = \dfrac{1}{xy}$

**3.** $\dfrac{\partial^2 z}{\partial x \partial y} = 2x + 2y$

**4.** $\dfrac{\partial^2 z}{\partial y^2} = \sin (xy)$

**5.** $\dfrac{\partial^2 u}{\partial y \partial x} = 4x \sin (3xy)$

**6.** $\log \left[\dfrac{\partial^2 z}{\partial x \partial y}\right] = x + y$

**7.** $\dfrac{\partial^3 z}{\partial x^2 \partial y} = \cos (2x + 3y)$

**8.** $\dfrac{\partial^2 u}{\partial x \partial t} = e^{-t} \cos x$

**9.** $\dfrac{\partial^2 z}{\partial x^2} = a^2 z$ given that when $x = 0$, $\dfrac{\partial z}{\partial x} = a \sin y$ and $\dfrac{\partial z}{\partial y} = 0$.

**Answers**

**1.** $z = \frac{1}{6} x^3 y + x f(y) + \phi(y)$ **2.** $z = \log x \log y + g(y) + \phi(x)$ **3.** $z = xy(x+y) + g(y) + \phi(x)$

**4.** $z = -\dfrac{1}{x^2} \sin xy + y f(x) + \phi(x)$ **5.** $u = -\dfrac{4}{9y} \sin(3xy) + f(x) + \phi(y)$ **6.** $z = e^{x+y} + g(y) + \phi(x)$

**7.** $z = f(x) + x\phi(y) + g(y) - \dfrac{1}{12} \sin(2x + 3y)$ **8.** $u = -e^{-t} \sin x + f(x) + g(t)$

**9.** $A \cosh ax + \sin y \sinh ax$.

## 3.5. LINEAR PARTIAL DIFFERENTIAL EQUATIONS OF THE FIRST ORDER

A differential equation involving first order partial derivatives $p$ and $q$ only is called a *partial differential equation of the first order*. If $p$ and $q$ both occur in the first degree only and are not multiplied together, then it is called a *linear partial differential equation of the first order*.

## 3.6. LAGRANGE'S LINEAR EQUATION

The partial differential equation of the form $Pp + Qq = R$, where P, Q and R are functions of $x, y, z$ is the standard form of a linear partial differential equation of the first order and is called *Lagrange's Linear Equation*.

Now Lagrange's linear equation $\qquad Pp + Qq = R \qquad$ ...(1)

is obtained by eliminating an arbitrary function $\phi$ from $\qquad \phi(u, v) = 0 \qquad$ ...(2)

where $u, v$ are some definite functions of $x, y, z$.

Differentiating (2) partially w.r.t. $x$ and $y$

$$\frac{\partial \phi}{\partial u}\left(\frac{\partial u}{\partial x} + \frac{\partial u}{\partial z} p\right) + \frac{\partial \phi}{\partial v}\left(\frac{\partial v}{\partial x} + \frac{\partial v}{\partial z} p\right) = 0$$

and

$$\frac{\partial \phi}{\partial u}\left(\frac{\partial u}{\partial y} + \frac{\partial u}{\partial z} q\right) + \frac{\partial \phi}{\partial v}\left(\frac{\partial v}{\partial y} + \frac{\partial v}{\partial z} q\right) = 0$$

Eliminating $\dfrac{\partial \phi}{\partial u}$ and $\dfrac{\partial \phi}{\partial v}$, we get

$$\left(\frac{\partial u}{\partial x} + \frac{\partial u}{\partial z} p\right)\left(\frac{\partial v}{\partial y} + \frac{\partial v}{\partial z} q\right) - \left(\frac{\partial v}{\partial x} + \frac{\partial v}{\partial z} p\right)\left(\frac{\partial u}{\partial y} + \frac{\partial u}{\partial z} q\right) = 0$$

or

$$\left(\frac{\partial u}{\partial y} \cdot \frac{\partial v}{\partial z} - \frac{\partial u}{\partial z} \cdot \frac{\partial v}{\partial y}\right) p + \left(\frac{\partial u}{\partial z} \cdot \frac{\partial v}{\partial x} - \frac{\partial u}{\partial x} \cdot \frac{\partial v}{\partial z}\right) q = \frac{\partial u}{\partial x} \cdot \frac{\partial v}{\partial y} - \frac{\partial u}{\partial y} \cdot \frac{\partial v}{\partial x}$$

which is the same as (1) with

$$P = \frac{\partial u}{\partial y} \cdot \frac{\partial v}{\partial z} - \frac{\partial u}{\partial z} \cdot \frac{\partial v}{\partial y}, \quad Q = \frac{\partial u}{\partial z} \cdot \frac{\partial v}{\partial x} - \frac{\partial u}{\partial x} \cdot \frac{\partial v}{\partial z}, \quad R = \frac{\partial u}{\partial x} \cdot \frac{\partial v}{\partial y} - \frac{\partial u}{\partial y} \cdot \frac{\partial v}{\partial x}.$$

To determine $u, v$ from P, Q, R, suppose $u = a$ and $v = b$, where $a, b$ are constants, so that

$$\frac{\partial u}{\partial x} dx + \frac{\partial u}{\partial y} dy + \frac{\partial u}{\partial z} dz = du = 0$$

$$\frac{\partial v}{\partial x}dx + \frac{\partial v}{\partial y}dy + \frac{\partial v}{\partial z}dz = dv = 0$$

By cross-multiplication, we have

$$\frac{dx}{\frac{\partial u}{\partial y}\cdot\frac{\partial v}{\partial z} - \frac{\partial u}{\partial z}\cdot\frac{\partial v}{\partial y}} = \frac{dy}{\frac{\partial u}{\partial z}\cdot\frac{\partial v}{\partial x} - \frac{\partial u}{\partial x}\cdot\frac{\partial v}{\partial z}} = \frac{dz}{\frac{\partial u}{\partial x}\cdot\frac{\partial v}{\partial y} - \frac{\partial u}{\partial y}\cdot\frac{\partial v}{\partial x}}$$

or $$\frac{dx}{P} = \frac{dy}{Q} = \frac{dz}{R} \quad ...(3)$$

The solutions of these equations are $u = a$ and $v = b$. Thus determining $u, v$ from the simultaneous equations (3), we have the solution of the partial differential equation.

$$Pp + Qq = R \quad \text{as} \quad \phi(u, v) = 0 \quad \text{or} \quad u = f(v).$$

**Note.** Equations (3) are called **Lagrange's auxiliary equations** or **subsidiary equations.**

### 3.7. WORKING METHOD

To solve the equation $\quad Pp + Qq = R$

(*i*) form the auxiliary equations $\quad \frac{dx}{P} = \frac{dy}{Q} = \frac{dz}{R}$

(*ii*) solve the auxiliary equations by the method of grouping or the method of multipliers or both to get two independent solutions $u = a$ and $v = b$, where $a, b$ are arbitrary constants.

(*iii*) then $\phi(u, v) = 0$ or $u = f(v)$ is the general solution of the equation $Pp + Qq = R$.

## ILLUSTRATIVE EXAMPLES

**Example 1.** *Solve the following differential equations :*

(*i*) $\frac{y^2 z}{x} p + xzq = y^2$ (*ii*) $pz - qz = z^2 + (x + y)^2$

(*iii*) $(x^2 - yz)p + (y^2 - zx)q = z^2 - xy.$ (M.G.U. June 2006)

**Sol.** (*i*) The given equation can be written as $\quad y^2zp + x^2zq = xy^2$

Comparing with $Pp + Qq = R$, we have $\quad P = y^2z, \quad Q = x^2z, \quad R = xy^2$

$\therefore$ The auxiliary equations are $\frac{dx}{y^2 z} = \frac{dy}{x^2 z} = \frac{dz}{xy^2}$

Taking the first two members, we have $\quad x^2dx = y^2dy$

which on integration gives $\quad x^3 - y^3 = a$ ...(1)

Again taking the first and third members, we have $\quad xdx = zdz$

which on integration gives $\quad x^2 - z^2 = b$ ...(2)

From (1) and (2), the general solution is $\quad \phi(x^3 - y^3, x^2 - z^2) = 0.$

(*ii*) Here the auxiliary equations are $\quad \frac{dx}{z} = \frac{dy}{-z} = \frac{dz}{z^2 + (x + y)^2}$

Taking the first two members, we have $\quad dx + dy = 0$

which on integration gives $\quad x + y = a$ ...(1)

Again taking the first and third members, we have

$$dx = \frac{zdz}{z^2 + a^2}, \text{ since } x + y = a$$

or $$\frac{2z\,dz}{z^2 + a^2} = 2dx$$

which on integration gives $\log(z^2 + a^2) = 2x + b$ or $\log[z^2 + (x + y)^2] - 2x = b$ ...(2)

From (1) and (2), the general solution is

$$\phi[x + y, \log(x^2 + y^2 + z^2 + 2xy) - 2x] = 0.$$

(*iii*) Here the auxiliary equations are

$$\frac{dx}{x^2 - yz} = \frac{dy}{y^2 - zx} = \frac{dz}{z^2 - xy} \quad ...(1)$$

$$\therefore \quad \frac{dx - dy}{(x - y)(x + y + z)} = \frac{dy - dz}{(y - z)(x + y + z)}$$

or $$\frac{dx - dy}{x - y} = \frac{dy - dz}{y - z}$$

which on integration gives $\log(x - y) = \log(y - z) + \log a$

or $$\log\left(\frac{x - y}{y - z}\right) = \log a \quad \text{or} \quad \frac{x - y}{y - z} = a \quad ...(2)$$

Using $x, y, z$ as multipliers,

each fraction of (1) $$= \frac{x\,dx + y\,dy + z\,dz}{x^3 + y^3 + z^3 - 3xyz}$$

$$= \frac{x\,dx + y\,dy + z\,dz}{(x + y + z)(x^2 + y^2 + z^2 - xy - yz - zx)} \quad ...(3)$$

Also, each fraction of (1)

$$= \frac{dx + dy + dz}{x^2 + y^2 + z^2 - xy - yz - zx} \quad ...(4)$$

From (3) and (4), $$\frac{x\,dx + y\,dy + z\,dz}{x + y + z} = dx + dy + dz$$

or $$xdx + ydy + zdz = (x + y + z)\,d(x + y + z)$$

Integrating $$\frac{x^2}{2} + \frac{y^2}{2} + \frac{z^2}{2} = \frac{(x + y + z)^2}{2} + c$$

or $$x^2 + y^2 + z^2 = (x + y + z)^2 + 2c$$

or $$2xy + 2yz + 2zx + 2c = 0$$

or $$xy + yz + zx = b, \quad \text{where } b = -c \quad ...(5)$$

From (2) and (5), the general solution is

$$\phi\left(\frac{x - y}{y - z}, xy + yz + zx\right) = 0.$$

**Example 2.** *Solve the following differential equations :*

(*i*) $(mz - ny)p + (nx - lz)q = ly - mx$

(*ii*) $x^2(y - z)p + y^2(z - x)q = z^2(x - y)$. (M.G.U. Dec. 2007)

**Sol.** (*i*) Here the auxiliary equations are $\dfrac{dx}{mz - ny} = \dfrac{dy}{nx - lz} = \dfrac{dz}{ly - mx}$

Using $x, y, z$ as multipliers, we get

$$\text{each fraction} = \frac{x\,dx + y\,dy + z\,dz}{0}$$

$$\therefore \qquad xdx + ydy + zdz = 0$$

which on integration gives $x^2 + y^2 + z^2 = a$ ...(1)

Again using $l, m, n$ as multipliers, we get

$$\text{each fraction} = \frac{ldx + mdy + ndz}{0}$$

$$\therefore \qquad ldx + mdy + ndz = 0$$

which on integration gives $lx + my + nz = b$ ...(2)

From (1) and (2), the general solution is

$$x^2 + y^2 + z^2 = f(lx + my + nz).$$

(*ii*) Here the auxiliary equations are

$$\frac{dx}{x^2(y - z)} = \frac{dy}{y^2(z - x)} = \frac{dz}{z^2(x - y)}$$

Using $\dfrac{1}{x^2}, \dfrac{1}{y^2}, \dfrac{1}{z^2}$ as multipliers, we get

$$\text{each fraction} = \frac{\dfrac{1}{x^2}dx + \dfrac{1}{y^2}dy + \dfrac{1}{z^2}dz}{0}$$

$$\therefore \qquad \frac{dx}{x^2} + \frac{dy}{y^2} + \frac{dz}{z^2} = 0$$

which on integration gives $\dfrac{1}{x} + \dfrac{1}{y} + \dfrac{1}{z} = a$ ...(1)

Again using $\dfrac{1}{x}, \dfrac{1}{y}, \dfrac{1}{z}$ as multipliers, we get

$$\text{each fraction} = \frac{\dfrac{1}{x}dx + \dfrac{1}{y}dy + \dfrac{1}{z}dz}{0}$$

$$\therefore \qquad \frac{dx}{x} + \frac{dy}{y} + \frac{dz}{z} = 0$$

which on integration gives $\log x + \log y + \log z = \log b$

or $\log (xyz) = \log b$ or $xyz = b$ ...(2)

From (1) and (2), the general solution is $\phi\left(\dfrac{1}{x} + \dfrac{1}{y} + \dfrac{1}{z}, xyz\right) = 0.$

**Example 3.** *Solve the following differential equations :*

(*i*) $(x^2 - y^2 - z^2)p + 2xyq = 2xz$

(*ii*) $(z^2 - 2yz - y^2)p + (xy + zx)q = xy - zx.$ (M.G.U. May 2010)

**Sol.** (*i*) Here the auxiliary equations are

$$\frac{dx}{x^2 - y^2 - z^2} = \frac{dy}{2xy} = \frac{dz}{2xz}$$

Taking the last two members, we have

$$\frac{dy}{y} = \frac{dz}{z}$$

which on integration gives $\log y = \log z + \log a$

or $$\log \frac{y}{z} = \log a \quad \text{or} \quad \frac{y}{z} = a \qquad ...(1)$$

Using $x, y, z$ as multipliers, we get

$$\text{each fraction} = \frac{x\,dx + y\,dy + z\,dz}{x(x^2 + y^2 + z^2)}$$

$$\therefore \quad \frac{x\,dx + y\,dy + z\,dz}{x(x^2 + y^2 + z^2)} = \frac{dz}{2xz} \quad \text{or} \quad \frac{2x\,dx + 2y\,dy + 2z\,dz}{x^2 + y^2 + z^2} = \frac{dz}{z}$$

which on integration gives $\log (x^2 + y^2 + z^2) = \log z + \log b$

or $$\log \left(\frac{x^2 + y^2 + z^2}{z}\right) = \log b \quad \text{or} \quad \frac{x^2 + y^2 + z^2}{z} = b \qquad ...(2)$$

From (1) and (2), the general solution is

$$\frac{x^2 + y^2 + z^2}{z} = f\left(\frac{y}{z}\right) \quad \text{or} \quad x^2 + y^2 + z^2 = z\, f\left(\frac{y}{z}\right).$$

(*ii*) Here the auxiliary equations are

$$\frac{dx}{z^2 - 2yz - y^2} = \frac{dy}{xy + zx} = \frac{dz}{xy - zx}$$

Taking $x, y, z$ as multipliers, we have

$$\text{each fraction} = \frac{x\,dx + y\,dy + z\,dz}{0}$$

$$\therefore \qquad x\,dx + y\,dy + z\,dz = 0$$

which on integration gives $x^2 + y^2 + z^2 = a$ ...(1)

Again, taking the last two members, we have

$$\frac{dy}{y + z} = \frac{dz}{y - z} \quad \text{or} \quad (y - z)dy = (y + z)dz$$

or $$y\,dy - (z\,dy + y\,dz) - z\,dz = 0 \quad \text{or} \quad y\,dy - d(yz) - z\,dz = 0$$

which on integration gives $y^2 - 2yz - z^2 = b$ ...(2)

From (1) and (2), the general solution is

$$\phi(x^2 + y^2 + z^2, y^2 - 2yz - z^2) = 0.$$

**Example 4.** *Solve* $x\dfrac{\partial u}{\partial x} + y\dfrac{\partial u}{\partial y} + z\dfrac{\partial u}{\partial z} = xyz$.

**Sol.**[In the differential equation P$p$ + Q$q$ = R, there are **two independent variables** $x$ and $y$. To solve it, we have to find **two independent solutions** satisfying the equation $\dfrac{dx}{P} = \dfrac{dy}{Q} = \dfrac{dz}{R}$. This procedure can be extended to linear partial differential equations of the first order involving more than two independent variables.

If $u_1 = c_1, u_2 = c_2, \ldots\ldots, u_n = c_n$ are $n$ independent solutions of the equations

$$\frac{dx_1}{P_1} = \frac{dx_2}{P_2} = \ldots\ldots = \frac{dx_n}{P_n} = \frac{dz}{R}$$

then the general solution of the partial differential equation

$$P_1 \frac{\partial z}{\partial x_1} + P_2 \frac{\partial z}{\partial x_2} + \ldots\ldots + P_n \frac{\partial z}{\partial x_n} = R$$

is $\phi(u_1, u_2, \ldots\ldots, u_n) = 0$, where $\phi$ is an arbitrary function.]

Here the auxiliary equations are $\dfrac{dx}{x} = \dfrac{dy}{y} = \dfrac{dz}{z} = \dfrac{du}{xyz}$

Taking first and second members, we have

$$\frac{dx}{x} = \frac{dy}{y}$$

which on integration gives $\log x = \log y + \log c_1$

or $\log \dfrac{x}{y} = \log c_1$ or $\dfrac{x}{y} = c_1$ ...(1)

Similarly, taking second and third members, we have

$$\frac{y}{z} = c_2 \qquad \ldots(2)$$

Also, we have $\dfrac{yz\,dx + zx\,dy + xy\,dz}{3xyz} = \dfrac{du}{xyz}$

or $d(xyz) = 3du$

which on integration gives $xyz - 3u = c_3$ ...(3)

From (1), (2) and (3), the general solution is $\phi\left(\dfrac{x}{y}, \dfrac{y}{z}, xyz - 3u\right) = 0$.

## TEST YOUR KNOWLEDGE

*Solve the following equations :*

1. $2p + 3q = 1$
2. $xp + yq = 3z$
3. $(y - z)p + (x - y)q = z - x$
4. $p \tan x + q \tan y = \tan z$ *(M.G.U. July 2007)*
5. $p\sqrt{x} + q\sqrt{y} = \sqrt{z}$
6. $(z - y)p + (x - z)q = y - x$
7. $yzp + zxq = xy$
8. $(y + z)p + (z + x)q = x + y$

9. $y^2p - xyq = x(z - 2y)$

10. $x(y - z)p + y(z - x)q = z(x - y)$

11. $\left(\frac{y - z}{yz}\right) p + \left(\frac{z - x}{zx}\right) q = \frac{x - y}{xy}$

12. $x(z^2 - y^2)p + y(x^2 - z^2)q = z(y^2 - x^2)$

13. $x^2p + y^2q = (x + y)z$

14. $z(xp - yq) = y^2 - x^2$

15. $(y^3x - 2x^4)\, p - (2y^4 - x^3y)q = 9z(x^3 - y^3)$

16. $x_1p_1 + 2x_2p_2 + 3x_3p_3 + 4x_4p_4 = 0$

17. Solve the partial differential equation $(y + z)p - (x + z)\, q = x - y$.

## Answers

1. $\phi\,(3x - 2y, y - 3z) = 0$

2. $\phi\left(\frac{x}{y}, \frac{x^3}{z}\right) = 0$

3. $\phi\left(x + y + z, \frac{x^2}{2} + yz\right) = 0$

4. $\phi\left(\frac{\sin x}{\sin y}, \frac{\sin y}{\sin z}\right) = 0$

5. $\sqrt{x} - \sqrt{y} = f(\sqrt{x} - \sqrt{z})$

6. $x^2 + y^2 + z^2 = f\,(x + y + z)$

7. $\phi\,(x^2 - y^2, x^2 - z^2) = 0$

8. $\phi\left[\frac{x - y}{y - z}, (x - y)^2\,(x + y + z)\right] = 0$

9. $\phi\,(x^2 + y^2, yz - y^2) = 0$

10. $\phi\,(x + y + z, xyz) = 0$

11. $\phi\,(x + y + z, xyz) = 0$

12. $\phi\,(x^2 + y^2 + z^2, xyz) = 0$

13. $\phi\left(\frac{x - y}{z}, \frac{1}{y} - \frac{1}{x}\right) = 0$

14. $\phi\,(xy, x^2 + y^2 + z^2) = 0$

15. $\phi\left(\frac{y}{x^2} + \frac{x}{y^2}, xyz^{1/3}\right) = 0$

16. $\phi\left(\frac{x_1^2}{x_2}, \frac{x_1^3}{x_3}, \frac{x_1^4}{x_4}\right) = 0$

17. $\phi\,(x + y + z, x^2 + y^2 - z^2) = 0.$

[**Hint.** The auxiliary equations are $\frac{dx_1}{x_1} = \frac{dx_2}{2x_2} = \frac{dx_3}{3x_3} = \frac{dx_4}{4x_4} = \frac{dz}{0}$.]

### 3.8. CHARPIT'S METHOD

This is a general method for finding the complete solution of non-linear partial differential equations of the first order.

Let the given equation be $\quad f\,(x, y, z, p, q) = 0 \quad$ ...(1)

If we can find another relation $\quad F\,(x, y, z, p, q) = 0 \quad$ ...(2)

involving $x, y, z, p$ and $q$, then we can solve (1) and (2) for $p$ and $q$ and substitute in

$$dz = pdx + qdy \quad \text{...(3)}$$

Solution of (3), if it exists, is the complete solution of (1).

To determine F, we differentiate (1) and (2) partially with respect to $x$ and $y$. Thus

$$\frac{\partial f}{\partial x} + \frac{\partial f}{\partial z} \cdot p + \frac{\partial f}{\partial p} \cdot \frac{\partial p}{\partial x} + \frac{\partial f}{\partial q} \cdot \frac{\partial q}{\partial x} = 0 \quad \text{...(4)}$$

$$\frac{\partial F}{\partial x} + \frac{\partial F}{\partial z} \cdot p + \frac{\partial F}{\partial p} \cdot \frac{\partial p}{\partial x} + \frac{\partial F}{\partial q} \cdot \frac{\partial q}{\partial x} = 0 \quad \text{...(5)}$$

$$\frac{\partial f}{\partial y} + \frac{\partial f}{\partial z} \cdot q + \frac{\partial f}{\partial p} \cdot \frac{\partial p}{\partial y} + \frac{\partial f}{\partial q} \cdot \frac{\partial q}{\partial y} = 0 \quad \text{...(6)}$$

$$\frac{\partial F}{\partial y} + \frac{\partial F}{\partial z} \cdot q + \frac{\partial F}{\partial p} \cdot \frac{\partial p}{\partial y} + \frac{\partial F}{\partial q} \cdot \frac{\partial q}{\partial y} = 0 \quad \text{...(7)}$$

Eliminating $\frac{\partial p}{\partial x}$ between (4) and (5), we get

$$\left(\frac{\partial f}{\partial x}\cdot\frac{\partial F}{\partial p}-\frac{\partial F}{\partial x}\cdot\frac{\partial f}{\partial p}\right)+\left(\frac{\partial f}{\partial z}\cdot\frac{\partial F}{\partial p}-\frac{\partial F}{\partial z}\cdot\frac{\partial f}{\partial p}\right)p+\left(\frac{\partial f}{\partial q}\cdot\frac{\partial F}{\partial p}-\frac{\partial F}{\partial q}\cdot\frac{\partial f}{\partial p}\right)\frac{\partial q}{\partial x}=0 \qquad ...(8)$$

Eliminating $\frac{\partial q}{\partial y}$ between (6) and (7), we get

$$\left(\frac{\partial f}{\partial y}\cdot\frac{\partial F}{\partial q}-\frac{\partial F}{\partial y}\cdot\frac{\partial f}{\partial q}\right)+\left(\frac{\partial f}{\partial z}\cdot\frac{\partial F}{\partial q}-\frac{\partial F}{\partial z}\cdot\frac{\partial f}{\partial q}\right)q+\left(\frac{\partial f}{\partial p}\cdot\frac{\partial F}{\partial q}-\frac{\partial F}{\partial p}\cdot\frac{\partial f}{\partial q}\right)\frac{\partial p}{\partial y}=0 \qquad ...(9)$$

Since $\frac{\partial q}{\partial x}=\frac{\partial^2 z}{\partial x\partial y}=\frac{\partial^2 z}{\partial y\partial x}=\frac{\partial p}{\partial y}$, the last terms in (8) and (9) differ in sign only. Adding (8) and (9), we get

$$\left(\frac{\partial f}{\partial x}+p\frac{\partial f}{\partial z}\right)\frac{\partial F}{\partial p}+\left(\frac{\partial f}{\partial y}+q\frac{\partial f}{\partial z}\right)\frac{\partial F}{\partial q}+\left(-p\frac{\partial f}{\partial p}-q\frac{\partial f}{\partial q}\right)\frac{\partial F}{\partial z}+\left(-\frac{\partial f}{\partial p}\right)\frac{\partial F}{\partial x}+\left(-\frac{\partial f}{\partial q}\right)\frac{\partial F}{\partial y}=0 \qquad ...(10)$$

which is a linear partial differential equation of the first order with $x, y, z, p, q$ as independent variables and F as the dependent variable.

∴ The auxiliary equations are

$$\frac{dp}{\frac{\partial f}{\partial x}+p\frac{\partial f}{\partial z}}=\frac{dq}{\frac{\partial f}{\partial y}+q\frac{\partial f}{\partial z}}=\frac{dz}{-p\frac{\partial f}{\partial p}-q\frac{\partial f}{\partial q}}=\frac{dx}{-\frac{\partial f}{\partial p}}=\frac{dy}{-\frac{\partial f}{\partial q}}=\frac{\partial F}{0} \qquad ...(11)$$

Any integral of (11) which involves $p$ or $q$ or both can be taken as the assumed relation (2). In practice, we choose the simplest of the integrals of (11).

## ILLUSTRATIVE EXAMPLES

**Example 1.** *Solve :* $2zx - px^2 - 2qxy + pq = 0.$

**Sol.** Here $f = 2zx - px^2 - 2qxy + pq = 0$ ...(1)

∴ $\frac{\partial f}{\partial x}=2z-2px-2qy,\ \frac{\partial f}{\partial y}=-2qx,\ \frac{\partial f}{\partial z}=2x,\ \frac{\partial f}{\partial p}=-x^2+q,\ \frac{\partial f}{\partial q}=-2xy+p$

Charpit's auxiliary equations are

$$\frac{dp}{\frac{\partial f}{\partial x}+p\frac{\partial f}{\partial z}}=\frac{dq}{\frac{\partial f}{\partial y}+q\frac{\partial f}{\partial z}}=\frac{dz}{-p\frac{\partial f}{\partial p}-q\frac{\partial f}{\partial q}}=\frac{dx}{-\frac{\partial f}{\partial p}}=\frac{dy}{-\frac{\partial f}{\partial q}}=\frac{dF}{0}$$

or
$$\frac{dp}{2z-2qy}=\frac{dq}{0}=\frac{dz}{px^2-2pq+2qxy}=\frac{dx}{x^2-q}=\frac{dy}{2xy-p}=\frac{dF}{0}$$

∴ $dq = 0$ or $q = a$

Putting $q = a$ in (1), we get $p=\frac{2x(z-ay)}{x^2-a}$

∴ $$dz = pdx + qdy = \frac{2x(z-ay)}{x^2-a}\,dx + a\,dy$$

or $$\frac{dz - ady}{z - ay} = \frac{2x}{x^2 - a}\, dx$$

Integrating, $\log (z - ay) = \log (x^2 - a) + \log b$ or $z - ay = b\,(x^2 - a)$

$\therefore$ $z = ay + b(x^2 - a)$ which is the required complete integral.

**Example 2.** *Solve* $(p^2 + q^2)y = qz.$ (M.G.U. June 2006 ; May 2010)

**Sol.** Here $f = (p^2 + q^2)y - qz = 0$ ...(1)

$$\therefore \quad \frac{\partial f}{\partial x} = 0, \frac{\partial f}{\partial y} = p^2 + q^2, \frac{\partial f}{\partial z} = -q, \frac{\partial f}{\partial p} = 2py, \frac{\partial f}{\partial q} = 2qy - z$$

Charpit's auxiliary equations are

$$\frac{dp}{\frac{\partial f}{\partial x} + p\frac{\partial f}{\partial z}} = \frac{dq}{\frac{\partial f}{\partial y} + q\frac{\partial f}{\partial z}} = \frac{dz}{-p\frac{\partial f}{\partial p} - q\frac{\partial f}{\partial q}} = \frac{dx}{-\frac{\partial f}{\partial p}} = \frac{dy}{-\frac{\partial f}{\partial q}} = \frac{dF}{0}$$

or $$\frac{dp}{-pq} = \frac{dq}{p^2} = \frac{dz}{-qz} = \frac{dx}{-2py} = \frac{dy}{-2qy + z} = \frac{dF}{0}$$

From the first two members, we have $pdp + qdq = 0$

Integrating, $p^2 + q^2 = a^2$ ...(2)

Putting in (1), $$q = \frac{a^2 y}{z}$$

$\therefore$ From (2), $$p = \sqrt{a^2 - q^2} = \sqrt{a^2 - \frac{a^4 y^2}{z^2}} = \frac{a}{z}\sqrt{z^2 - a^2 y^2}$$

$$\therefore \quad dz = pdx + qdy = \frac{a}{z}\sqrt{z^2 - a^2 y^2}\, dx + \frac{a^2 y}{z}\, dy$$

or $$zdz - a^2 ydy = a\sqrt{z^2 - a^2 y^2}\, dx \quad \text{or} \quad \frac{\frac{1}{2}d(z^2 - a^2 y^2)}{\sqrt{z^2 - a^2 y^2}} = a\, dx$$

Integrating, we get $\sqrt{z^2 - a^2 y^2} = ax + b$

or $$z^2 = (ax + b)^2 + a^2 y^2$$

which is the required complete solution.

## TEST YOUR KNOWLEDGE

*Solve the following equations by Charpit's method :*

1. $px + qy = pq$
2. $z^2 = pqxy$
3. $pxy + pq + qy = yz$ (*M.G.U. July 2007*)
4. $z = p^2 x + q^2 y$
5. $2(z + px + qy) = yp^2$
6. $q + xp = p^2$.

### Answers

1. $az = \frac{1}{2}(y + ax)^2 + b$
2. $z = ax^b y^{1/b}$
3. $\log (z - ax) = y - a \log (a + y) + b$
4. $\sqrt{(1 + a)z} = \sqrt{ax} + \sqrt{y} + b$
5. $z = \frac{ax}{y^2} - \frac{a^2}{4y^3} + \frac{b}{y}$
6. $z = axe^{-y} - \frac{1}{2}a^2 e^{-2y} + b.$

## 3.9. HOMOGENEOUS LINEAR EQUATIONS WITH CONSTANT CO-EFFICIENTS

An equation of the form

$$a_0 \frac{\partial^n z}{\partial x^n} + a_1 \frac{\partial^n z}{\partial x^{n-1} \partial y} + a_2 \frac{\partial^n z}{\partial x^{n-2} \partial y^2} + \ldots\ldots + a_n \frac{\partial^n z}{\partial y^n} = \mathrm{F}(x, y) \qquad \ldots(1)$$

where $a_0, a_1, a_2, \ldots\ldots, a_n$ are constants, is called a *homogeneous linear partial differential equation of the nth order with constant co-efficients.*

Here, all the partial derivatives are of the $n$th order

Writing D for $\frac{\partial}{\partial x}$ and D′ for $\frac{\partial}{\partial y}$, (1) can be written as

$$(\mathrm{D}^n + a_1\mathrm{D}^{n-1}\mathrm{D}' + a_2\mathrm{D}^{n-2}\mathrm{D}'^2 + \ldots + a_n\mathrm{D}'^n)z = \mathrm{F}(x, y)$$

or

$$\phi(\mathrm{D}, \mathrm{D}')z = \mathrm{F}(x, y) \qquad \ldots(2)$$

As in the case of ordinary linear differential equations with constant co-efficients the complete solution of (2) consists of two parts :

(*i*) the **complementary function** (C.F.) which is the complete solution of the equation $\phi(\mathrm{D}, \mathrm{D}')z = 0$. It must contain $n$ arbitrary functions, where $n$ is the order of the differential equation.

(*ii*) the **particular integral** (P.I.) which is a particular solution (free from arbitrary constants) of

$$\phi(\mathrm{D}, \mathrm{D}')z = \mathrm{F}(x, y)$$

The complete solution of (2) is $z$ = C.F. + P.I.

## 3.10. RULES FOR FINDING THE C.F.

We explain the procedure for finding the complementary function of a differential equation of the second order. It can be easily extended to differential equations of higher order.

Consider the equation $\frac{\partial^2 z}{\partial x^2} + a_1 \frac{\partial^2 z}{\partial x \partial y} + a_2 \frac{\partial^2 z}{\partial y^2} = 0$

which in symbolic form is $\quad (\mathrm{D}^2 + a_1\mathrm{DD}' + a_2\mathrm{D}'^2)z = 0 \qquad \ldots(1)$

Its symbolic operator equated to zero, *i.e.*, $\mathrm{D}^2 + a_1\mathrm{DD}' + a_2\mathrm{D}'^2 = 0 \qquad \ldots(2)$

is called the **auxiliary equation** (A.E.)

Considered as a quadratic in D/D′, let its roots be $m_1, m_2$.

**Case I.** *When the A.E. has distinct roots i.e.,* $m_1 \neq m_2$, then (2) can be written as

$$(\mathrm{D} - m_1\mathrm{D}')(\mathrm{D} - m_2\mathrm{D}')z = 0 \qquad \ldots(3)$$

Now the solution of $(\mathrm{D} - m_2\mathrm{D}')z = 0$ will also be a solution of (3).

But $\quad (\mathrm{D} - m_2\mathrm{D}')z = 0 \;\Rightarrow\; p - m_2 q = 0$

which is of Lagrange's form and the auxiliary equations are $\frac{dx}{1} = \frac{dy}{-m_2} = \frac{dz}{0}$

The first two members give $dy + m_2 dx = 0$ or $y + m_2 x = a$

Also $\quad dz = 0$ or $z = b$

$\therefore \quad z = f_2(y + m_2 x)$ is a solution of $(\mathrm{D} - m_2\mathrm{D}')z = 0$

Similarly, (3) will also be satisfied by the solution of

$(\mathrm{D} - m_1\mathrm{D}')z = 0$ *i.e.,* by $z = f_1(y + m_1 x)$.

Hence the complete solution of (2) is

$$z = f_1(y + m_1x) + f_2(y + m_2x).$$

**Case II.** *When the A.E. has equal roots,* each = $m$, then (2) can be written as

$$(D - mD')(D - mD')z = 0 \quad ...(4)$$

Let $(D - mD')z = u$, then (4) becomes $(D - mD')u = 0$

Its solution is $u = f(y + mx)$, as proved in Case I.

$\therefore$ $(D - mD')z = u$ takes the form $(D - mD')z = f(y + mx)$

or $p - mq = f(y + mx)$ [Lagrange's form]

The Auxiliary equations are $\dfrac{dx}{1} = \dfrac{dy}{-m} = \dfrac{dz}{f(y+mx)}$

Now $\dfrac{dx}{1} = \dfrac{dy}{-m}$ gives $dy + mdx = 0$ or $y + mx = a$

Also $\dfrac{dx}{1} = \dfrac{dz}{f(a)}$ gives $dz = f(a)\,dx$ or $z = f(a)\,x + b$ *i.e.,* $z - xf(y + mx) = b$

$\therefore$ The complete solution of (2) is

$$z - x\phi(y + mx) = \phi(y + mx) \quad \text{or} \quad z = f(y + mx) + xf(y + mx).$$

**Note 1.** We know that for the differential equation

$$(D^2 + a_1DD' + a_2D'^2)\,z = 0,$$

the A.E. is $D^2 + a_1DD' + a_2D'^2 = 0$ ...(1)

Now the roots of (1), considered as a quadratic in D/D′, are the same as those of

$$m^2 + a_1m + a_2 = 0 \quad ...(2)$$

$\therefore$ This quadratic in $m$ can also be called the A.E. Henceforth we shall write the A.E. in terms of $m$.

Thus the A.E. is obtained by putting $D = m$ and $D' = 1$ in $\phi(D, D') = 0$.

Hence the A.E. of the differential equation $\phi(D, D')z = F(x, y)$ is $\phi(m, 1) = 0$.

**Note 2.** Generalising the results of Case I and Case II, we have (*i*) if the roots of A.E. are $m_1, m_2, m_3, ......$ (all distinct roots), then

$$\text{C.F.} = f_1(y + m_1x) + f_2(y + m_2x) + f_3(y + m_3x) + ......$$

(*ii*) if the roots of A.E. are $m_1, m_1, m_2, ...$ (two equal roots), then

$$\text{C.F.} = f_1(y + m_1x) + xf_2(y + m_1x) + f_3(y + m_2x) + ......$$

(*iii*) if the roots of A.E. are $m_1, m_1, m_1, ...$ (three equal roots), then

$$\text{C.F.} = f_1(y + m_1x) + xf_2(y + m_1x) + x^2f_3(y + m_1x) + ......$$

**Example.** *Solve :*

(*i*) $\dfrac{\partial^2 z}{\partial x^2} - \dfrac{\partial^2 z}{\partial x \partial y} - 6\dfrac{\partial^2 z}{\partial y^2} = 0$ (*ii*) $(D + 2D')(D - 3D')^2z = 0$ (*iii*) $4r - 12s + 9t = 0$.

**Sol.** (*i*) The given equation in symbolic form is

$$(D^2 - DD' - 6D'^2)z = 0$$

Its A.E. is $m^2 - m - 6 = 0$ or $(m - 3)(m + 2) = 0$ $\therefore$ $m = 3, -2$

Hence the complete solution is

$$z = f_1(y + 3x) + f_2(y - 2x).$$

(*ii*) The given equation is

$$(D + 2D')(D - 3D')^2z = 0$$

Its A.E. is $(m + 2)(m - 3)^2 = 0$ which gives $m = -2, 3, 3$

Hence the complete solution is

$$z = f_1(y - 2x) + f_2(y + 3x) + xf_3(y + 3x).$$

(*iii*) The given equation in symbolic form is $(4D^2 - 12DD' + 9D'^2)z = 0$

Since $r = \dfrac{\partial^2 z}{\partial x^2} = D^2 z, s = \dfrac{\partial^2 z}{\partial x \partial y} = DD' z, t = \dfrac{\partial^2 z}{\partial y^2} = D'^2 z$

Its A.E. is $4m^2 - 12m + 9 = 0$ or $(2m - 3)^2 = 0$ $\therefore$ $m = 3/2, 3/2$

Hence the complete solution is

$$z = \phi_1\left(y + \frac{3}{2}x\right) + x\phi_2\left(y + \frac{3}{2}x\right)$$

which may be written as $z = f_1(2y + 3x) + xf_2(2y + 3x)$.

### 3.11. RULES FOR FINDING THE P.I.

The P.I. of the equation $\phi(D, D')z = F(x, y)$ is given by $\dfrac{1}{\phi(D, D')} F(x, y)$.

**I. Short methods to find the P.I.**

Analogous to the short methods for finding the P.I. of an ordinary linear differential equation with constant co-efficients, we have short methods for finding the P.I. of homogeneous linear partial differential equations. We give below, without proof, the short methods for the P.I.

(*i*) When $F(x, y) = e^{ax+by}$

$$\text{P.I.} = \frac{1}{\phi(D, D')} e^{ax+by} = \frac{1}{\phi(a, b)} e^{ax+by}$$ (*i.e.*, put $D = a$ and $D' = b$) provided $\phi(a, b) \neq 0$.

If $\phi(a, b) = 0$, then it is called a case of failure.

(*ii*) When $F(x, y) = \sin(ax + by)$

$$\text{P.I.} = \frac{1}{\phi(D^2, DD', D'^2)} \sin(ax + by) = \frac{1}{\phi(-a^2, -ab, -b^2)} \sin(ax + by)$$

(*i.e.* put $D^2 = -a^2$, $DD' = -ab$, $D'^2 = -b^2$) provided $\phi(-a^2, -ab, -b^2) \neq 0$.

If $\phi(-a^2, -ab, -b^2) = 0$, then it is called a case of failure.

A similar rule holds when $F(x, y) = \cos(ax + by)$.

(*iii*) When $F(x, y) = x^p y^q$, where $p, q$ are positive integers.

$$\text{P.I.} = \frac{1}{\phi(D, D')} x^p y^q = [\phi(D, D')]^{-1} x^p y^q$$

If $p < q$, expand $[\phi(D, D')]^{-1}$ in powers of $\dfrac{D}{D'}$

If $q < p$ expand $[\phi(D, D')]^{-1}$ in powers of $\dfrac{D'}{D}$

Also, we have $\dfrac{1}{D} F(x, y) = \displaystyle\int_{y \text{ constant}} F(x, y)$ and $\dfrac{1}{D'} F(x, y) = \displaystyle\int_{x \text{ constant}} F(x, y)\, dy$

**II. General method to find the P.I.**

$F(x, y)$ is not always of the forms given before. Moreover, there are cases of failure in the short methods. The general method is applicable to all cases where $F(x, y)$ is not of the forms given before or the short methods fail.

Now, $\phi(D, D')$ can be factorised, in general, into $n$ linear factors.

$$\therefore \quad \text{P.I.} = \frac{1}{\phi(D, D')} F(x, y)$$

$$= \frac{1}{(D - m_1D')(D - m_2D')\ldots(D - m_nD')} F(x, y)$$

$$= \frac{1}{D - m_1D'} \cdot \frac{1}{D - m_2D'} \cdots\cdots \frac{1}{D - m_nD'} F(x, y)$$

Let us evaluate $\frac{1}{D - mD'} F(x, y)$

Consider the equation, $(D - mD')z = F(x, y)$ or $p - mq = F(x, y)$ [Lagrange's form]

The auxiliary equations are $\frac{dx}{1} = \frac{dy}{-m} = \frac{dz}{F(x, y)}$

From the first two members $dy + mdx = 0$ or $y + mx = c$

From the first and last members, we have

$$dz = F(x, y)dx = F(x, c - mx)dx$$

$$\therefore \quad z = \int F(x, c - mx)dx \quad \text{or} \quad \frac{1}{D - mD'} F(x, y) = \int F(x, c - mx)\, dx$$

where $c$ is replaced by $y + mx$ after integration.

By repeated application of the above rule, the P.I. can be evaluated.

## ILLUSTRATIVE EXAMPLES

**Example 1.** *Solve* $\frac{\partial^3 z}{\partial x^3} - 3\frac{\partial^3 z}{\partial x^2 \partial y} + 4\frac{\partial^3 z}{\partial y^3} = e^{x+2y}$. (M.G.U. May 2010)

**Sol.** The given equation in symbolic form is $(D^3 - 3D^2D' + 4D'^3)z = e^{x+2y}$

Its A.E. is $m^3 - 3m^2 + 4 = 0$

or $(m + 1)(m^2 - 4m + 4) = 0$ or $(m + 1)(m - 2)^2 = 0$

$$\therefore \quad m = -1, 2, 2$$

$$\text{C.F.} = f_1(y - x) + f_2(y + 2x) + xf_3(y + 2x)$$

$$\text{P.I.} = \frac{1}{D^3 - 3D^2D' + 4D'^3} e^{x+2y} = \frac{1}{1^3 - 3.1^2.2 + 4.2^3} e^{x+2y}$$

(Putting $D = 1$, $D' = 2$)

$$= \frac{1}{27} e^{x+2y}$$

$\therefore$ The complete solution is $z = f_1(y - x) + f_2(y + 2x) + xf_3(y + 2x) + \frac{1}{27} e^{x+2y}$.

**Example 2.** *Solve* $\frac{\partial^2 z}{\partial x^2} - \frac{\partial^2 z}{\partial x \partial y} = \sin x \cos 2y.$ (M.G.U. May 2010)

**Sol.** The given equation in symbolic form is $(D^2 - DD')z = \sin x \cos 2y$

Its A.E. is $m^2 - m = 0$ or $m(m-1) = 0$ $\therefore$ $m = 0, 1$

$$\text{C.F.} = f_1(y) + f_2(y + x)$$

$$\text{P.I.} = \frac{1}{D^2 - DD'} \sin x \cos 2y = \frac{1}{D^2 - DD'}\left[\frac{1}{2}(2 \sin x \cos 2y)\right]$$

$$= \frac{1}{2} \cdot \frac{1}{D^2 - DD'} [\sin(x + 2y) + \sin(x - 2y)]$$

$$= \frac{1}{2}\left[\frac{1}{D^2 - DD'} \sin(x + 2y) + \frac{1}{D^2 - DD'} \sin(x - 2y)\right]$$

$$= \frac{1}{2}\left[\frac{1}{-1^2 - (-1.2)} \sin(x + 2y) + \frac{1}{-1^2 - (-1.(-2))} \sin(x - 2y)\right]$$

$$= \frac{1}{2} \sin(x + 2y) - \frac{1}{6} \sin(x - 2y)$$

$\therefore$ The complete solution is $z = f_1(y) + f_2(y + x) + \frac{1}{2} \sin(x + 2y) - \frac{1}{6} \sin(x - 2y).$

**Example 3.** *Solve* $(D^3 - 7DD'^2 - 6D'^3)z = \sin(x + 2y) + e^{2x+y}.$

**Sol.** The A.E. is $m^3 - 7m - 6 = 0$

or $(m + 1)(m^2 - m - 6) = 0$ or $(m + 1)(m - 3)(m + 2) = 0$

$\therefore$ $m = -1, 3, -2$

$$\text{C.F.} = f_1(y - x) + f_2(y + 3x) + f_3(y - 2x)$$

$$\text{P.I.} = \frac{1}{D^3 - 7DD'^2 - 6D'^3} [\sin(x + 2y) + e^{2x+y}]$$

$$= \frac{1}{D^3 - 7DD'^2 - 6D'^3} \sin(x + 2y) + \frac{1}{D^3 - 7DD'^2 - 6D'^3} e^{2x+y}$$

$$= \frac{1}{D(D^2) - 7D(D'^2) - 6D'(D'^2)} \sin(x + 2y) + \frac{1}{2^3 - 7(2)(1)^2 - 6.1^3} e^{2x+y}$$

$$= \frac{1}{D(-1^2) - 7D(-2^2) - 6D'(-2^2)} \sin(x + 2y) - \frac{1}{12} e^{2x+y}$$

$$= \frac{1}{27D + 24D'} \sin(x + 2y) - \frac{1}{12} e^{2x+y} = \frac{D}{27D^2 + 24DD'} \sin(x + 2y) - \frac{1}{12} e^{2x+y}$$

$$= \frac{D}{27(-1^2) + 24(-1.2)} \sin(x + 2y) - \frac{1}{12} e^{2x+y} = -\frac{1}{75} \cos(x + 2y) - \frac{1}{12} e^{2x+y}$$

$\therefore$ The complete solution is

$$z = f_1(y - x) + f_2(y + 3x) + f_3(y - 2x) - \frac{1}{75} \cos(x + 2y) - \frac{1}{12} e^{2x+y}.$$

**Example 4.** *Solve* $\dfrac{\partial^2 z}{\partial x^2} + 3\dfrac{\partial^2 z}{\partial x \partial y} + 2\dfrac{\partial^2 z}{\partial y^2} = x + y.$

**Sol.** The given equation in symbolic form is $(D^2 + 3DD' + 2D'^2)z = x + y$

Its A.E. is $m^2 + 3m + 2 = 0$ or $(m + 1)(m + 2) = 0 \quad \therefore \quad m = -1, -2$

$$\text{C.F.} = f_1(y - x) + f_2(y - 2x)$$

$$\text{P.I.} = \frac{1}{D^2 + 3DD' + 2D'^2}(x + y) = \frac{1}{D^2\left(1 + 3\dfrac{D'}{D} + 2\dfrac{D'^2}{D^2}\right)}(x + y)$$

$$= \frac{1}{D^2}\left[1 + \left(\frac{3D'}{D} + \frac{2D'^2}{D^2}\right)\right]^{-1}(x + y) = \frac{1}{D^2}\left(1 - \frac{3D'}{D} \ldots\ldots\right)(x + y)$$

$$= \frac{1}{D^2}\left[x + y - \frac{3}{D}(1)\right] = \frac{1}{D^2}(x + y - 3x)$$

$$= \frac{1}{D^2}(y - 2x) = \frac{1}{D}(yx - x^2) = \frac{yx^2}{2} - \frac{x^3}{3}$$

Hence the complete solution is $z = f_1(y - x) + f_2(y - 2x) + \dfrac{x^2 y}{2} - \dfrac{x^3}{3}$.

**Example 5.** *Solve* $r - 4s + 4t = e^{2x+y}$.

**Sol.** The equation is $\dfrac{\partial^2 z}{\partial x^2} - 4\dfrac{\partial^2 z}{\partial x \partial y} + 4\dfrac{\partial^2 z}{\partial y^2} = e^{2x+y}$.

Its symbolic form is $(D^2 - 4DD' + 4D'^2)z = e^{2x+y}$

Its A.E. is $m^2 - 4m + 4 = 0$ or $(m - 2)^2 = 0 \quad \therefore \quad m = 2, 2$

$$\text{C.F.} = f_1(y + 2x) + xf_2(y + 2x)$$

$$\text{P.I.} = \frac{1}{(D - 2D')^2} e^{2x+y}$$

Putting D = 2 and D′ = 1, the denominator vanishes.

∴ It is a case of failure.

Since $\dfrac{1}{D - mD'} F(x, y) = \displaystyle\int F(x, c - mx)dx$, where $c$ is to be replaced by $(y + mx)$ after integration.

∴ $$\text{P.I.} = \frac{1}{D - 2D'} \cdot \frac{1}{D - 2D'} e^{2x+y} = \frac{1}{D - 2D'}\int e^{2x+(c-2x)}\,dx \quad | \text{Here } m = 2$$

$$= \frac{1}{D - 2D'}\int e^c\,dx = \frac{1}{D - 2D'} xe^c = \frac{1}{D - 2D'} xe^{y+2x}$$

$$= \int x\,e^{(c-2x)+2x}\,dx = e^c \int x\,dx = \frac{1}{2}x^2 e^c = \frac{1}{2}x^2 e^{y+2x}$$

Hence the complete solution is $\quad z = f_1(y + 2x) + xf_2(y + 2x) + \dfrac{1}{2}x^2 e^{y+2x}$.

**Example 6.** *Solve* $\quad (2D^2 - 5DD' + 2D'^2)z = 5 \sin (2x + y)$.

**Sol.** The A.E. is $2m^2 - 5m + 2 = 0$ or $(2m - 1)(m - 2) = 0 \quad \therefore \quad m = \dfrac{1}{2}, 2$

$$\text{C.F.} = f_1(2y + x) + f_2(y + 2x)$$

$$\text{P.I.} = 5.\frac{1}{2D^2 - 5DD' + 2D'^2}\sin(2x+y)$$

Putting $D^2 = -2^2$, $DD' = -2.1$, $D'^2 = -1^2$

Denominator $= 2(-4) - 5(-2) + 2(-1) = 0$

$\therefore$ It is a case of failure.

Now
$$\text{P.I.} = 5.\frac{1}{(2D - D')(D - 2D')}\sin(2x+y)$$

$$= 5.\frac{1}{2D - D'}\cdot\frac{1}{D - 2D'}\sin(2x+y)$$

$$= 5.\frac{1}{2D - D'}\int \sin[2x + (c - 2x)]dx \qquad [\text{Here } m = 2]$$

$$= \frac{5}{2}\cdot\frac{1}{D - \frac{1}{2}D'}\int \sin c\, dx = \frac{5}{2}\cdot\frac{1}{D - \frac{1}{2}D'} x \sin c$$

$$= \frac{5}{2}\cdot\frac{1}{D - \frac{1}{2}D'} x \sin(y + 2x)$$

$$= \frac{5}{2}\int x \sin\left[\left(c - \frac{1}{2}x\right) + 2x\right]dx \qquad [\text{Here } m = 1/2]$$

$$= \frac{5}{2}\int x \sin\left(c + \frac{3}{2}x\right)dx$$

$$= \frac{5}{2}\left[x.\frac{-\cos\left(c + \frac{3}{2}x\right)}{\frac{3}{2}} - \int 1.\frac{-\cos\left(c + \frac{3}{2}x\right)}{\frac{3}{2}}dx\right]$$

$$= -\frac{5}{3}x\cos\left(c + \frac{3}{2}x\right) + \frac{10}{9}\sin\left(c + \frac{3}{2}x\right)$$

$$= -\frac{5}{3}x\cos\left[\left(y + \frac{1}{2}x\right) + \frac{3}{2}\right] + \frac{10}{9}\sin\left[\left(y + \frac{1}{2}x\right) + \frac{3}{2}x\right]$$

$$= -\frac{5}{3}x\cos(y + 2x) + \frac{10}{9}\sin(y + 2x)$$

Hence the complete solution is

$$z = f_1(2y + x) + f_2(y + 2x) - \frac{5}{3}x\cos(y + 2x) + \frac{10}{9}\sin(y + 2x)$$

or
$$z = f_1(2y + x) + F_2(y + 2x) - \frac{5}{3}x\cos(y + 2x)$$

Since
$$f_2(y + 2x) + \frac{10}{9}\sin(y + 2x) = f_2(y + 2x) + \phi(y + 2x) = F_2(y + 2x).$$

**Note.** If we write

$$\text{P.I.} = 5.\frac{1}{(D - 2D')(2D - D')}\sin(2x + y) = \frac{5}{2}\cdot\frac{1}{D - 2D'}\cdot\frac{1}{D - \frac{1}{2}D'}\sin(2x + y)$$

$$= \frac{5}{2} \cdot \frac{1}{D - 2D'} \int \sin\left[2x + \left(c - \frac{1}{2}x\right)\right] dx$$

$$= \frac{5}{2} \cdot \frac{1}{D - 2D'} \left[-\frac{2}{3} \cos\left(\frac{3}{2}x + c\right)\right]$$

$$= -\frac{5}{3} \cdot \frac{D}{D - 2D'} \cos\left(\frac{3}{2}x + y + \frac{1}{2}x\right) = -\frac{5}{3} \cdot \frac{1}{D - 2D'} \cos(y + 2x)$$

$$= -\frac{5}{3} \int \cos[(c - 2x) + 2x]dx = -\frac{5}{3}x \cos c = -\frac{5}{3}x \cos(y + 2x)$$

we directly get the result.

**Example 7.** *Solve* $\frac{\partial^2 z}{\partial x^2} + \frac{\partial^2 z}{\partial x \partial y} - 6\frac{\partial^2 z}{\partial y^2} = y \cos x.$ (M.G.U. Dec., 2007)

**Sol.** The equation in symbolic form is $(D^2 + DD' - 6D'^2)z = y \cos x$

The A.E. is $m^2 + m - 6 = 0$ so that $m = -3, 2$

$\therefore$ C.F. $= f_1(y - 3x) + f_2(y + 2x)$

$$\text{P.I.} = \frac{1}{D^2 + DD' - 6D'^2} y \cos x = \frac{1}{(D + 3D')(D - 2D')} y \cos x$$

$$= \frac{1}{D + 3D'} \cdot \frac{1}{D - 2D'} y \cos x = \frac{1}{D + 3D'} \int (c - 2x) \cos x dx$$

| Here $m = 2$

where $c$ is to be replaced by $y + mx = y + 2x$ after integration.

$$= \frac{1}{D + 3D}\left[(c - 2x) \sin x - \int -2 \sin x\, dx\right]$$

$$= \frac{1}{D + 3D}[(y + 2x - 2x) \sin x - 2 \cos x] = \frac{1}{D + 3D'}(y \sin x - 2 \cos x)$$

$$= \int [(c + 3x) \sin x - 2 \cos x]\, dx$$ | Here $m = -3$

where $c$ is to be replaced by $y + mx = y - 3x$ after integration.

$$= (c + 3x)(-\cos x) - \int 3(-\cos x)\, dx - 2 \sin x$$

$$= (y - 3x + 3x)(-\cos x) + 3 \sin x - 2 \sin x = -y \cos x + \sin x$$

$\therefore$ The complete solution is $z = f_1(y - 3x) + f_2(y + 2x) - y \cos x + \sin x.$

## TEST YOUR KNOWLEDGE

*Solve the following equations :*

**1.** $2\frac{\partial^2 z}{\partial x^2} + 5\frac{\partial^2 z}{\partial x \partial y} + 2\frac{\partial^2 z}{\partial y^2} = 0$

**2.** $\frac{\partial^3 z}{\partial x^3} - 4\frac{\partial^3 z}{\partial x^2 \partial y} + 4\frac{\partial^3 z}{\partial x \partial y^2} = 0$

**3.** $\frac{\partial^3 z}{\partial x^3} - 7\frac{\partial^3 z}{\partial x \partial y^2} + 6\frac{\partial^3 z}{\partial y^3} = 0$

**4.** $25r - 40s + 16t = 0$

**5.** $\frac{\partial^2 z}{\partial x^2} - 7\frac{\partial^2 z}{\partial x \partial y} + 12\frac{\partial^2 z}{\partial y^2} = e^{x-y}$

**6.** $(D^2 + 2DD' + D'^2)z = e^{2x+3y}$

**7.** $\frac{\partial^2 z}{\partial x^2} + \frac{\partial^2 z}{\partial x \partial y} - 6\frac{\partial^2 z}{\partial y^2} = \cos(3x + y)$

**8.** $(D^3 - 4D^2D' + 4DD'^2)z = 6\sin(3x + 2y)$

**9.** $\frac{\partial^2 z}{\partial x^2} - 2\frac{\partial^2 z}{\partial x \partial y} + \frac{\partial^2 z}{\partial y^2} = \sin x$

**10.** $\frac{\partial^2 y}{\partial t^2} - a^2\frac{\partial^2 y}{\partial x^2} = E\sin pt$

**11.** $\frac{\partial^2 z}{\partial x^2} - \frac{\partial^2 z}{\partial x \partial y} = \cos x \cos 2y$ *(M.G.U. July 2007, Nov. 2009)*

**12.** $\frac{\partial^2 z}{\partial x^2} - 3\frac{\partial^2 z}{\partial x \partial y} + 2\frac{\partial^2 z}{\partial y^2} = e^{2x+3y} + \sin(x - 2y)$

**13.** $\frac{\partial^2 z}{\partial x^2} + 3\frac{\partial^2 z}{\partial x \partial y} + 2\frac{\partial^2 z}{\partial y^2} = 12xy$

**14.** $\frac{\partial^2 z}{\partial x^2} + 2\frac{\partial^2 z}{\partial x \partial y} + \frac{\partial^2 z}{\partial y^2} = x^2 + xy + y^2$

**15.** $(D^2 - 6DD' + 9D'^2)z = 6x + 2y$

**16.** $\frac{\partial^3 z}{\partial x^3} - 2\frac{\partial^3 z}{\partial x^2 \partial y} = 2e^{2x} + 3x^2 y$

**17.** $(D^2 - 6DD' + 9D'^2)z = 12x^2 + 36xy$

**18.** $(D^2 - 2DD' + D'^2)z = e^{x+y}$

**19.** $4r + 12s + 9t = e^{3x-2y}$

**20.** $\frac{\partial^3 z}{\partial x^2 \partial y} - 5\frac{\partial^3 z}{\partial x \partial y^2} + 6\frac{\partial^3 z}{\partial y^3} = e^x$

**21.** $r + 2s + t = 2(y - x) + \sin(x - y)$

**22.** $r + s - 6t = \cos(2x + y)$

**23.** $\frac{\partial^3 z}{\partial x^3} - 4\frac{\partial^3 z}{\partial x^2 \partial y} + 4\frac{\partial^3 z}{\partial x \partial y^2} = 4\sin(2x + y)$

**24.** $(D^2 - DD' - 2D'^2)z = (y - 1)e^x$

**25.** $(D^2 + 2DD' + D'^2)z = 2\cos y - x\sin y$

**26.** $4r - 4s + t = 16\log(x + 2y)$.

## Answers

**1.** $z = f_1(y - 2x) + f_2(2y - x)$

**2.** $z = f_1(y) + f_2(y + 2x) + xf_3(y + 2x)$

**3.** $z = f_1(y + x) + f_2(y + 2x) + f_3(y - 3x)$

**4.** $z = f_1(5y + 4x) + xf_2(5y + 4x)$

**5.** $z = f_1(y + 3x) + f_2(y + 4x) + \frac{1}{20}e^{x-y}$

**6.** $z = f_1(y - x) + xf_2(y - x) + \frac{1}{25}e^{2x+3y}$

**7.** $z = f_1(y - 3x) + f_2(y + 2x) - \frac{1}{6}\cos(3x + y)$

**8.** $z = f_1(y) + f_2(y + 2x) + xf_3(y + 2x) + 2\cos(3x + 2y)$

**9.** $z = f_1(y + x) + xf_2(y + x) - \sin x$

**10.** $y = f_1(x - at) + f_2(x - at) - \frac{E}{p^2}\sin pt$

**11.** $z = f_1(y) + f_2(y + x) + \frac{1}{2}\cos(x + 2y) - \frac{1}{6}\cos(x - 2y)$

**12.** $z = f_1(y + x) + f_2(y + 2x) + \frac{1}{4}e^{2x+3y} - \frac{1}{15}\sin(x - 2y)$

**13.** $z = f_1(y - x) + f_2(y - 2x) + 2x^3y - \frac{3}{2}x^4$

**14.** $z = f_1(y - x) + xf_2(y - x) + \frac{1}{4}(x^4 - 2x^3y + 2x^2y^2)$

**15.** $z = f_1(y + 3x) + xf_2(y + 3x) + x^2(3x + y)$

**16.** $z = f_1(y) + xf_2(y) + f_3(y + 2x) + \frac{1}{4} e^{2x} + \frac{1}{60} (3x^5y + x^6)$

**17.** $z = f_1(y + 3x) + xf_2(y + 3x) + 10x^4 + 6x^3y$

**18.** $z = f_1(y + x) + xf_2(y + x) + \frac{1}{2} x^2 e^{x+y}$

**19.** $z = f_1(2y - 3x) + xf_2(2y - 3x) + \frac{1}{8} x^2 e^{3x-2y}$

**20.** $z = f_1(x) + f_2(y + 2x) + f_3(y + 3x) + ye^x$

**21.** $z = f_1(y - x) + xf_2(y - x) + x^2y - x^3 + \frac{1}{2} x^2 \sin (x - y)$

**22.** $z = f_1(y - 3x) + f_2(y + 2x) + \frac{1}{5} x \sin (2x + y)$

**23.** $z = f_1(y) + f_2(y + 2x) + xf_3(y + 2x) - x^2 \cos (2x + y)$

**24.** $z = f_1(y - x) + f_2(y + 2x) + ye^x$

**25.** $z = f_1(y - x) + xf_2(y - x) + x \sin y$

**26.** $z = f_1(2y + x) + xf_2(2y + x) + 2x^2 \log (x + 2y)$.

# 4

# Probability Distribution

## 4.1. RANDOM VARIABLE

If the numerical values assumed by a variable are the result of some chance factors, so that a particular value cannot be exactly predicted in advance, the variable is then called a *random variable*. A random variable is also called '*chance variable*' or '*stochastic variable*'.

Random variables are denoted by capital letters, usually, from the last part of the alphabet, for instance, X, Y, Z etc.

**Continuous and Discrete Random Variables**

A *continuous random variable* is one which can assume any value within an interval, *i.e.*, all values of a continuous scale. For example (*i*) the weights (in kg) of a group of individuals, (*ii*) the heights of a group of individuals.

A *discrete random variable* is one which can assume only isolated values. For example,

(*i*) the number of heads in 4 tosses of a coin is a discrete random variable as it cannot assume values other than 0, 1, 2, 3, 4.

(*ii*) the number of aces in a draw of 2 cards from a well shuffled deck is a random variable as it can take the values 0, 1, 2 only.

## 4.2. DISCRETE PROBABILITY DISTRIBUTION

Let a random variable X assume values $x_1, x_2, x_3, ......, x_n$ with probabilities $p_1, p_2, p_3, ......, p_n$ respectively, where $P(X = x_i) = p_i \geq 0$ for each $x_i$ and $p_1 + p_2 + p_3 + ...... + p_n = \sum_{i=1}^{n} p_i = 1$.

Then

$$\begin{array}{lllll} X & : & x_1, & x_2, & x_3, ......, x_n \\ P(X) & : & p_1, & p_2, & p_3, ......, p_n \end{array}$$

is called the discrete probability distribution for X and it spells out how a total probability of 1 is distributed over several values of the random variable.

## 4.3. MEAN AND VARIANCE OF RANDOM VARIABLES

Let
$$\begin{array}{llll} X : x_1, & x_2, & x_3, ......, x_n \\ P(X) : p_1, & p_2, & p_3, ......, p_n \end{array}$$

be a discrete probability distribution.

We denote the *mean* by μ and define $\mu = \dfrac{\Sigma p_i x_i}{\Sigma p_i} = \Sigma p_i x_i$ $\quad (\because \ \Sigma p_i = 1)$

Other names for the mean are *average or expected value E(X).*
We denote the *variance* by $\sigma^2$ and define $\sigma^2 = \Sigma p_i(x_i - \mu)^2$
If $\mu$ is not a whole number, then $\sigma^2 = \Sigma p_i x_i^2 - \mu^2$

**Standard deviation** $\sigma = + \sqrt{\text{Variance}}$.

## ILLUSTRATIVE EXAMPLES

**Example 1.** *Five defective bulbs are accidentally mixed with twenty good ones. It is not possible to just look at a bulb and tell whether or not it is defective. Find the probability distribution of the number of defective bulbs, if four bulbs are drawn at random from this lot.*

**Sol.** Let X denote the number of defective bulbs in 4. Clearly X can take the values 0, 1, 2, 3 or 4.

Number of defective bulbs = 5
Number of good bulbs = 20
Total number of bulbs = 25

$$P(X = 0) = P \text{ (no defective)} = P \text{ (all 4 good ones)}$$
$$= \frac{^{20}C_4}{^{25}C_4} = \frac{20 \times 19 \times 18 \times 17}{25 \times 24 \times 23 \times 22} = \frac{969}{2530}$$

$$P(X = 1) = P\text{(one defective and 3 good ones)} = \frac{^5C_1 \times {^{20}C_3}}{^{25}C_4} = \frac{1140}{2530}$$

$$P(X = 2) = P \text{ (2 defectives and 2 good ones)} = \frac{^5C_2 \times {^{20}C_2}}{^{25}C_4} = \frac{380}{2530}$$

$$P(X = 3) = P\text{(3 defectives and 1 good one)} = \frac{^5C_3 \times {^{20}C_1}}{^{25}C_4} = \frac{40}{2530}$$

$$P(X = 4) = P \text{ (all 4 defectives)} = \frac{^5C_4}{^{25}C_4} = \frac{1}{2530}$$

$\therefore$ The probability distribution of the random variable X is

| X : | 0 | 1 | 2 | 3 | 4 |
|---|---|---|---|---|---|
| P(X) : | $\frac{969}{2530}$ | $\frac{1140}{2530}$ | $\frac{380}{2530}$ | $\frac{40}{2530}$ | $\frac{1}{2530}$. |

**Example 2.** *A die is tossed thrice. A success is 'getting 1 or 6' on a toss. Find the mean and the variance of the number of successes.*

**Sol.** Let X denote the number of success. Clearly X can take the values 0, 1, 2 or 3.

Probability of success $= \frac{2}{6} = \frac{1}{3}$; Probability of failure $= 1 - \frac{1}{3} = \frac{2}{3}$

$$P(X = 0) = P \text{ (no success)} = P \text{ (all 3 failures)} = \frac{2}{3} \times \frac{2}{3} \times \frac{2}{3} = \frac{8}{27}$$

$$P(X = 1) = P \text{ (one success and 2 failures)} = {^3C_1} \times \frac{1}{3} \times \frac{2}{3} \times \frac{2}{3} = \frac{12}{27}$$

$$P(X = 2) = P \text{ (two successes and one failure)} = {^3C_2} \times \frac{1}{3} \times \frac{1}{3} \times \frac{2}{3} = \frac{6}{27}$$

$$P(X = 3) = P \text{ (all 3 successes)} = \frac{1}{3} \times \frac{1}{3} \times \frac{1}{3} = \frac{1}{27}$$

∴ The probability distribution of the random variable X is

| X | : | 0 | 1 | 2 | 3 |
|---|---|---|---|---|---|
| P(X) | : | $\frac{8}{27}$ | $\frac{12}{27}$ | $\frac{6}{27}$ | $\frac{1}{27}$ |

To find the mean and variance

| $x_i$ | $p_i$ | $p_i x_i$ | $p_i x_i^2$ |
|---|---|---|---|
| 0 | $\frac{8}{27}$ | 0 | 0 |
| 1 | $\frac{12}{27}$ | $\frac{12}{27}$ | $\frac{12}{27}$ |
| 2 | $\frac{6}{27}$ | $\frac{12}{27}$ | $\frac{24}{27}$ |
| 3 | $\frac{1}{27}$ | $\frac{3}{27}$ | $\frac{9}{27}$ |
| | | 1 | $\frac{5}{3}$ |

Mean $\mu = \Sigma p_i x_i = 1$

Variance $\sigma^2 = \Sigma p_i x_i^2 - \mu^2 = \frac{5}{3} - 1 = \frac{2}{3}$.

**Example 3.** *A random variable X has the following probability function :*

| *Values of X,* | $x$ | : | 0 | 1 | 2 | 3 | 4 | 5 | 6 | 7 |
|---|---|---|---|---|---|---|---|---|---|---|
| | $p(x)$ | : | 0 | $k$ | $2k$ | $2k$ | $3k$ | $k^2$ | $2k^2$ | $7k^2 + k$ |

*(i) Find k,*

*(ii) Evaluate* $P(X < 6)$, $P(X \geq 6)$, $P(3 < X \leq 6)$

*(iii) Find the minimum value of x so that* $P(X \leq x) > \frac{1}{2}$.

**Sol.** (*i*) Since $\sum_{x=0}^{7} p(x) = 1$, we have

$$0 + k + 2k + 2k + 3k + k^2 + 2k^2 + 7k^2 + k = 1$$

$$\Rightarrow \quad 10k^2 + 9k - 1 = 0 \quad \Rightarrow \quad (10k - 1)(k + 1) = 0$$

$$\Rightarrow \quad k = \frac{1}{10} \qquad [\because \; p(x) \geq 0]$$

(*ii*) $P(X < 6) = P(X = 0) + P(X = 1) + \ldots\ldots + P(X = 5)$

$$= 0 + k + 2k + 2k + 3k + k^2 = 8k + k^2 = \frac{8}{10} + \frac{1}{100} = \frac{81}{100}$$

$P(X \geq 6) = P(X = 6) + P(X = 7)$

$$= 2k^2 + 7k^2 + k = \frac{9}{100} + \frac{1}{10} = \frac{19}{100}$$

$P(3 < X \leq 6) = P(X = 4) + P(X = 5) + P(X = 6)$

$$= 3k + k^2 + 2k^2 = \frac{3}{10} + \frac{3}{100} = \frac{33}{100}$$

(*iii*) $P(X \le 1) = k = \frac{1}{10} < \frac{1}{2}$ ; $P(X \le 2) = k + 2k = \frac{3}{10} < \frac{1}{2}$

$P(X \le 3) = k + 2k + 2k = \frac{5}{10} = \frac{1}{2}$ ; $P(X \le 4) = k + 2k + 2k + 3k = \frac{8}{10} > \frac{1}{2}$

$\therefore$ The maximum value of $x$ so that $P(X \le x) > \frac{1}{2}$ is 4.

## TEST YOUR KNOWLEDGE

1. Find the probability distribution of the number of doublets in four throws of a pair of dice.
2. Two bad eggs are mixed accidently with 10 good ones. Find the probability distribution of the number of bad eggs in 3, drawn at random, without replacement, from this lot.
3. A die is tossed twice. Getting a number greater than 4 is considered a success. Find the variance of the probability distribution of the number of successes.
4. Two cards are drawn simultaneously from a well-shuffled deck of 52 cards. Compute the variance for the number of aces.
5. An urn contains 4 white and 3 red balls. Three balls are drawn, with replacement, from this urn. Find $\mu$, $\sigma^2$ and $\sigma$ for the number of red balls drawn.
6. A random variable X has the following probability distribution :

| Values of X, $x$ : | 0 | 1 | 2 | 3 | 4 | 5 | 6 | 7 | 8 |
|---|---|---|---|---|---|---|---|---|---|
| $p(x)$ : | $a$ | $3a$ | $5a$ | $7a$ | $9a$ | $11a$ | $13a$ | $15a$ | $17a$ |

(*i*) Determine the value of $a$. (*ii*) Find $P(X < 3)$, $P(X \ge 3)$, $P(2 \le X < 5)$

(*iii*) What is the smallest value of $x$ for which $P(X \le x) > 0.5$ ?

7. Find the standard deviation for the following discrete distribution :

| $x$ : | 8 | 12 | 16 | 20 | 24 |
|---|---|---|---|---|---|
| $p(x)$ : | $\frac{1}{8}$ | $\frac{1}{6}$ | $\frac{3}{8}$ | $\frac{1}{4}$ | $\frac{1}{12}$. |

### Answers

1.

| X : | 0 | 1 | 2 | 3 | 4 |
|---|---|---|---|---|---|
| P(X) : | $\frac{625}{1296}$ | $\frac{500}{1296}$ | $\frac{150}{1296}$ | $\frac{20}{1296}$ | $\frac{1}{1296}$ |

2.

| X : | 0 | 1 | 2 |
|---|---|---|---|
| P(X) : | $\frac{12}{22}$ | $\frac{9}{22}$ | $\frac{1}{22}$ |

3. $\frac{4}{9}$ 4. $\frac{400}{2873}$ 5. $\frac{9}{7}, \frac{36}{49}, \frac{6}{7}$

6. (*i*) $a = \frac{1}{81}$ (*ii*) $\frac{1}{9}, \frac{8}{9}, \frac{7}{27}$ (*iii*) 5 7. $2\sqrt{5}$.

## 4.4. THEORETICAL DISTRIBUTIONS

Frequency distributions can be classified under two heads :

(*i*) Observed Frequency Distributions.

(*ii*) Theoretical or Expected Frequency Distributions.

Observed frequency distributions are based on actual observation and experimentation. If certain hypothesis is assumed, it is sometimes possible to derive mathematically what the frequency distribution of certain universe should be. Such distributions are called **Theoretical Distributions**.

There are many types of theoretical frequency distributions but we shall consider only three which are of great importance :

(*i*) Binomial Distribution (or Bernoulli's Distribution) ;

(*ii*) Poisson's Distribution ;

(*iii*) Normal Distribution.

# BINOMIAL (OR BERNOULLI'S) DISTRIBUTION

## 4.5. BINOMIAL PROBABILITY DISTRIBUTION

Let there be $n$ independent trials in an experiment. Let a random variable X denote the number of successes in these $n$ trials. Let $p$ be the probability of a success and $q$ that of a failure in a single trial so that $p + q = 1$. Let the trials be independent and $p$ be constant for every trial.

**Let us find the probability of r successes in n trials.**

$r$ successes can be obtained in $n$ trials in ${}^nC_r$ ways.

$$\therefore \quad P(X = r) = {}^nC_r P(\underbrace{S\,S\,S\ldots\ldots S}_{r \text{ times}} \quad \underbrace{F\,F\,F\ldots\ldots F}_{(n-r) \text{ times}})$$

$$= {}^nC_r \underbrace{P(S)\,P(S)\ldots\ldots P(S)}_{r \text{ factors}} \quad \underbrace{P(F)\,P(F)\ldots\ldots P(F)}_{(n-r) \text{ factors}}$$

$$= {}^nC_r \underbrace{p\,p\,p\ldots\ldots p}_{r \text{ factors}} \quad \underbrace{q\,q\,q\ldots\ldots q}_{(n-r) \text{ factors}}$$

$$= {}^nC_r p^r q^{n-r} \qquad \ldots(1)$$

Hence $\quad$ **P(X = r) =** $\mathbf{{}^nC_r\, q^{n-r}\, p^r}$, where $\mathbf{p + q = 1}$ **and** $\mathbf{r = 0, 1, 2, \ldots, n}$.

The distribution (1) is called the *binomial probability distribution* and X is called the *binomial variate*.

**Note 1.** $P(X = r)$ is usually written as $P(r)$.

**Note 2.** The successive probabilities $P(r)$ in (1) for $r = 0, 1, 2, \ldots\ldots, n$ are

$${}^nC_0 q^n,\ {}^nC_1 q^{n-1} p,\ {}^nC_2 q^{n-2} p^2,\ \ldots\ldots,\ {}^nC_n p^n$$

which are the successive terms of the binomial expansion of $(q + p)^n$. That is why this distribution is called "binomial" distribution.

**Note 3.** $n$ and $p$ occurring in the binomial distribution are called the *parameters* of the distribution.

**Note 4.** In a binomial distribution :

(*i*) $n$, the number of trials is finite.

(*ii*) each trial has only two possible outcomes usually called success and failure.

(*iii*) all the trials are independent.

(*iv*) $p$ (and hence $q$) is constant for all the trials.

## 4.6. RECURRENCE OR RECURSION FORMULA FOR THE BINOMIAL DISTRIBUTION

In a binomial distribution,

$$P(r) = {}^nC_r\, q^{n-r}\, p^r = \frac{n!}{(n-r)!\,r!}\, q^{n-r}\, p^r$$

$$P(r+1) = {}^nC_{r+1}\, q^{n-r-1}\, p^{r+1} = \frac{n!}{(n-r-1)!\,(r+1)!}\, q^{n-r-1}\, p^{r+1}$$

$$\therefore \quad \frac{P(r+1)}{P(r)} = \frac{(n-r)!}{(n-r-1)!} \times \frac{r!}{(r+1)!} \times \frac{p}{q}$$

$$= \frac{(n-r)\times(n-r-1)!}{(n-r-1)!} \times \frac{r!}{(r+1)\times r!} \times \frac{p}{q} \times = \left(\frac{n-r}{r+1}\right) \cdot \frac{p}{q}$$

$$\Rightarrow \quad P(r+1) = \frac{n-r}{r+1} \cdot \frac{p}{q}\, P(r)$$

which is the required recurrence formula. Applying this formula successively, we can find P(1), P(2), P(3), ......, if P(0) is known.

## 4.7. MEAN AND VARIANCE OF THE BINOMIAL DISTRIBUTION

For the binomial distribution, $P(r) = {}^nC_r\, q^{n-r}\, p^r$ *(M.G.U. May 2010)*

$$\text{Mean } \mu = \sum_{r=0}^{n} rP(r) = \sum_{r=0}^{n} r\,.\,{}^nC_r q^{n-r}\, p^r$$

$$= 0 + 1\,.\,{}^nC_1\, q^{n-1}\, p + 2\,.\,{}^nC_2\, q^{n-2}\, p^2 + 3\,.\,{}^nC_3\, q^{n-3}\, p^3 + \ldots\ldots + n\,.\,{}^nC_n\, p^n$$

$$= nq^{n-1}\, p + 2\,.\,\frac{n(n-1)}{2\,.\,1}\, q^{n-2}p^2 + 3\,.\,\frac{n(n-1)(n-2)}{3\,.\,2\,.\,1}\, q^{n-3}\, p^3 + \ldots\ldots + n.p^n$$

$$= nq^{n-1}p + n(n-1)\, q^{n-2}p^2 + \frac{n(n-1)(n-2)}{2\,.\,1}\, q^{n-3}p^3 + \ldots\ldots + np^n$$

$$= np\left[q^{n-1} + (n-1)q^{n-2}\, p + \frac{(n-1)(n-2)}{2\,.\,1}\, q^{n-3}\, p^2 + \ldots\ldots + p^{n-1}\right]$$

$$= np[{}^{n-1}C_0 q^{n-1} + {}^{n-1}C_1 q^{n-2}p + {}^{n-1}C_2 q^{n-3}p^2 + \ldots + {}^{n-1}C_{n-1} p^{n-1}]$$

$$= np(q+p)^{n-1} = np \qquad (\because\ p + q = 1)$$

**Hence the mean of the binomial distribution is np.**

$$\text{Variance } \sigma^2 = \sum_{r=0}^{n} r^2 P(r) - \mu^2 = \sum_{r=0}^{n} [r + r(r-1)]\, P(r) - \mu^2$$

$$= \sum_{r=0}^{n} rP(r) + \sum_{r=0}^{n} r(r-1)\, P(r) - \mu^2 = \mu + \sum_{r=2}^{n} r(r-1)\, {}^nC_r q^{n-r}p^r - \mu^2$$

(since the contribution due to $r = 0$ and $r = 1$ is zero)

$$= \mu + [2\,.1\,.\,{}^nC_2 q^{n-2}p^2 + 3.2\,.\,{}^nC_3 q^{n-3}p^3 + \ldots + n(n-1)\,{}^nC_n p^n] - \mu^2$$

$$= \mu + \left[2\,.\,1.\frac{n(n-1)}{2\,.\,1}\, q^{n-2}p^2 + 3\,.\,2\,.\frac{n(n-1)(n-2)}{3\,.\,2\,.\,1}\, q^{n-3}p^3 + \ldots + n(n-1)p^n\right] - \mu^2$$

$$= \mu + [n(n-1)q^{n-2}p^2 + n(n-1)(n-2)q^{n-3}p^3 + ... + n(n-1)p^n] - \mu^2$$
$$= \mu + n(n-1)\, p^2[q^{n-2} + (n-2)q^{n-3}p + ... + p^{n-2}] - \mu^2$$
$$= \mu + n\,(n-1)p^2\,[{}^{n-2}C_0 q^{n-2} + {}^{n-2}C_1 q^{n-3}p + ... + {}^{n-2}C_{n-2}p^{n-2}] - \mu^2$$
$$= \mu + n(n-1)p^2(q+p)^{n-2} - \mu^2 = \mu + n(n-1)p^2 - \mu^2 \qquad [\because \; q+p=1]$$
$$= np + n(n-1)p^2 - n^2p^2 \qquad [\because \; \mu = np]$$
$$= np[1 + (n-1)p - np] = np[1-p] = npq.$$

**Hence the variance of the binomial distribution is npq.**

Standard deviation of the binomial distribution is $\sqrt{npq}$.

Similarly, we can prove that

$$\beta_1 = \frac{{\mu_3}^2}{{\mu_2}^3} = \frac{(q-p)^2}{npq} = \frac{(1-2p)^2}{npq} \;; \qquad \beta_2 = \frac{\mu_4}{{\mu_2}^2} = 3 + \frac{1-6pq}{npq}$$

Hence $\quad \gamma_1 = \sqrt{\beta_1} = \dfrac{q-p}{\sqrt{npq}} = \dfrac{1-2p}{\sqrt{npq}} \;; \qquad \gamma_2 = \beta_2 - 3 = \dfrac{1-6pq}{\sqrt{npq}}.$

**Note.** $\gamma_1 = \dfrac{q-p}{\sqrt{npq}} = \dfrac{1-2p}{\sqrt{npq}}$ gives a **measure of skewness** of the binomial distribution. If $p < \frac{1}{2}$, skewness is positive, if $p > \frac{1}{2}$, skewness is negative and if $p = \frac{1}{2}$, it is zero.

$\beta_2 = 3 + \dfrac{1-6pq}{npq}$ gives a **measure of the kurtosis** of the binomial distribution.

## ILLUSTRATIVE EXAMPLES

**Example 1.** *During war, 1 ship out of 9 was sunk on an average in making a certain voyage. What was the probability that exactly 3 out of a convoy of 6 ships would arrive safely ?*

**Sol.** $p$, the probability of a ship arriving safely $= 1 - \dfrac{1}{9} = \dfrac{8}{9}$ ; $q = \dfrac{1}{9}$, $n = 6$

Binomial distribution is $\left(\dfrac{1}{9} + \dfrac{8}{9}\right)^6$

The probability that exactly 3 ships arrive safely $= {}^6C_3 \left(\dfrac{1}{9}\right)^3 \left(\dfrac{8}{9}\right)^3 = \dfrac{10240}{9^6}.$

**Example 2.** *Assume that on the average one telephone number out of fifteen called between 2 P.M. and 3 P.M. on week-days is busy. What is the probability that if 6 randomly selected telephone numbers are called (i) not more than three, (ii) at least three of them will be busy ?*

**Sol.** $p$, the probability of a telephone number being busy between 2 P.M. and 3 P.M. on week-days $= \dfrac{1}{15}$

$$q = 1 - \frac{1}{15} = \frac{14}{15}, \quad n = 6 \text{ ; Binomial distribution is } \left(\frac{14}{15} + \frac{1}{15}\right)^6$$

The probability that not more than three will be busy

$$= p(0) + p(1) + p(2) + p(3)$$

$$= {}^6C_0\left(\frac{14}{15}\right)^6 + {}^6C_1\left(\frac{14}{15}\right)^5\left(\frac{1}{15}\right) + {}^6C_2\left(\frac{14}{15}\right)^4\left(\frac{1}{15}\right)^2 - {}^6C_3\left(\frac{14}{15}\right)^3\left(\frac{1}{15}\right)^3$$

$$= \frac{(14)^3}{(15)^6}[2744 + 1176 + 210 + 20] = \frac{2744 \times 4150}{(15)^6} = 0.9997$$

The probability that at least three of them will be busy

$$= p(3) + p(4) + p(5) + p(6)$$

$$= {}^6C_3\left(\frac{14}{15}\right)^3\left(\frac{1}{15}\right)^3 + {}^6C_4\left(\frac{14}{15}\right)^2\left(\frac{1}{15}\right)^4 + {}^6C_5\left(\frac{14}{15}\right)\left(\frac{1}{15}\right)^5 + {}^6C_6\left(\frac{1}{15}\right)^6 = 0.005.$$

**Example 3.** *Six dice are thrown 729 times. How many times do you expect at least three dice to show a five or six ?*

**Sol.** $p$ = the chance of getting 5 or 6 with one die $= \frac{2}{6} = \frac{1}{3}$

$$q = 1 - \frac{1}{3} = \frac{2}{3},\ n = 6,\ N = 729$$

since dice are in sets of 6 and there are 729 sets.

The binomial distribution is $N(q + p)^n = 729\left(\frac{2}{3} + \frac{1}{3}\right)^6$

The expected number of times *at least three* dice showing five or six

$$= 729\left[{}^6C_3\left(\frac{2}{3}\right)^3\left(\frac{1}{3}\right)^3 + {}^6C_4\left(\frac{2}{3}\right)^2\left(\frac{1}{3}\right)^4 + {}^6C_5\left(\frac{2}{3}\right)\left(\frac{1}{3}\right)^5 + {}^6C_6\left(\frac{1}{3}\right)^6\right]$$

$$= \frac{729}{3^6}[160 + 60 + 12 + 1] = 233.$$

**Example 4.** *Out of 800 families with 4 children each, how many families would be expected to have (i) 2 boys and 2 girls (ii) at least one boy (iii) no girl (iv) at most two girls ? Assume equal probabilities for boys and girls.*

**Sol.** Since probabilities for boys and girls are equal

$p$ = probability of having a boy $= \frac{1}{2}$; $q$ = probability of having a girl $= \frac{1}{2}$

$n = 4$, $N = 800$ $\therefore$ The binomial distribution is $800\left(\frac{1}{2} + \frac{1}{2}\right)^4$.

(*i*) The expected number of families having 2 *boys* and 2 girls

$$= 800\ {}^4C_2\left(\frac{1}{2}\right)^2\left(\frac{1}{2}\right)^2 = 800 \times 6 \times \frac{1}{16} = 300.$$

(*ii*) The expected number of families having *at least one boy*

$$= 800\left[{}^4C_1\left(\frac{1}{2}\right)^3\left(\frac{1}{2}\right) + {}^4C_2\left(\frac{1}{2}\right)^2\left(\frac{1}{2}\right)^2 + {}^4C_3\left(\frac{1}{2}\right)\left(\frac{1}{2}\right)^3 + {}^4C_4\left(\frac{1}{2}\right)^4\right]$$

$$= 800 \times \frac{1}{16} [4 + 6 + 4 + 1] = 750.$$

(*iii*) The expected number of families having no girl, *i.e.*, having 4 boys

$$= 800 \,.\, {}^4C_4 \left(\frac{1}{2}\right)^4 = 50.$$

(*iv*) The expected number of families having *at most two girls i.e.*, having *at least 2 boys*

$$= 800 \left[ {}^4C_2 \left(\frac{1}{2}\right)^2 \left(\frac{1}{2}\right)^2 + {}^4C_3 \left(\frac{1}{2}\right)\left(\frac{1}{2}\right)^3 + {}^4C_4 \left(\frac{1}{2}\right)^4 \right] = 800 \times \frac{1}{16} [6 + 4 + 1] = 550.$$

## TEST YOUR KNOWLEDGE

1. Ten coins are tossed simultaneously. Find the probability of getting at least seven heads.
2. The probability of any ship of a company being destroyed on a certain voyage is 0.02. The company owns 6 ships for the voyage. What is the probability of :
   (*i*) losing one ship (*ii*) losing at most two ships (*iii*) losing none.
3. The probability that a man aged 60 will live to be 70 is 0.65. What is the probability that out of ten men now 60, at least 7 would live to be 70 ?
4. The incidence of occupational disease in an industry is such that the workers have a 20% chance of suffering from it. What is the probability that out of six workers chosen at random, four or more will suffer from the disease ?
5. The probability that a pen manufactured by a company will be defective is $\frac{1}{10}$. If 12 such pens are manufactured, find the probability that
   (*i*) exactly two will be defective (*ii*) at least two will be defective
   (*iii*) none will be defective.
6. If the chance that one of the ten telephone lines is busy at an instant is 0.2.
   (*i*) What is the chance that 5 of the lines are busy ?
   (*ii*) What is the probability that all the lines are busy ?
7. If on an average 1 vessel in every 10 is wrecked, find the probability that out of 5 vessels expected to arrive, at least 4 will arrive safely.
8. A product is 0.5% defective and is packed in cartons of 100. What percentage contains not more than 3 defectives ?
9. A bag contains 5 white, 7 red and 8 black balls. If four balls are drawn, one by one, with replacement, what is the probability that
   (*i*) none is white (*ii*) all are white
   (*iii*) at least one is white (*iv*) only 2 are white ?
10. In a hurdle race, a player has to cross 10 hurdles. The probability that he will clear each hurdle is $\frac{5}{6}$. What is the probability that he will knock down fewer than 2 hurdles ?
11. Fit a binomial distribution for the following data and compare the theoretical frequencies with the actual ones :

| $x$ : | 0 | 1 | 2 | 3 | 4 | 5 |
|---|---|---|---|---|---|---|
| $f$ : | 2 | 14 | 20 | 34 | 22 | 8 |

**12.** If the sum of mean and variance of a binomial distribution is 4.8 for five trials, find the distribution.

**13.** If the mean of a binomial distribution is 3 and the variance is $\frac{3}{2}$, find the probability of obtaining at least 4 success.

**14.** In 800 families with 5 children each, how many families would be expected to have (*i*) 3 boys and 2 girls, (*ii*) 2 boys and 3 girls, (*iii*) no girl (*iv*) at the most two girls. (Assume probabilities for boys and girls to be equal.)

**15.** In 100 sets of ten tosses of an unbiased coin, in how many cases do you expect to get
(*i*) 7 heads and 3 tails (*ii*) at least 7 heads ?

**16.** The following data are the number of seeds germinating out of 10 on damp filter for 80 sets of seeds. Fit a binomial distribution to this data :

| $x$ : | 0 | 1 | 2 | 3 | 4 | 5 | 6 | 7 | 8 | 9 | 10 | Total |
|---|---|---|---|---|---|---|---|---|---|---|---|---|
| $f$ : | 6 | 20 | 28 | 12 | 8 | 6 | 0 | 0 | 0 | 0 | 0 | 80 |

[**Hint.** Here $n = 10$, N = 80, Mean $= \frac{\Sigma fx}{\Sigma f} = 2.175 \quad \therefore \quad np = 2.175$ etc.]

**17.** A bag contains 10 balls each marked with one of the digits 0 to 9. If four falls are drawn successively with replacement from the bag, what is the probability that none is marked with the digit 0 ?

**18.** A box contains 100 tickets each bearing one of the numbers from 1 to 100. If 5 tickets are drawn successively with replacement from the box, find the probability that all the tickets bear numbers divisible by 10.

**19.** The probability that a bomb dropped from a plane will strike the target is $\frac{1}{5}$. If six bombs are dropped, find the probability that (*i*) exactly two will strike the target, (*ii*) at least two will strike the target. (*M.G.U. Jan. 2007*)

**20.** In sampling a large number of parts manufactured by a machine, the mean number of defectives in a sample of 20 is 2. Out of 1000 such samples, how many would be expected to contain at least 3 defective parts.

**21.** Fit a binomial distribution to the following distribution.

| $x$ | 0 | 1 | 2 | 3 | 4 | 5 |
|---|---|---|---|---|---|---|
| $f$ | 27 | 14 | 6 | 3 | 0 | 0 |

**22.** If the probability of a defective bolt is 0.1, find (*a*) the mean (*b*) the standard deviation, for the number of defective bolt in a total of 400 bolts.

## Answers

**1.** $\frac{11}{64}$ **2.** (*i*) 0.1085, (*ii*) 0.9997, (*iii*) 0.8858 **3.** 0.514

**4.** $\frac{53}{3125}$ **5.** (*i*) 0.2301 (*ii*) 0.3412 (*iii*) 0.2833

**6.** (*i*) 0.02579 (*ii*) $1.024 \times 10^{-7}$ **7.** 0.91854 **8.** 99.83

**9.** (*i*) $\frac{81}{256}$ (*ii*) $\frac{1}{256}$ (*iii*) $\frac{175}{256}$ (*iv*) $\frac{27}{128}$ **10.** $\frac{5}{2}\left(\frac{5}{6}\right)^9$

**11.** $100\,(0.432 + 0.568)^5$ **12.** $\left(\frac{1}{5}+\frac{4}{5}\right)^5$ **13.** $\frac{11}{32}$

**14.** (*i*) 250, (*ii*) 250, (*iii*) 25, (*iv*) 400 **15.** (*i*) 12 nearly (*ii*) 17 nearly

**16.** 80 $(0.7825 + 0.2175)^{10}$ **17.** $\left(\frac{9}{10}\right)^4$ **18.** 0.00001

**19.** (*i*) 0.246 (*ii*) 0.345 **20.** 323 **21.** 50 $(.86 + 0.14)^5$

**22.** (*a*) mean = 40 (*b*) variance = 36, standard deviation = 6.

# POISSON DISTRIBUTION

## 4.8. POISSON DISTRIBUTION AS A LIMITING CASE OF BINOMIAL DISTRIBUTION

If the parameters $n$ and $p$ of a binomial distribution are known, we can find the distribution. But in situations where $n$ is very large and $p$ is very small, application of binomial distribution is very labourious. However, if we assume that as $n \to \infty$ and $p \to 0$ such that $np$ always remains finite, say $\lambda$, we get the Poisson approximation to the binomial distribution.

Now, for a binomial distribution

$$P(X = r) = {}^nC_r q^{n-r} p^r$$

$$= \frac{n(n-1)(n-2)\dots(n-r+1)}{r!} \times (1-p)^{n-r} \times p^r$$

$$= \frac{n(n-1)(n-2)\dots(n-r+1)}{r!} \times \left(1-\frac{\lambda}{n}\right)^{n-r} \times \left(\frac{\lambda}{n}\right)^r \quad \text{since } np = \lambda \quad \therefore \quad p = \frac{\lambda}{n}$$

$$= \frac{\lambda^r}{r!} \times \frac{n(n-1)(n-2)\dots(n-r+1)}{n^r} \times \frac{\left(1-\frac{\lambda}{n}\right)^n}{\left(1-\frac{\lambda}{n}\right)^r}$$

$$= \frac{\lambda^r}{r!}\left(\frac{n}{n}\right)\left(\frac{n-1}{n}\right)\left(\frac{n-2}{n}\right)\dots\dots\left(\frac{n-r+1}{n}\right) \times \frac{\left(1-\frac{\lambda}{n}\right)^n}{\left(1-\frac{\lambda}{n}\right)^r}$$

$$= \frac{\lambda^r}{r!}\left(1-\frac{1}{n}\right)\left(1-\frac{2}{n}\right)\dots\dots\left(1-\frac{r-1}{n}\right) \times \frac{\left[\left(1-\frac{\lambda}{n}\right)^{-\frac{n}{\lambda}}\right]^{-\lambda}}{\left(1-\frac{\lambda}{n}\right)^r}$$

As $n \to \infty$, each of the $(r-1)$ factors

$\left(1-\frac{1}{n}\right), \left(1-\frac{2}{n}\right), \dots\dots, \left(1-\frac{r-1}{n}\right)$ tends to 1. Also $\left(1-\frac{\lambda}{n}\right)^r$ tends to 1.

Since $\underset{x \to \pm\infty}{\text{Lt}} \left(1+\frac{1}{x}\right)^x = e$, the Naperian base. $\therefore \left[\left(1-\frac{\lambda}{n}\right)^{-\frac{n}{\lambda}}\right]^{-\lambda} \longrightarrow e^{-\lambda}$ as $n \to \infty$

Hence in the limiting case when $n \to \infty$, we have

$$P(X = r) = \frac{\lambda^r e^{-\lambda}}{r!} \quad (r = 0, 1, 2, 3, \ldots) \qquad \ldots(A)$$

where $\lambda$ is a finite number $= np$.

(A) Represents probability distribution which is called the Poisson probability distribution.

**Note 1.** $\lambda$ is called the parameter of the distribution.

**Note 2.** $e^x = 1 + \frac{x}{1!} + \frac{x^2}{2!} + \ldots\ldots + \frac{x^n}{n!} + \ldots\ldots$ to $\infty$.

**Note 3.** The sum of the probabilities $P(r)$ for $r = 0, 1, 2, 3, \ldots\ldots$ is 1, since

$$P(0) + P(1) + P(2) + P(3) + \ldots\ldots = e^{-\lambda} + \frac{\lambda e^{-\lambda}}{1!} + \frac{\lambda^2 e^{-\lambda}}{2!} + \frac{\lambda^3 e^{-\lambda}}{3!} + \ldots\ldots$$

$$= e^{-\lambda}\left(1 + \frac{\lambda}{1!} + \frac{\lambda^2}{2!} + \frac{\lambda^3}{3!} + \ldots\ldots\right) = e^{-\lambda} . e^{\lambda} = 1.$$

## 4.9. RECURRENCE FORMULA FOR THE POISSON DISTRIBUTION

For Poisson distribution, $P(r) = \frac{\lambda^r e^{-\lambda}}{r!}$ and $P(r+1) = \frac{\lambda^{r+1} e^{-\lambda}}{(r+1)!}$

$$\therefore \quad \frac{P(r+1)}{P(r)} = \frac{\lambda r!}{(r+1)!} = \frac{\lambda}{r+1} \quad \text{or} \quad P(r+1) = \frac{\lambda}{r+1} P(r),\ r = 0, 1, 2, 3, \ldots\ldots$$

This is called the recurrence formula for the Poisson distribution.

## 4.10. MEAN AND VARIANCE OF THE POISSON DISTRIBUTION

For the Poisson distribution, $P(r) = \frac{\lambda^r e^{-\lambda}}{r!}$

$$\text{Mean } \mu = \sum_{r=0}^{\infty} rP(r) = \sum_{r=0}^{\infty} r . \frac{\lambda^r e^{-\lambda}}{r!}$$

$$= e^{-\lambda} \sum_{r=1}^{\infty} \frac{\lambda^r}{(r-1)!} = e^{-\lambda}\left(\lambda + \frac{\lambda^2}{1!} + \frac{\lambda^3}{2!} + \ldots\ldots\right)$$

$$= \lambda e^{-\lambda}\left(1 + \frac{\lambda}{1!} + \frac{\lambda^2}{2!} + \ldots\ldots\right) = \lambda e^{-\lambda} . e^{\lambda} = \lambda$$

**Thus, the mean of the Poisson distribution is equal to the parameter $\lambda$.**

$$\text{Variance } \sigma^2 = \sum_{r=0}^{\infty} r^2 P(r) - \mu^2 = \sum_{r=0}^{\infty} r^2 . \frac{\lambda^r e^{-\lambda}}{r!} - \lambda^2 = e^{-\lambda} \sum_{r=1}^{\infty} \frac{r^2 \lambda^r}{r!} - \lambda^2$$

$$= e^{-\lambda}\left[\frac{1^2 . \lambda}{1!} + \frac{2^2 . \lambda^2}{2!} + \frac{3^2 \lambda^3}{3!} + \frac{4^2 \lambda^4}{4!} + \ldots\ldots\right] - \lambda^2$$

$$= \lambda e^{-\lambda}\left[1+\frac{2\lambda}{1!}+\frac{3\lambda^2}{2!}+\frac{4\lambda^3}{3!}+\ldots\ldots\right]-\lambda^2$$

$$= \lambda e^{-\lambda}\left[1+\frac{(1+1)\lambda}{1!}+\frac{(1+2)\lambda^2}{2!}+\frac{(1+3)\lambda^3}{3!}+\ldots\ldots\right]-\lambda^2$$

$$= \lambda e^{-\lambda}\left[\left(1+\frac{\lambda}{1!}+\frac{\lambda^2}{2!}+\frac{\lambda^3}{3!}+\ldots\ldots\right)+\left(\frac{\lambda}{1!}+\frac{2\lambda^2}{2!}+\frac{3\lambda^3}{3!}+\ldots\ldots\right)\right]-\lambda^2$$

$$= \lambda e^{-\lambda}\left[e^{\lambda}+\lambda\left(1+\frac{\lambda}{1!}+\frac{\lambda^2}{2!}+\ldots\ldots\right)\right]-\lambda^2$$

$$= \lambda e^{-\lambda}\,[e^{\lambda}+\lambda e^{\lambda}]-\lambda^2 = \lambda e^{-\lambda}\,.\,e^{\lambda}\,(1+\lambda)-\lambda^2 = \lambda(1+\lambda)-\lambda^2 = \lambda.$$

**Hence, the variance of the Poisson distribution is also $\lambda$.**

**Thus, the mean and the variance of the Poisson distribution are each equal to the parameter $\lambda$.**

**Note.** The mean and the variance of the Poisson distribution can also be derived from those of the binomial distribution in the limiting case when $n \to \infty$, $p \to 0$ and $np = \lambda$.

Mean of binomial distribution is $np$.

$\therefore$ Mean of Poisson distribution $= \underset{n\to\infty}{\text{Lt}}\ np = \underset{n\to\infty}{\text{Lt}}\ \lambda = \lambda$

Variance of binomial distribution is $npq = np\,(1-p)$

$\therefore$ Variance of Poisson distribution $= \underset{n\to\infty}{\text{Lt}}\ np\,(1-p) = \underset{n\to\infty}{\text{Lt}}\ \lambda\left(1-\frac{\lambda}{n}\right) = \lambda.$

## ILLUSTRATIVE EXAMPLES

**Example 1.** *If the variance of the Poisson distribution is 2, find the probabilities for $r = 1, 2, 3, 4$ from the recurrence relation of the Poisson distribution.*

**Sol.** $\lambda$, the parameter of Poisson distribution = Variance = 2

Recurrence relation for the Poisson distribution is

$$P(r+1) = \frac{\lambda}{r+1}\,P(r) = \frac{2}{r+1}\,P(r) \qquad \ldots(1)$$

Now $\quad P(r) = \dfrac{\lambda^r e^{-\lambda}}{r!} \Rightarrow P(0) = \dfrac{e^{-2}}{0!} = e^{-2} = 0.1353$

Putting $r = 0, 1, 2, 3$ in (1), we get

$$P(1) = 2P(0) = 2 \times 0.1353 = 0.2706\ ; \qquad P(2) = \frac{2}{2}\,P(1) = 0.2706$$

$$P(3) = \frac{2}{3}\,P(2) = \frac{2}{3} \times 0.2706 = 0.1804\ ; \qquad P(4) = \frac{2}{4}\,P(3) = \frac{1}{2} \times 0.1804 = .0902.$$

**Example 2.** *Assume that the probability of an individual coalminer being killed in a mine accident during a year is* $\frac{1}{2400}$. *Use Poisson's distribution to calculate the probability that in a mine employing 200 miners there will be at least one fatal accident in a year.*

**Sol.** Here $p = \frac{1}{2400}, n = 200$; $\therefore \quad \lambda = np = \frac{200}{2400} = \frac{1}{12} = 0.083$

$$\therefore \quad P(r) = \frac{\lambda^r e^{-\lambda}}{r!} = \frac{(0.083)^r e^{-.083}}{r!}$$

P(at least one fatal accident) = 1 – P (no fatal accident)

$$= 1 - P(0) = 1 - \frac{(0.083)^0 e^{-0.83}}{0!} = 1 - .92 = 0.08.$$

**Example 3.** *Data was collected over a period of 10 years, showing number of deaths from horse kicks in each of the 200 army corps. The distribution of deaths was as follows :*

| *No. of deaths* : | *0* | *1* | *2* | *3* | *4* | *Total* |
|---|---|---|---|---|---|---|
| *Frequency* : | *109* | *65* | *22* | *3* | *1* | *200* |

*Fit a Poisson distribution to the data and calculate the theoretical frequencies :*

**Sol.** Mean of given distribution $= \frac{\Sigma fx}{\Sigma f} = \frac{65 + 44 + 9 + 4}{200} = \frac{122}{200} = 0.61$

This is the parameter $(m)$ of the Poisson distribution.

$\therefore$ Required Poisson distribution is $N . \frac{m^r e^{-m}}{r!}$ where $N = \Sigma f = 200$

$$= 200e^{-0.61} . \frac{(0.61)^r}{r!} = 200 \times 0.5435 \frac{(0.61)^r}{r!} = 108.7 \times \frac{(0.61)^2}{r!}.$$

| *r* | *P(r)* | *Theoretical Frequency* |
|---|---|---|
| 0 | 108.7 | 109 |
| 1 | 108.7 × 0.61 = 66.3 | 66 |
| 2 | $108.7 \times \frac{(0.61)^2}{2!} = 20.2$ | 20 |
| 3 | $108.7 \times \frac{(0.61)^3}{3!} = 4.1$ | 4 |
| 4 | $108.7 \times \frac{(0.61)^4}{4!} = 0.7$ | 1 |
| | | Total = 200 |

**Example 4.** *A car-hire firm has two cars, which it hires out day by day. The number of demands for a car on each day is distributed as a Poisson distribution with mean 1.5. Calculate the proportion of days on which neither car is used and the proportion of days on which some demand is refused.* $(e^{-1.5} = 0.2231)$

**Sol.** Since the number of demands for a car is distributed as a Poisson distribution with mean $m = 1.5$.

$\therefore$ Proportion of days on which neither car is used

= Probability of there being no demand for the car

$$= \frac{m^0 e^{-m}}{0!} = e^{-1.5} = 0.2231$$

Proportion of days on which some demand is refused

= probability for the number of demands to be more than two

$$= 1 - P(x \le 2) = 1 - \left(e^{-m} + \frac{me^{-m}}{1!} + \frac{m^2 e^{-m}}{2!}\right)$$

$$= 1 - e^{-1.5}\left(1 + 1.5 + \frac{(1.5)^2}{2}\right) = 1 - 0.2231\,(1 + 1.5 + 1.125)$$

$$= 1 - 0.2231 \times 3.625 = 1 - 0.8087375 = 0.1912625.$$

**Example 5.** *Six coins are tossed 6400 times. Using the Poisson distribution, determine the approximate probability of getting six heads x times.*

**Sol.** Probability of getting one head with one coin $= \frac{1}{2}$.

$\therefore$ The probability of getting six heads with six coins $= \left(\frac{1}{2}\right)^6 = \frac{1}{64}$

$\therefore$ Average number of six heads with six coins in 6400 throws $= np = 6400 \times \frac{1}{64} = 100$

$\therefore$ The mean of the Poisson distribution = 100.

Approximate probability of getting six heads $x$ times when the distribution is Poisson

$$= \frac{m^x e^{-m}}{x!} = \frac{(100)^x \cdot e^{-100}}{(100)!}.$$

## TEST YOUR KNOWLEDGE

1. Fit a Poisson distribution to the following :

| $x$ : | 0 | 1 | 2 | 3 | 4 |
|---|---|---|---|---|---|
| $f$ : | 192 | 100 | 24 | 3 | 1 |

2. If the probability of a bad reaction from a certain injection is 0.001, determine the chance that out of 2000 individuals more than two will get a bad reaction.
3. If X is a Poisson variate such that P(X = 2) = 9P(X = 4) + 90P(X = 6), find the standard deviation.
4. If a random variable has a Poisson distribution such that P(1) = P(2), find
   (*i*) mean of the distribution (*ii*) P(4).
5. Suppose that X has a Poisson distribution. If P(X = 2) = $\frac{2}{3}$ P(X = 1) find, (*i*) P(X = 0) (*ii*) P(X = 3).
6. A certain screw making machine produces on average 2 defective screws out of 100, and packs them in boxes of 500. Find the probability that a box contains 15 defective screws.
7. The incidence of occupational disease in an industry is such that the workmen have a 10% chance of suffering from it. What is the probability that in a group of 7, five or more will suffer from it ?

**8.** Fit a Poisson distribution to the following and calculate theoretical frequencies :

| $x$ : | 0 | 1 | 2 | 3 | 4 |
|---|---|---|---|---|---|
| $f$ : | 122 | 60 | 15 | 2 | 1 |

**9.** Fit a Poisson distribution to the following data given the number of yeast cells per square for 400 squares :

| *No. of cells per sq.* : | 0 | 1 | 2 | 3 | 4 | 5 | 6 | 7 | 8 | 9 | 10 |
|---|---|---|---|---|---|---|---|---|---|---|---|
| *No. of squares* : | 103 | 143 | 98 | 42 | 8 | 4 | 2 | 0 | 0 | 0 | 0 |

**10.** Show that in a Poisson distribution with unit mean, mean deviation about mean is $\left(\frac{2}{e}\right)$ times the standard deviation.

**11.** In a certain factory turning razor blades, there is a small chance of 0.002 for any blade to be defective. The blades are supplied in packets of 10. Use Poisson distribution to calculate the approximate number of packets containing no defective, one defective and two defective blades respectively in a consignment of 10000 packets.

**12.** The probability that a man aged 35 years will die before reaching the age of 40 years may be taken as 0.018. Out of a group of 400 men, now aged 35 years, what is the probability that 2 men will die within the next 5 years ?

**13.** Suppose a book of 585 pages contains 43 typographical errors. If these errors are randomly distributed throughout the book, what is the probability that 10 pages, selected at random, will be free from errors ?

**14.** If $x$ has a Poisson distribution with parameter $\lambda$, and if $P(x = 0) = 0.2.$, evaluate $P(x > 2)$ *(M.G.U. Dec. 2007)*

**15.** If 3% of the electric bulbs manufactured by a company are defective, find the probability that in a sample of 100 bulbs (*a*) 0, (*b*) 1, (*c*) 2, (*d*) 3, (*e*) 4 bulbs will be defective.

**16.** The probabilities of a poisson variate taking values 3 and 4 are equal. Calculate the probabilities of the variate taking the values 0 and 1. *(M.G.U. Jan. 2007)*

**17.** Fit a Poisson distribution for the following data and hence calculate the theoretical frequencies :

| $x$ : | 0 | 1 | 2 | 3 | 4 | 5 |
|---|---|---|---|---|---|---|
| $f$ : | 142 | 156 | 69 | 27 | 5 | 1 |

*(M.G.U. May 2010)*

## Answers

**1.** $320 \times \dfrac{e^{0.503}(9.503)^r}{r!}$ **2.** 0.32 **3.** 1 **4.** (*i*) 2 (*ii*) $\dfrac{2}{3e^2}$

**5.** (*i*) $e^{-4}$ (*ii*) $4e^{-4}$ **6.** $\dfrac{(10)^{15}e^{-10}}{(15)!} = 0.035$ **7.** 0.0008

**8.** $121.36 \times \dfrac{(0.5)^r}{r!}$, where $r = 0, 1, 2, 3, 4$

Theoretical frequencies are 121, 61, 15, 3, 0 respectively

**9.** Theoretical frequencies are 109, 142, 92, 40, 13, 3, 1, 0, 0, 0, 0

**11.** 9802, 196, 2 **12.** 0.01936 **13.** 0.4795

**14.** $P(x > 2) = 1 - (0.2)\left(1 + \ln 5 + \dfrac{(\ln 5)^2}{2}\right).$

**15.** (*a*) 0.04979 (*b*) 0.1494 (*c*) 0.2241
(*d*) 0.2241 (*e*) 0.1680

**16.** $P(0) = e^{-4}$, $P(1) = 4e^{-4}$.

**17.** $P(x) = \dfrac{147.1517}{x!}$, $x = 0, 1, 2, 3, 4, 5$ theoretical frequencies are 147, 147, 74, 25, 6, 1.

## 4.11. UNIFORM DISTRIBUTION

The uniform distribution is a continuous distribution. The probability density function of the uniform distribution is given by $f(x) = \begin{cases} \dfrac{1}{\beta - \alpha} \end{cases}$ for $\alpha < x < \beta$ elsewhere $\alpha$ and $\beta$ are the parameters in the function. The graph of uniform distribution is as follows :

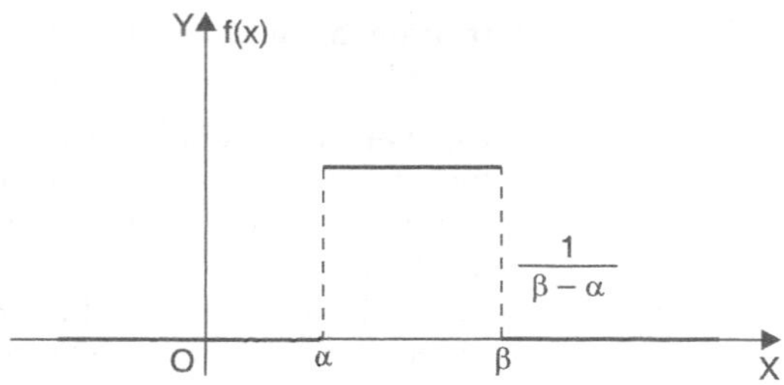


The mean of uniform distribution is

$$\mu = \int_{\alpha}^{\beta} x \frac{1}{\beta - \alpha}\, dx = \frac{\alpha + \beta}{2}$$

The variance of uniform distribution is $\sigma^2 = \dfrac{1}{12} (\beta - \alpha)^2$

**Proof :** Let $\qquad \mu_2^1 = \displaystyle\int_{\alpha}^{\beta} x^2 \frac{1}{\beta - \alpha}\, dx = \frac{\alpha^2 + \alpha\beta + \beta^2}{3}.$

The variance $\qquad \sigma^2 = \displaystyle\int_{\alpha}^{\beta} (x - \mu)^2 \frac{1}{\beta - \alpha}\, dx$

$$= \int_{\alpha}^{\beta} x^2 \frac{1}{\beta - \alpha}\, dx + \mu^2 \int_{\alpha}^{\beta} \frac{1}{\beta - \alpha}\, dx - \mu \int_{\alpha}^{\beta} 2x \frac{1}{\beta - \alpha}\, dx$$

$$= \frac{\alpha^2 + \beta\alpha + \beta^2}{3} + \mu^2 - 2\mu\left(\frac{\alpha + \beta}{2}\right)$$

$$= \frac{\alpha^2 + \beta\alpha + \beta^2}{3} + \mu^2 - 2\mu^2$$

$$= \frac{\alpha^2 + \beta\alpha + \beta^2}{3} - \mu^2$$

$$= \frac{\alpha^2 + \beta\alpha + \beta^2}{3} - \left(\frac{\alpha + \beta}{2}\right)^2$$

$$= \frac{1}{12} (\beta - \alpha)^2.$$

## 4.12. EXPONENTIAL DISTRIBUTION

The exponential distribution is a continuous distribution. A continuous random variable X assuming non-negative values is said to have an exponential distribution with parameter $\alpha > 0$, if its probability density function is given by

$$f(x) = \begin{cases} \alpha e^{-\alpha x}, & x \geq 0 \\ 0, & \text{otherwise} \end{cases}$$

The mean of the distribution

$$\mu = \int_0^\infty x \alpha e^{-\alpha x} dx = \frac{1}{\alpha}$$

The variance of the distribution

$$\sigma^2 = \int_0^\infty (x - \mu)^2 \alpha e^{-\alpha x} dx$$

$$= \int_0^\infty x^2 \alpha e^{-\alpha x} dx - \mu^2$$

$$= \frac{2}{\alpha^2} - \frac{1}{\alpha^2} = \frac{1}{\alpha^2}.$$

## 4.13. NORMAL DISTRIBUTION

The normal distribution is a continuous distribution. It can be derived from the binomial distribution in the limiting case when $n$, the number of trials is very large and $p$, the probability of a success, is close to $\frac{1}{2}$. The general equation of the normal distribution is given by

$$f(x) = \frac{1}{\sigma\sqrt{2\pi}} e^{-\frac{1}{2}\left(\frac{x-\mu}{\sigma}\right)^2}$$

where the variable $x$ can assume all values from $-\infty$ to $+\infty$. $\mu$ and $\sigma$, called the parameters of the distribution, are respectively the mean and the standard deviation of the distribution and $-\infty < \mu < \infty$, $\sigma > 0$. $x$ is called the normal variate and $f(x)$ is called probability density function of the normal distribution.

If a variable $x$ has the normal distribution with mean $\mu$ and standard deviation $\sigma$, we briefly write $x : N(\mu, \sigma^2)$.

The graph of the normal distribution is called the *normal curve*. It is bell-shapped and symmetrical about the mean $\mu$. The two tails of the curve extend to $+\infty$ and $-\infty$ towards the positive and negative directions of the $x$-axis respectively and gradually approach the $x$-axis without ever metting it. The curve is unimodal and the mode of the normal distribution coincides with its mean $\mu$. The line $x = \mu$ divides the area under the normal curve above $x$-axis into two equal parts. Thus, the median of the distribution also coincides with its mean and mode. The area under the normal curve between any two given ordinates $x = x_1$ and $x = x_2$ represents the probability of values falling into the given interval. The total area under the normal curve above the $x$-axis is 1.

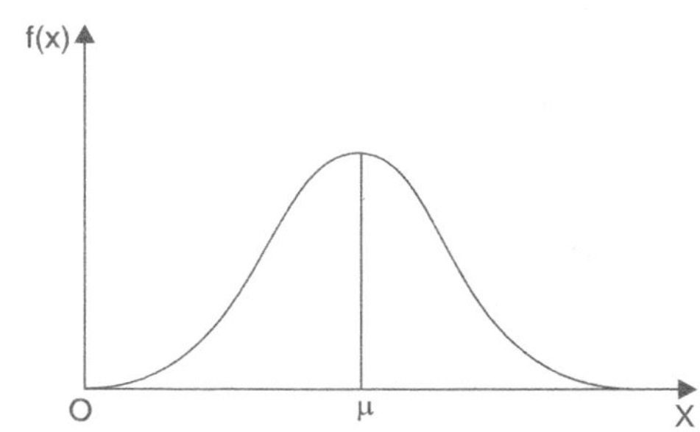

## 4.14. BASIC PROPERTIES OF THE NORMAL DISTRIBUTION

The probability density function of the normal distribution is given by

$$f(x) = \frac{1}{\sigma\sqrt{2\pi}} e^{-\frac{1}{2}\left(\frac{x-\mu}{\sigma}\right)^2}$$

(*i*) $f(x) \geq 0$ (*ii*) $\int_{-\infty}^{\infty} f(x)\, dx = 1,$

*i.e.,* the total area under the normal curve above the $x$-axis is 1.

(*iii*) The normal distribution is symmetrical about its mean.

(*iv*) It is a unimodal distribution. The mean, mode and median of this distribution coincide.

## 4.15. STANDARD FORM OF THE NORMAL DISTRIBUTION

If X is a normal random variable with mean μ and standard deviation σ, then the random variable $Z = \frac{X - \mu}{\sigma}$ has the normal distribution with mean 0 and standard deviation 1. The random variable Z is called the *standardized* (or *standard*) normal random variable.

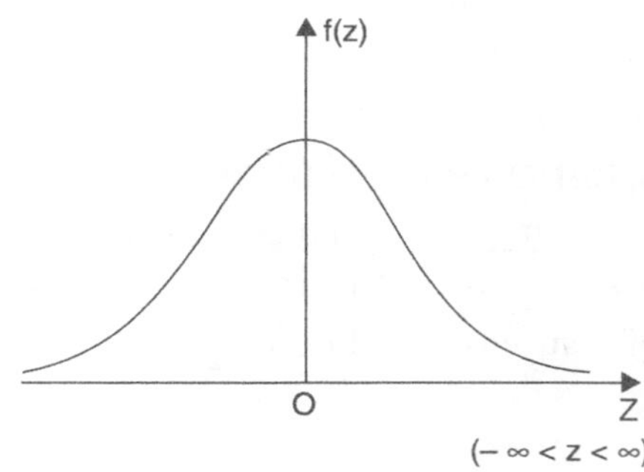


The probability density function for the normal distribution in standard form is given by

$$f(z) = \frac{1}{\sqrt{2\pi}} e^{-\frac{1}{2}z^2}$$

It is free from any parameter. This helps us to compute areas under the normal probability curve by making use of standard tables.

**Note 1.** If $f(z)$ is the probability density function for the normal distribution, then

$$P(z_1 \leq Z \leq z_2) = \int_{z_1}^{z_2} f(z)\, dz = F(z_2) - F(z_1), \quad \text{where} \quad F(z) = \int_{-\infty}^{z} f(z)\, dz = P(Z \leq z)$$

The function F($z$) defined above is called the *distribution function* for the normal distribution.

**Note 2.** The probabilities $P(z_1 \leq Z \leq z_2)$, $P(z_1 < Z \leq z_2)$, $P(z_1 \leq Z < z_2)$ and $P(z_1 < Z < z_2)$ are all regarded to be the same.

**Note 3.** $F(-z_1) = 1 - F(z_1)$.

## ILLUSTRATIVE EXAMPLES

**Example 1.** *A sample of 100 dry battery cells tested to find the length of life produced the following results :*

$$\bar{x} = 12 \text{ hours}, \sigma = 3 \text{ hours}.$$

*Assuming the data to be normally distributed, what percentage of battery cells are expected to have life*

(*i*) *more than 15 hours* (*ii*) *less than 6 hours*

(*iii*) *between 10 and 14 hours ?*

**Sol.** Here $x$ denotes the length of life of dry battery cells.

Also $$z = \frac{x - \bar{x}}{\sigma} = \frac{x - 12}{3}.$$

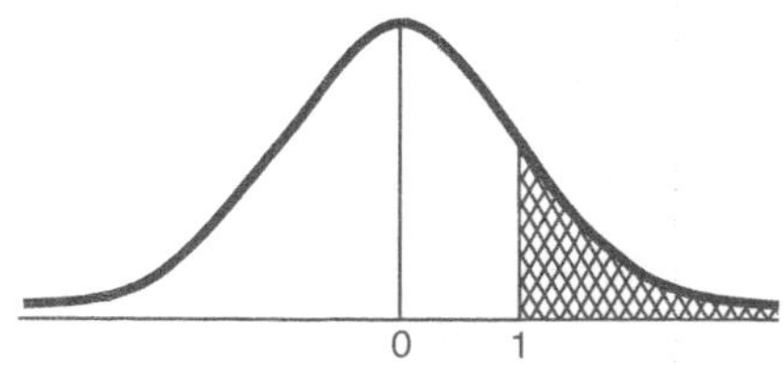


(*i*) When $x = 15$, $z = 1$

$\therefore$ $P(x > 15) = P(z > 1)$

$= P(0 < z < \infty) - P(0 < z < 1)$

$= 0.5 - 0.3413 = 0.1587 = 15.87\%$.

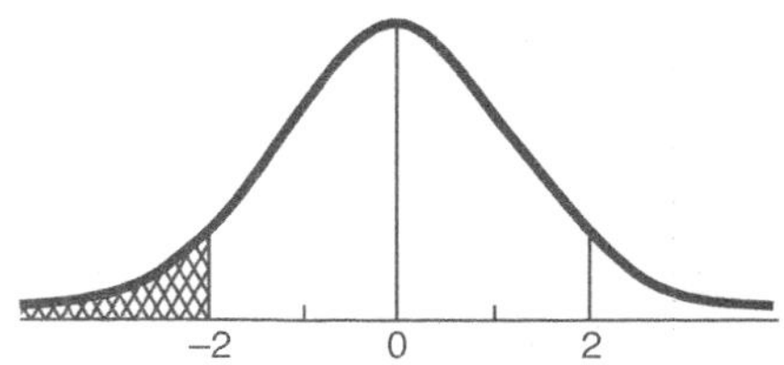


(*ii*) When $x = 6$, $z = -2$

$\therefore$ $P(x < 6) = P(z < -2)$

$= P(z > 2) = P(0 < z < \infty) - P(0 < z < 2)$

$= 0.5 - 0.4772 = 0.0228 = 2.28\%$.

(*iii*) When $x = 10$, $z = -\frac{2}{3} = -0.67$

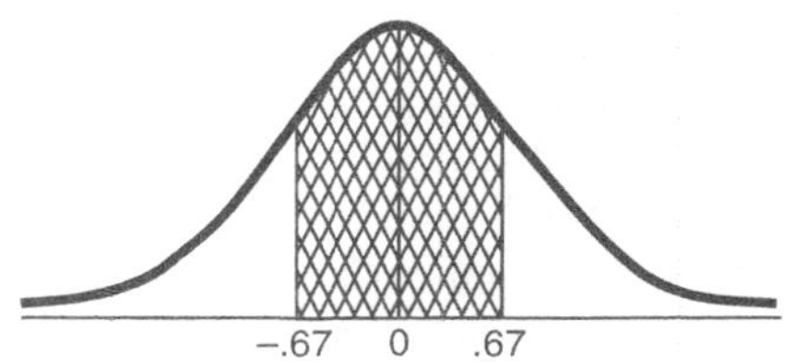


When $x = 14$, $z = \frac{2}{3} = 0.67$

$P(10 < x < 14)$

$= P(-0.67 < z < 0.67)$

$= 2P(0 < z < 0.67) = 2 \times 0.2487$

$= 0.4974 = 49.74\%$.

**Example 2.** *In a normal distribution, 31% of the items are under 45 and 8% are over 64. Find the mean and standard deviation of the distribution.*

**Sol.** Let $\bar{x}$ and $\sigma$ be the mean and S.D. respectively.

31% of the items are under 45.

$\Rightarrow$ Area to the left of the ordinate $x = 45$ is 0.31

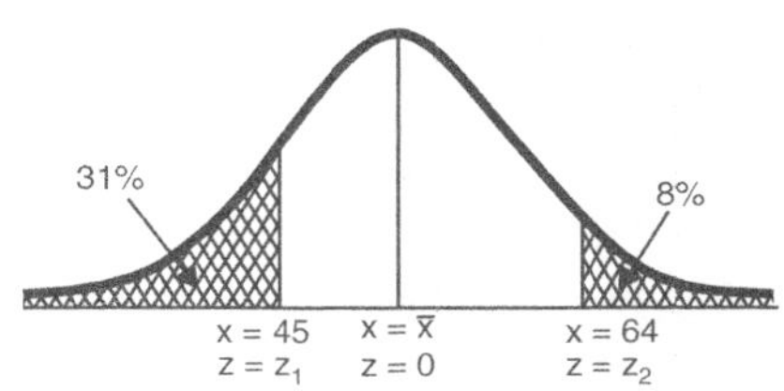


When $x = 45$, let $z = z_1$

$P(z_1 < z < 0) = 0.5 - 0.31 = 0.19$

From the tables, the value of $z$ corresponding to this area is 0.5

$\therefore$ $z_1 = -0.5 [z_1 < 0]$

When $x = 64$, let $z = z_2$

$P(0 < z < z_2) = 0.5 - 0.08 = 0.42$

From the tables, the value of $z$ corresponding to this area is 1.4.

$z_2 = 1.4$

Since $$z = \frac{x - \bar{x}}{\sigma}$$

$$-0.5 = \frac{45 - \bar{x}}{\sigma} \quad \text{and} \quad 1.4 = \frac{64 - \bar{x}}{\sigma}$$

$\Rightarrow$ $45 - \bar{x} = -0.5\sigma$ ...(1)

and $64 - \bar{x} = 1.4\sigma$ ...(2)

Subtracting $-19 = -1.9\sigma$ $\therefore$ $\sigma = 10$

From (1), $45 - \bar{x} = -0.5 \times 10 = -5$ $\therefore$ $\bar{x} = 50$.

**Example 3.** *If X has normal distribution with mean* $\mu$ *and variance* $\sigma^2$, *find* $P[\mu - \sigma < X < \mu + \sigma]$. (M.G.U. Dec 2007)

**Sol.** Let $X$ follows $N(\mu, \sigma)$.

Then $\dfrac{X-\mu}{\sigma} = T$ follows $N(0, 1)$

When $\mu - \sigma < X < \mu + \sigma$, the variable T lies between – 1 and 1.

So $\quad p[\mu - \sigma < X < \mu + \sigma]$

$$= p\left[-1 < \frac{X-\mu}{\sigma} < 1\right]$$

$$= \int_{-1}^{1} \frac{1}{\sqrt{2\pi}} e^{-\frac{t^2}{2}}\, dt = .6826$$

## TEST YOUR KNOWLEDGE

1. In a certain examination, the percentage of candidate passing and getting distinctions were 45 and 9 respectively. Estimate the average marks obtained by the candidates, if the minimum pass and distinction marks being 40 and 75 respectively. (Assume the distribution of marks to be normal).
2. A random variable has a normal distribution with $\sigma = 10$. If the probability is 0.8212 that it will take on a value less than 82.5. What is the probability that it will take on a value greater than 58.3.
3. Fit a Binomial distribution to the following data :

| $x$ : | 0 | 1 | 2 | 3 | 4 |
|---|---|---|---|---|---|
| $f$ : | 4 | 30 | 36 | 25 | 5 |

4. The mean weight of 500 students is 52 kgs and SD is 15 kgs . Assume the weights are normally distributed find how many students weight lie between 40 kgs and 50 kgs.
5. The mean height of 500 male students in a certain college is 151 cm and the standard deviation is 15 cm. Assuming the heights are normally distributed, find how many students have heights between 120 and 155 cm ?
6. An aptitude test for selecting officers in a bank is conducted on 1000 candidates. The average score is 42 and the standard deviation of score is 24. Assuming normal distribution for the scores, find

   (*i*) The number of candidates whose scores exceed 60

   (*ii*) The number of candidates whose scores lie between 30 and 60.
7. In a normal distribution, 7% of the items are under 35 and 89% are under 63. What are the mean and standard deviation of the distribution ?
8. Let X denote the number of scores on a test. If X is normally distributed with mean 100 and standard deviation 15, find the probability that X does not exceed 130.
9. It is known from the past experience that the number of telephone calls made daily in a certain community between 3 p.m. and 4 p.m. have a mean of 352 and a standard deviation of 31. What percentage of the time will there be more than 400 telephone calls made in this community between 3 p.m. and 4 p.m. ?
10. Students of a class were given a mechanical aptitude test. Their marks were found to be normally distributed with mean 60 and standard deviation 5. What per cent of students scored

    (*i*) more than 60 marks ? (*ii*) less than 56 marks ?

    (*iii*) between 45 and 65 marks ?

**11.** In an examination taken by 500 candidates, the average and the standard deviation of marks obtained (normally distributed) are 40% and 10%. Find approximately :

(*i*) How many will pass, if 50% is fixed as a minimum ?

(*ii*) What should be the minimum if 350 candidates are to pass ?

(*iii*) How many have scored marks above 60% ?

**12.** If $X$ is normally distributed with mean 5 and standard deviation 2, find $p(X > 8)$.

**13.** In a distribution exactly normal, 10.03% of the items are under 25 kgs weight and 97% of the items are under 70 kgs weight. What are the mean and standard deviation of the distribution ?

**14.** The mean and standard deviation of marks obtained by 1000 students in an examination are respectively 34.4 and 16.5. Assuming the normality of the distribution find the approximate number of students expected to obtain marks between 30 and 60.

**15.** In a normal distribution, 7% of the items are under 35 and 10% of the items are above 55. Find the mean and variance of the distribution. (*M.G.U. May 2010*)

**16.** In a normal distribution 9% of the items are under 30 and 85% are under 65. Find the mean and standard deviation. (*M.G.U. Nov. 2009*)

**17.** A normal population has mean 0.1 and SD, $\sigma = 2.1$. Find the probability that the mean of a sample of size 900 will be negative.

## Answers

**1.** Average = 36.4

**2.** $\mu = 73.48$, Required probability = .9357

**3.** $\overline{X} = 1.97$, $f(x) = {}^4C_x\,(.4925)^x\,(.5075)^{4-x}$

**4.** 118.

**5.** 300

**6.** (*i*) 252 (*ii*) 533

**7.** $\bar{x} = 50.3$, $\sigma = 10.33$

**8.** 0.9772

**9.** 6.06%

**10.** (*i*) 50% (*ii*) 21.2% (*iii*) 84%

**11.** (*i*) 79 (*ii*) 35% (*iii*) 11.

**12.** 0.0668

**13.** $\mu = 47.5$, $\sigma = 15.578$

**14.** 543

**15.** mean $\mu = 45.69$, variance $\sigma^2 = 52.128$

**16.** mean $\mu = 49.7058$, standard deviation $\sigma = 14.706$

**17.** Probability = 0.0764.

# 5

# Testing of Hypothesis

## SAMPLING AND TESTS OF SIGNIFICANCE

### 5.1. POPULATION OR UNIVERSE

An aggregate of objects (animate or inanimate) under study is called **population or universe**. It is thus a collection of individuals or of their attributes (qualities) or of results of operations which can be numerically specified.

A universe containing a finite number of individuals or members is called a **finite inverse**. For example, the universe of the weights of students in a particular class or the universe of smokes in Rohtak district.

A universe with infinite number of members is known as an **infinite universe**. For example, the universe of pressures at various points in the atmosphere.

In some cases, we may be even ignorant whether or not a particular universe is infinite, *e.g.*, the universe of stars.

The universe of concrete objects is an **existent universe**. The collection of all possible ways in which a specified event can happen is called a **hypothetical universe**. The universe of heads and tails obtained by tossing a coin an infinite number of times (provided that it does not wear out) is a hypothetical one.

### 5.2. SAMPLING

The statistician is often confronted with the problem of discussing universe of which he cannot examine every member *i.e.*, of which complete enumeration is impracticable. For example, if we want to have an idea of the average per capita income of the people of India, enumeration of every earning individual in the country is a very difficult task. Naturally, the question arises : What can be said about a universe of which we can examine only a limited number of members ? This question is the origin of the Theory of Sampling.

A finite sub-set of a universe is called a **sample**. A sample is thus a small portion of the universe. The number of individuals in a sample is called the **sample size**. The process of selecting a sample from a universe is called **sampling**.

The theory of sampling is a study of relationship existing between a population and samples drawn from the population. The fundamental object of sampling is to get as much information as possible of the whole universe by examining only a part of it. An attempt is thus made through sampling to give the maximum information about the parent universe with the minimum effort.

Sampling is quite often used in our day-to-day practical life. For example, in a shop we asses the quality of sugar, rice or any other commodity by taking only a handful of it from the bag and then decide whether to purchase it or not. A housewife normally tests the cooked products to find if they are properly cooked and contain the proper quantity of salt or sugar, by taking a spoonful of it.

### 5.3. PARAMETERS OF STATISTICS

The statistical constants of the population such as mean, the variance etc. are known as the parameters. The statistical concepts of the sample from the members of the sample to estimate the parameters of the population from which the sample has been drawn are known as *statistic*.

Population mean and variance are denoted by $\mu$ and $\sigma^2$, while those of the sample are given by $\bar{x}$, $s^2$.

### 5.4. STANDARD ERROR (S.E.)

The standard deviation of the sampling distribution of a statistic is known as the standard error (S.E.).

It plays an important role in the theory of large samples and it forms a basis of the testing of hypothesis. If $t$ is any statistic, for large sample.

$$z = \frac{t - \mathrm{E}(t)}{\mathrm{S.E}(t)} \text{ is normally distributed with mean 0 and variance unity.}$$

For large sample, the standard errors of some of the well known statistic are listed below :

$n$—sample size ; $\sigma^2$—population variance ; $s^2$—sample variance ; $p$—population proportion ; $Q = 1 - p$ ; $n_1$, $n_2$—are sizes of two independent random sample.

| *No.* | *Statistic* | *Standard error* |
|---|---|---|
| 1. | $\bar{x}$ | $\sigma/\sqrt{n}$ |
| 2. | $s$ | $\sqrt{\sigma^2/2n}$ |
| 3. | Difference of two sample means $\bar{x}_1 - \bar{x}_2$ | $\sqrt{\frac{\sigma_1^2}{n_1} + \frac{\sigma_2^2}{n_2}}$ |
| 4. | Difference of two sample standard deviation $s_1 - s_2$ | $\sqrt{\frac{\sigma_1^2}{2n_1} + \frac{\sigma_2^2}{2n_2}}$ |
| 5. | Difference of two sample proportions $p_1 - p_2$ | $\sqrt{\frac{P_1Q_1}{n_1} + \frac{P_2Q_2}{n_2}}$ |
| 6. | Observed sample proportion $p$ | $\sqrt{PQ/n}$ |

### 5.5. TEST OF SIGNIFICANCE

An important aspect of the sampling theory is to study the test of significance. Which will enable us to decide, on the basis of the results of the sample, whether

(*i*) *the deviation between the observed sample statistic and the hypothetical parameter value or*

*(ii) the deviation between two sample statistics is significant or might be attributed due to chance or the fluctuations of the sampling.*

For applying the tests of significance, we first set up a hypothesis which is a definite statement about the population parameter called **Null hypothesis** denoted by $H_0$.

Any hypothesis which is complementary to the null hypothesis ($\mathbf{H_0}$) is called an **Alternative hypothesis** denoted by $\mathbf{H_1}$.

For example if we want to test the null hypothesis that the population has a specified mean $\mu_0$, then we have

$$\mathbf{H_0} : \mu = \mu_0$$

Alternative hypothesis will be

(*i*) $H_1 : \mu \neq \mu_0$ ($\mu > \mu_0$ *or* $\mu < \mu_0$) (two tailed alternative hypothesis).

(*ii*) $H_1 : \mu > \mu_0$ (right tailed alternative hypothesis (*or*) single tailed).

(*iii*) $H_1 : \mu < \mu_0$ (left tailed alternative hypothesis (*or*) single tailed).

Hence alternative hypothesis helps to know whether the test is two tailed test or one tailed test.

### 5.6. CRITICAL REGION

A region corresponding to a statistic $t$, in the sample space S which amounts to rejection of the null hypothesis $H_0$ is called as **critical region** or **region of rejection**. The region of the sample space S which amounts to the acceptance of $H_0$ is called *acceptance region*.

### 5.7. LEVEL OF SIGNIFICANCE

The probability of the value of the variate falling in the critical region is known as level of significance.

The probability $\alpha$ that a random value of the statistic $t$ belongs to the critical region is known as the level of significance.

$$P(t \in \omega \mid H_0) = \alpha$$

*i.e.*, the level of significance is the size of the type I error or the maximum producer's risk.

### 5.8. ERRORS IN SAMPLING

The main aim of the sampling theory is to draw a valid conclusion about the population parameters. On the basis of the sample results. In doing this we may commit the following two types of errors :

**Type I Error.** When $H_0$ is true, we may reject it.

P(Reject $H_0$ when it is true) = P(Reject $H_0/H_0$) = $\alpha$

$\alpha$ is called the size of the type I error also referred to as **producer's risk**.

**Type II Error.** When $H_0$ is wrong we may accept it P(Accept $H_0$ when it is wrong) = P(Accept $H_0/H_1$) = $\beta$. $\beta$ is called the size of the type II error, also referred to as **consumer's risk.**

**Critical values or significant values**

The values of the test statistic which separates the critical region and acceptance region is called the **critical values** or **significant value.**

This value is dependent on (*i*) the level of significance used and (*ii*) the alternative hypothesis, whether it is one tailed or two tailed.

For larger samples corresponding to the statistic $t$, the variable $z = \dfrac{t - E(t)}{S.E(t)}$ is normally distributed with mean 0 and variance 1. The value of $z$ given above under the null hypothesis is known as **test statistic.**

The critical value of $z_\alpha$ of the test statistic at level of significance $\alpha$ for a two tailed test is given by

$$p(|z| > z_\alpha) = \alpha \qquad \text{...(1)}$$

*i.e.,* $z_\alpha$ is the value of $z$ so that the total area of the critical region on both tails is $\alpha$. Since the normal curve is a symmetrical, from equation (1), we get

$$p(z > z_\alpha) + p(z < -z_\alpha) = \alpha \;;\; i.e.,\ 2p(z > z_\alpha) = \alpha \;;\; p(z > z_\alpha) = \alpha/2$$

*i.e.,* the area of each tail is $\alpha/2$.

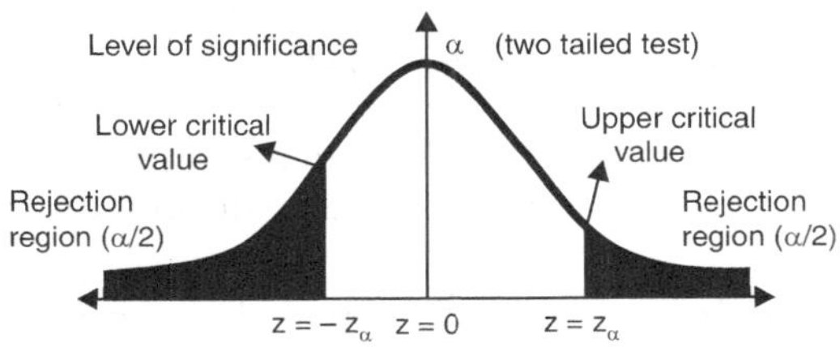


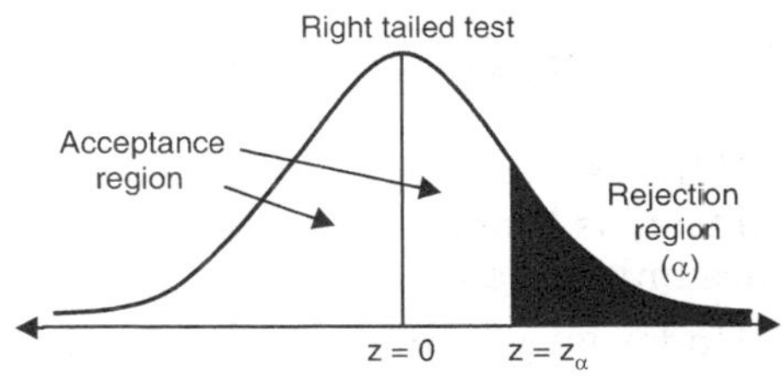


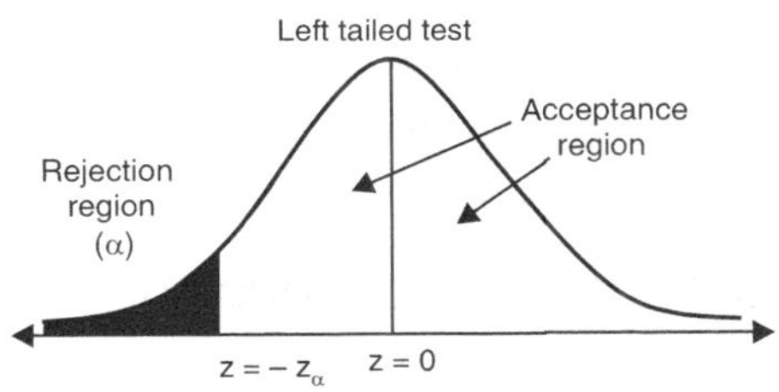


The critical value $z_\alpha$ is that value such that the area to the right of $z_\alpha$ is $\alpha/2$ and the area to the left of $-z_\alpha$ is $\alpha/2$.

In the case of one tailed test

$$p(z > z_\alpha) = \alpha \text{ if it is right tailed ; } p(z < -z_\alpha) = \alpha \text{ if it is left tailed.}$$

The critical value of $z$ for a single—tailed test (right or left) at level of significance $\alpha$ is same as the critical value of $z$ for two-tailed test at level of significance $2\alpha$.

Using the equation, also using the normal tables, the critical value of $z$ at different level of significance ($\alpha$) for both single tailed and two tailed test are calculated and listed below. The equations are

$$p(|z| > z_\alpha) = \alpha \;;\; p(z > z_\alpha) = \alpha \;;\; p(z < -z_\alpha) = \alpha$$

| | *Level of significance* | | |
|---|---|---|---|
| | *1% (0.01)* | *5% (0.05)* | *10% (0.1)* |
| Two tailed test | $\lvert z_\alpha \rvert = 2.58$ | $\lvert z \rvert = 1.966$ | $\lvert z \rvert = 0.645$ |
| Right tailed | $z_\alpha = 2.33$ | $z_\alpha = 1.645$ | $z_\alpha = 1.28$ |
| Left tailed | $z_\alpha = -2.33$ | $z_\alpha = -1.645$ | $z_\alpha = -1.28$ |

**Note.** The following steps may be adopted in testing of statistical hypothesis :

**Step 1 : Null hypothesis.** Set up $H_0$ is clear terms.

**Step 2 : Alternative hypothesis.** Set up $H_1$, so that we could decide whether we should used one-tailed test or two tailed test.

**Step 3 : Level of significance.** Select the appropriate level of significance in advance depending on the reliability of the estimates.

**Step 4 : Test statistic.** Compute the test statistic $z = \dfrac{t - E(t)}{S.E(t)}$ under the null hypothesis.

**Step 5 : Conclusion.** Compare the computed value of $z$ with the critical value $z_\alpha$ at level of significance ($\alpha$).

If $|z| > z_\alpha$, we reject $H_0$ and conclude that there is significant difference. If $|z| < z_\alpha$, we accept $H_0$ and conclude that there is no significant difference.

## TEST OF SIGNIFICANCE FOR LARGE SAMPLES

If the sample size $n > 30$, the sample is taken as large sample. For such sample we apply normal test, as Binomial, Poisson, chisquare etc. are closely approximated by normal distributions assuming the population as normal.

Under large sample test, the following are the important tests to test the significance.

1. *Testing of significance for single proportion.*
2. *Testing of significance for difference of proportions.*
3. *Testing of significance for single mean.*
4. *Testing of significance for difference of means.*

### 5.9. TESTING OF SIGNIFICANCE FOR SINGLE PROPORTION

This test is used to find the significant difference between proportion of the sample and the population.

Let X be the number of successes in $n$ independent trials with constant probability P of success for each trial.

$$E(X) = nP\ ;\ V(X) = nPQ\ ;\ Q = 1 - P = \text{Probability of failure.}$$

Let $p = X/n$ called the observed proportion of success.

$$E(p) = E(X/n) = \frac{1}{n}\,E(X) = \frac{nP}{n} = P\ ;\ E(p) = P$$

$$V(p) = V(X/n) = \frac{1}{n^2}\,V(X) = \frac{n(PQ)}{n^2} = \frac{PQ}{n}$$

$$S.E(p) = \sqrt{\frac{PQ}{n}}\ ;\ z = \frac{p - E(p)}{SE(p)} = \frac{p - P}{\sqrt{PQ/n}} \sim N(0, 1)$$

This $z$ is called test statistic which is used to test the significant difference of sample and population proportion.

**Note** 1. The probable limit for the observed proportion of successes are $p \pm z_\alpha \sqrt{PQ/n}$, where $z_\alpha$ is the significant value at level of significance $\alpha$.

2. If $p$ is not known, the limits for the proportion in the population are $p \pm z_\alpha \sqrt{pq/n}$, $q = 1 - p$.

3. If $\alpha$ is not given, we can take safely $3\sigma$ limits.

Hence, confidence limits for observed proportion $p$ are $p \pm 3\sqrt{\dfrac{PQ}{n}}$.

The confidence limits for the population proportion $p$ are $p \pm \sqrt{\dfrac{pq}{n}}$.

## ILLUSTRATIVE EXAMPLES

**Example 1.** *A coin was tossed 400 times and the head turned up 216 times. Test the hypothesis that the coin is unbiased.*

**Sol.** $H_0$ : The coin is unbiased *i.e.,* P = 0.5.

$H_1$ : The coin is not unbiased. (biased) ; $P \neq 0.5$

Here $n = 400$ ; X = No. of success = 216

$$p = \text{proportion of success in the sample } \frac{X}{n} = \frac{216}{400} = 0.54$$

population proportion = 0.5 = P ; Q = 1 – P = 1 – 0.5 = 0.5

under $H_0$, test statistic $z = \dfrac{p - P}{\sqrt{PQ/n}}$

$$|z| = \left| \frac{0.54 - 0.5}{\sqrt{\dfrac{0.5 \times 0.5}{400}}} \right| = 1.6$$

we use two tailed test.

**Conclusion.** Since $|z| = 1.6 < 1.96$

*i.e.,* $|z| < z_\alpha$, $z_\alpha$ is the significant value of $z$ at 5% level of significance.

*i.e.,* the coin is unbiased in P = 0.5.

**Example 2.** *A certain cubical die was thrown 9000 times and 5 or 6 was obtained 3240 times. On the assumption of certain throwing, do the data indicate an unbiased die ?*

**Sol.** Here $n = 9000$

P = probability of success (*i.e.,* getting 5 or 6 in die)

P = 2/6 = 1/3, Q = 1 – 1/3 = 2/3

$$p = \frac{X}{n} = \frac{3240}{9000} = 0.36$$

$H_0$ : is unbiased, *i.e.,* P = 1/3

$H_1$ : $P \neq 1/3$ (two tailed test)

The test statistic
$$z = \frac{p - P}{\sqrt{\dfrac{PQ}{n}}} = \frac{0.36 - 0.33}{\sqrt{\dfrac{1}{3} \times \dfrac{2}{3} \times \dfrac{1}{9000}}} = 0.03496$$

$$|z| = 0.03496 < 1.96$$

**Conclusion.** Accept the hypothesis

As $|z| < z_\alpha$, $z_\alpha$ is the tabulated value of $z$ at 5% level of significance.

$\because$ $H_0$ is accepted, we conclude that the die is unbiased.

**Example 3.** *A manufacturer claims that only 4% of his products supplied by him are defective. A random sample of 600 products contained 36 defectives. Test the claim of the manufacturer.*

**Sol.** (*i*) P = observed proportion of success.

*i.e.,* P = proportion of defective in the sample = $\frac{36}{600} = 0.06$

$p$ = proportion of defectives in the population = 0.04

$H_0 : p = 0.04$ is true.

*i.e.,* the claim of the manufacturer is accepted.

$H_1$ : (*i*) $P \neq 0.04$ (two tailed test)

(*ii*) If we want to reject, only if $p > 0.04$ then (right tailed).

Under $H_0$,
$$z = \frac{p - P}{\sqrt{PQ/n}} = \frac{0.06 - 0.04}{\sqrt{\frac{0.04 \times 0.96}{600}}} = 2.5.$$

**Conclusion.** Since $|z| = 2.5 > 1.96$, we reject the hypothesis $H_0$ at 5% level of significance two tailed.

If $H_1$ is taken as $p > 0.04$ we apply right tailed test.

$|z| = 2.5 > 1.645$ $(z_\alpha)$ we reject the null hypothesis here also.

In both cases, manufacturer's claim is not acceptable.

**Example 4.** *A machine is producing bolts of which a certain fraction is defective. A random sample of 400 is taken from a large batch and is found to contain 30 defective bolt. Does this indicate that the proportion of defectives is larger than that claimed by the manufacturer where the manufacturer claims that only 5% of his product are defective. Find 95% confidence limits of the proportion of defective bolts in batch.*

**Sol. Null hypothesis.** $H_0$ : The manufacturer claim is accepted *i.e.,* $P = \frac{5}{100} = 0.05$

$$Q = 1 - P = 1 - 0.05 = 0.95$$

**Alternative hypothesis.** $p > 0.05$ (Right tailed test).

$p$ = observed proportion of sample = $\frac{30}{400} = 0.075$

Under $H_0$, the test statistic $z = \frac{p - P}{\sqrt{PQ/n}}$ $\therefore$ $z = \frac{0.075 - 0.05}{\sqrt{\frac{0.05 \times 0.95}{400}}} = 2.2941.$

**Conclusion.** The tabulated value of $z$ at 5% level of significance for right tailed test is

$$z_\alpha = 1.645. \text{ Since } |z| = 2.2941 > 1.645,$$

$H_0$ is rejected at 5% level of significance. *i.e.,* the proportion of defective is larger than the manufacturer claim.

To find 95% confidence limits of the proportion.

It is given by $p \pm z_\alpha \sqrt{PQ/n}$

$$0.05 \pm 1.96\sqrt{\frac{0.05 \times 0.95}{400}} = 0.05 \pm 0.02135 = 0.07136, 0.02865$$

Hence 95% confidence limits for the proportion of defective bolt are (0.07136, 0.02865).

**Example 5.** *A bag contains defective article, the exact number of which is not known. A sample of 100 from the bag gives 10 defective articles. Find the limits for the proportion of defective articles in the bag.*

**Sol.** Here $p$ = proportion of defective articles = $\frac{10}{100} = 0.1$ ; $q = 1 - p = 1 - 0.1 = 0.9$

Since the confidence limits is not given, we assume it is 95%.

$\therefore$ level of significance is 5% $z_\alpha = 1.96$.

Also the proportion of population P is not given. To get the confidence limit, we use P and it is given by $P \pm z_\alpha \sqrt{pq/n} = 0.1 \pm 1.96\sqrt{\frac{0.1 \times 0.9}{100}} = 0.1 \pm 0.0588 = 0.1588, 0.0412$

Hence 95% confidence limits for defective article in the bag are (0.1588, 0.0412).

## TEST YOUR KNOWLEDGE

1. A sample of size of 600 persons selected at random from a large city shows that the percentage of males in the sample is 53. It is believed that the ratio of males to the total population in the city is 0.5. Test whether the belief is confirmed by the observation.
2. In a city a sample of 1000 people were taken and out of them 540 are vegetarian and the rest are non-vegetarian. Can we say that the both habits of eating (Vegetarion or non vegetarion) are equally popular in the city at (*i*) 1% level of significance (*ii*) 5% level of significance.
3. 325 men out of 600 men chosen from a big city were found to be smokers. Does this information support the conclusion that the majority of men in the city are smokers.
4. A random sample of 500 bolts was taken from a large consignment and 65 were found to be defective. Find the percentage of defective bolts in the consignment.
5. In a hospital 475 female and 525 male babies were born in a week. Do these figure confirm the hypothesis that males and females are born in equal number.
6. 400 apples are taken at random from a large basket and 40 are found to be bad. Estimate the proportion of bad apples in the basket and assign limits within which the percentage most probably lies.

### Answers

**1.** $H_0$ accepted at 5% level **2.** $H_0$ rejected at 5% level, accepted at 1% level

**3.** $H_0$ rejected at 5% level **4.** Between 17.51 and 8.49 **5.** $H_0$ accepted at 5% level

**6.** 8.5 : 11.5.

## 5.10. TEST OF DIFFERENCE BETWEEN PROPORTIONS

Consider two samples $X_1$ and $X_2$ of sizes $n_1$ and $n_2$ respectively taken from two different populations. To test the significance of the difference between the sample proportion $p_1$ and $p_2$. The test statistic under the null hypothesis $H_0$, that there is no significant difference between the two sample proportion, we have

$$z = \frac{p_1 - p_2}{\sqrt{PQ\left(\frac{1}{n_1} + \frac{1}{n_2}\right)}}, \quad \text{where } P = \frac{n_1 p_1 + n_2 p_2}{n_1 + n_2} \text{ and } Q = 1 - P.$$

## ILLUSTRATIVE EXAMPLES

**Example 1.** *Before an increase in excise duty on tea, 800 people out of a sample of 1000 persons were found to be tea drinkers. After an increase in the duty, 800 persons were known to be tea drinkers in a sample of 1200 people. Do you think that there has been a significant decrease in the consumption of tea after the increase in the excise duty.*

**Sol.** Here $n_1 = 800, n_2 = 1200$

$$p_1 = \frac{X_1}{n_1} = \frac{800}{1000} = \frac{4}{5} \; ; p_2 = \frac{X_2}{n_2} = \frac{800}{1200} = \frac{2}{3}$$

$$P = \frac{p_1 n_1 + p_2 n_2}{n_1 + n_2} = \frac{X_1 + X_2}{n_1 + n_2} = \frac{800 + 800}{1000 + 1200} = \frac{8}{11} \; ; Q = 1 - P = \frac{3}{11}$$

**Null hypothesis $H_0$.** $p_1 = p_2$ *i.e.*, there is no significant difference in the consumption of tea before and after increase of excise duty.

$H_1 : p_1 > p_2$ (right tailed test)

The test statistic $z = \dfrac{p_1 - p_2}{\sqrt{PQ\left(\dfrac{1}{n_1} + \dfrac{1}{n_2}\right)}} = \dfrac{0.8 - 0.6666}{\sqrt{\dfrac{8}{11} \times \dfrac{3}{11}\left(\dfrac{1}{1000} + \dfrac{1}{1200}\right)}} = 6.842.$

**Conclusion.** Since the calculated value of $|z| > 1.645$ also $|z| > 2.33$, both the significant value of $z$ at 5% and 1% level of significance. Hence $H_0$ is rejected *i.e.,* there is a significant decrease in the consumption of tea due to increase in excise duty.

**Example 2.** *A machine produced 16 defective articles in a batch of 500. After overhauling it produced 3 defectives in a batch of 100. Has the machine improved ?*

**Sol.** $p_1 = \dfrac{16}{500} = 0.032 \; ; n_1 = 500$ | $p_2 = \dfrac{3}{100} = 0.03 \; ; n_2 = 100$

**Null hypothesis $H_0$.** The machine has not improved due to overhauling. $p_1 = p_2$.

$H_1 : p_1 > p_2$ (right tailed) $\therefore$ $P = \dfrac{p_1 n_1 + p_2 n_2}{n_1 + n_2} = \dfrac{19}{600} \cong 0.032$

Under $H_0$, the test statistic

$$z = \frac{p_1 - p_2}{\sqrt{PQ\left(\dfrac{1}{n_1} + \dfrac{1}{n_2}\right)}} = \frac{0.032 - 0.03}{\sqrt{(0.032)(0.968)\left(\dfrac{1}{500} + \dfrac{1}{100}\right)}} = 0.104.$$

**Conclusion.** The calculated value of $|z| < 1.645$, the significant value of $z$ at 5% level of significance. $H_0$ is accepted. *i.e.*, the machine has not improved due to overhauling.

**Example 3.** *In two large populations there are 30% and 25% respectively of fair haired people. Is this difference likely to be hidden in samples of 1200 and 900 respectively from the two populations.*

**Sol.** $p_1$ = proportion of fair haired people in the first population = 30% = 0.3 ; $p_2$ = 25% = 0.25 ; $q_1 = 0.7, q_2 = 0.75$ ; $q_1 = 1 - p_1, q_2 = 1 - p_2$.

$H_0$ : Sample proportions are equal *i.e.*, the difference in population proportions is likely to be hidden in sampling.

$H_1 : p_1 \neq p_2$

$$z = \frac{p_1 - p_2}{\sqrt{\dfrac{p_1q_1}{n_1} + \dfrac{p_2q_2}{n_2}}} = \frac{0.3 - 0.25}{\sqrt{\dfrac{0.3 \times 0.7}{1200} + \dfrac{0.25 \times 0.75}{900}}} = 2.5376.$$

**Conclusion.** Since $|z| > 1.96$, the significant value of $z$ at 5% level of significance, $H_0$ is rejected. However $|z| < 2.58$, the significant value of $z$ at 1% level of significance. $H_0$ is accepted. At 5% level these samples will reveal the difference in the population proportions.

**Example 4.** *500 articles from a factory are examined and found to be 2% defective. 800 similar articles from a second factory are found to have only 1.5% defective. Can it reasonably be concluded that the product of the first factory are inferior to those of second ?*

**Sol.** $n_1 = 500, n_2 = 800$

$p_1$ = proportion of defective from first factory = 2% = 0.02

$p_2$ = proportion of defective from second factory = 1.5% = 0.015

$H_0$ : There is no significant difference between the two products *i.e.,* the products do not differ in quality.

$H_1 : p_1 < p_2$ (one tailed test)

Under $H_0$, $$z = \frac{p_1 - p_2}{\sqrt{PQ\left(\dfrac{1}{n_1} + \dfrac{1}{n_2}\right)}}$$

$$P = \frac{n_1p_1 + n_2p_2}{n_1 + n_2} = \frac{0.02(500) + (0.015)(800)}{500 + 800} = 0.01692 \text{ ; } Q = 1 - P = 0.9830$$

$$z = \frac{0.02 - 0.015}{\sqrt{0.01692 \times 0.983\left(\dfrac{1}{500} + \dfrac{1}{800}\right)}} = 0.68$$

**Conclusion.** As $|z| < 1.645$, the significant value of $z$ at 5% level of significance. $H_0$ is accepted. *i.e.,* the products do not differ in quality.

## TEST YOUR KNOWLEDGE

1. Random sample of 400 men and 600 women were asked whether they would to have a school near their residence. 200 men and 325 women were in favour of proposal. Test the hypothesis that the proportion of men and women in favour of the proposal are same at 5% level of significance.
2. In a town A, there were 956 births of which 52.5% was males while in towns A and B combined, this proportion in total of 1406 births was 0.496. Is there any significant difference in the proportion of male births in the two towns ?
3. In a referendum submitted to the students body at a university, 850 men and 560 women voted. 500 men and 320 women voted yes. Does this indicate a significant difference of opinion between men and women on this matter at 1% level.
4. A manufacturing firm claims that its brand A product outsells its brand B product by 8%. If it is found that 42 out of a sample of 200 person prefer brand A and 18 out of another sample of 100 person prefer brand B. Test whether the 8% difference is a valid claim.
5. In a large city A, 20% of a random sample of 900 school boys had a slight physical defect. In another city B, 5% of a random sample of 1600 school boys had the same defect. Is the difference between the proportion singificant. *(M.G.U. May 2010)*

**Answers**

**1.** $H_0$ : accepted **2.** $H_0$ : Rejected **3.** $H_0$ : accepted **4.** $H_0$ : accepted.

**5.** Let $H_0$ : "Sample proportions are equal." $H_0$ is rejected. The sample will reveal the differences in population proportions ; at 1% level of significance.

## 5.11. TEST OF SIGNIFICANCE FOR SINGLE MEAN

*To test whether the difference between sample mean and population mean is significant or not.*

Let $X_1, X_2, \ldots\ldots, X_n$ be a random sample of size $n$ from a large population $X_1, X_2, \ldots\ldots, X_N$ of size N with mean $\mu$ and variance $\sigma^2$. $\therefore$ the standard error of mean of a random sample of size $n$ from a population with variance $\sigma^2$ is $\sigma/\sqrt{n}$.

To test whether the given sample of size $n$ has been drawn from a population with mean $\mu$ *i.e.,* to test whether the difference between the sample mean and population mean is significant or not. Under the null hypothesis that there is no difference between the sample mean and population mean.

The test statistic is $z = \dfrac{\bar{x} - \mu}{\sigma/\sqrt{n}}$, where $\sigma$ is the standard deviation of the population.

If $\sigma$ is not known, we use the test statistic $z = \dfrac{\bar{X} - \mu}{s/\sqrt{n}}$, where $s$ is the standard deviation of the sample.

**Note.** If the level of significance is $\alpha$ and $z_\alpha$ is the critical value $-z_\alpha < | z | = \left| \dfrac{\bar{x} - \mu}{\sigma/\sqrt{n}} \right| < z_\alpha$

The limits of the population mean $\mu$ are given by $\bar{x} - z_\alpha \dfrac{\sigma}{\sqrt{n}} < \mu < \bar{x} + z_\alpha \sigma/\sqrt{n}$.

At 5% of level of significance, 95% confidence limits are $\bar{x} - 1.96 \dfrac{\sigma}{\sqrt{n}} < \mu < \bar{x} + 1.96 \dfrac{\sigma}{\sqrt{n}}$

At 1% level of significance, 99% confidence limits are $\bar{x} - 2.58 \dfrac{\sigma}{\sqrt{n}} < \mu < \bar{x} + 2.58 \dfrac{\sigma}{\sqrt{n}}$.

These limits are called confidence limits or fiducial limits.

## ILLUSTRATIVE EXAMPLES

**Example 1.** *A normal population has a mean of 6.8 and standard deviation of 1.5. A sample of 400 members gave a mean of 6.75. Is the difference significant ?*

**Sol.** $H_0$ : There is no significant difference between $\bar{x}$ and $\mu$.

$H_1$ : There is significant difference between $\bar{x}$ and $\mu$.

Given $\mu = 6.8$, $\sigma = 1.5$, $\bar{x} = 6.75$ and $n = 400$

$$| z | = \left| \frac{\bar{x} - \mu}{\sigma/\sqrt{n}} \right| = \left| \frac{6.75 - 6.8}{1.5/\sqrt{900}} \right| = | -0.67 | = 0.67$$

**Conclusion.** As the calculated value of $| z | < z_\alpha = 1.96$ at 5% level of significance, $H_0$ is accepted *i.e.,* there is no significant difference between $\bar{x}$ and $\mu$.

**Example 2.** *A random sample of 900 members has a mean 3.4 cms. Can it be reasonably regarded as a sample from a large population of mean 3.2 cms and S.D. 2.3 cms ?*

**Sol.** Here $n = 900$, $\bar{x} = 3.4$, $\mu = 3.2$, $\sigma = 2.3$

$H_0$ : Assume that the sample is drawn from a large population with mean 3.2 and S.D. = 2.3

$H_1 : \mu \neq 3.25$ (Apply two tailed test)

$$\text{Under } H_0\ ; \quad z = \frac{\bar{x} - \mu}{\sigma/\sqrt{n}} = \frac{3.4 - 3.2}{2.3/\sqrt{900}} = 0.261.$$

**Conclusion.** As the calculated value of $|z| = 0.261 < 1.96$ the significant value of $z$ at 5% level of significance. $H_0$ is accepted *i.e.,* the sample is drawn from the population with mean 3.2 and S.D. = 2.3.

**Example 3.** *The mean weight obtained from a random sample of size 100 is 64 gms. The S.D. of the weight distribution of the population is 3 gms. Test the statement that the mean weight of the population is 67 gms at 5% level of significance. Also set up 99% confidence limits of the mean weight of the population.*

**Sol.** Here $n = 100$, $\mu = 67$, $\bar{x} = 64$, $\sigma = 3$

$H_0$ : There is no significant difference between sample and population mean.

*i.e.,* $\mu = 67$, the sample is drawn from the population with $\mu = 67$

$H_1 : \mu \neq 67$ (Two tailed test)

$$\text{Under } H_0,\ z = \frac{\bar{x} - \mu}{\sigma/\sqrt{n}} = \frac{64 - 67}{3/\sqrt{100}} = -10 \quad \therefore \quad |z| = 10.$$

**Conclusion.** Since the calculated value of $|z| > 1.96$, the significant value of $z$ at 5% level of significance. $H_0$ is rejected *i.e.,* the sample is not drawn from the population with mean 67.

To find 99% confidence limits. It is given by $\bar{x} \pm 2.58\ \sigma/\sqrt{n} = 64 \pm 2.58 \times 3/\sqrt{100}$ = 64.774, 63.226.

**Example 4.** *The average marks in Mathematics of a sample of 100 students was 51 with a S.D. of 6 marks. Could this have been a random sample from a population with average marks 50 ?*

**Sol.** Here $n = 100$, $\bar{x} = 51$, $s = 6$, $\mu = 50$ ; $\sigma$ is unknown.

$H_0$ : The sample is drawn from a population with mean 50, $\mu = 50$

$H_1 : \mu \neq 50$

$$\text{Under } H_0,\ z = \frac{\bar{x} - \mu}{s/\sqrt{n}} = \frac{51 - 50}{6/\sqrt{100}} = \frac{10}{6} = 1.6666$$

**Conclusion.** Since $|z| = 1.666 < 1.96$, $z_\alpha$ the significant value of $z$ at 5% level of significance, $H_0$, is accepted *i.e.,* the sample is drawn from the population with mean 50.

## TEST YOUR KNOWLEDGE

1. A sample of 1000 students from a university was taken and their average weight was found to be 112 pounds with a S.D. of 20 pounds. Could the mean weight of students in the population be 120 pounds ?
2. A sample of 400 male students is found to have a mean height of 160 cms. Can it be reasonably regarded as a sample from a large population with mean height 162.5 cms and standard deviation 4.5 cms.
3. A random sample of 200 measurements from a large population gave a mean value of 50 and a S.D. of 9. Determine 95% confidence interval for the mean of population.

4. The guaranteed average life of certain type of bulbs is 1000 hours with a S.D. of 125 hours. It is decided to sample the output so as to ensure that 90% of the bulbs do not fall short of the guaranteed average by more than 2.5%. What must be the minimum size of the sample.
5. The heights of college students in a city are normally distributed with S.D. 6 cms. A sample of 1000 students has mean height 158 cms. Test the hypothesis that the mean height of college students in the city is 160 cms.
6. A random sample of size $n = 100$ is taken from a population with $\sigma = 5.1$. Given that the sample mean is $\bar{x} = 21.6$. Construct 95% confidence interval for the population mean $\mu$.

*(M.G.U. May 2009)*

**Answers**

**1.** $H_0$ is rejected **2.** $H_0$ accepted **3.** 48.8 and 51.2 **4.** $n = 4$
**5.** $H_0$ rejected both at 1% to 5% level of significance **6.** $20.6 < \mu < 22.6$.

## 5.12. TEST OF SIGNIFICANCE FOR DIFFERENCE OF MEANS OF TWO LARGE SAMPLES

Let $\bar{x}_1$ be the mean of a sample of size $n_1$ from a population with mean $\mu_1$, and variance $\sigma_1^2$. Let $\bar{x}_2$ be the mean of an independent sample of size $n_2$ from another population with mean $\mu_2$ and variance $\sigma_2^2$. The test statistic is given by $z = \dfrac{\bar{x}_1 - \bar{x}_2}{\sqrt{\dfrac{\sigma_1^2}{n_1} + \dfrac{\sigma_2^2}{n_2}}}$.

Under the null hypothesis that the samples are drawn from the same population where $\sigma_1 = \sigma_2 = \sigma$ *i.e.*, $\mu_1 = \mu_2$ the test statistic is given by $z = \dfrac{\bar{x}_1 - \bar{x}_2}{\sigma\sqrt{\dfrac{1}{n_1} + \dfrac{1}{n_2}}}$.

**Note 1.** If $\sigma_1, \sigma_2$ are not known and $\sigma_1 \neq \sigma_2$ the test statistic in this case is $z = \dfrac{\bar{x}_1 - \bar{x}_2}{\sqrt{\dfrac{s_1^2}{n_1} + \dfrac{s_2^2}{n_2}}}$.

**Note 2.** If $\sigma$ is not known and $\sigma_1 = \sigma_2$

We use $\sigma^2 = \dfrac{n_1 s_1^2 + n_2 s_2^2}{n_1 + n_2}$ to calculate $\sigma$;

$$z = \frac{\bar{x}_1 - \bar{x}_2}{\sqrt{\dfrac{n_1 s_1^2 + n_2 s_2^2}{n_1 + n_2}\left(\dfrac{1}{n_1} + \dfrac{1}{n_2}\right)}}.$$

## ILLUSTRATIVE EXAMPLES

**Example 1.** *The average income of persons was ₹210 with a S.D. of ₹10 in sample of 100 people of a city. For another sample of 150 persons, the average income was ₹220 with S.D. of ₹12. The S.D. of incomes of the people of the city was ₹11. Test whether there is any significant difference between the average incomes of the localities.*

**Sol.** Here $n_1 = 100$, $n_2 = 150$, $\bar{x}_1 = 210$, $\bar{x}_2 = 220$, $s_1 = 10$, $s_2 = 12$.

**Null hypothesis.** The difference is not significant. *i.e.*, there is no difference between the incomes of the localities.

$$H_0 : \bar{x}_1 = \bar{x}_2, \quad H_1 : \bar{x}_1 \neq \bar{x}_2$$

Under $H_0$, $z = \dfrac{\bar{x}_1 - \bar{x}_2}{\sqrt{\dfrac{s_1^2}{n_1} + \dfrac{s_2^2}{n_2}}} = \dfrac{210 - 220}{\sqrt{\dfrac{10^2}{100} + \dfrac{12^2}{150}}} = -7.1428 \quad \therefore \quad |z| = 7.1428.$

**Conclusion.** As the calculated value of $|z| > 1.96$, the significant value of $z$ at 5% level of significance, $H_0$ is rejected *i.e.,* there is significant difference between the average incomes of the localities.

**Example 2.** *Intelligent tests were given to two groups of boys and girls.*

| | *Mean* | *S.D.* | *Size* |
|---|---|---|---|
| *Girls* | *75* | *8* | *60* |
| *Boys* | *73* | *10* | *100* |

*Examine if the difference between mean scores is significant.*

**Sol. Null hypothesis $H_0$.** There is no significant difference between mean scores *i.e.,* $\bar{x}_1 = \bar{x}_2$.

$$H_1 : \bar{x}_1 \neq \bar{x}_2$$

Under the null hypothesis $z = \dfrac{\bar{x}_1 - \bar{x}_2}{\sqrt{\dfrac{s_1^2}{n_1} + \dfrac{s_2^2}{n_2}}} = \dfrac{75 - 73}{\sqrt{\dfrac{8^2}{60} + \dfrac{10^2}{100}}} = 1.3912.$

**Conclusion.** As the calculated value of $|z| < 1.96$, the significant value of $z$ at 5% level of significance, $H_0$ is accepted. *i.e.,* there is no significant difference between mean scores.

**Example 3.** *For sample I, $n_1 = 1000$, $\Sigma x = 49{,}000$, $\Sigma(x - \bar{x})^2 = 7{,}84{,}000$.*

*For sample II, $n_2 = 1{,}500$, $\Sigma x = 70{,}500$, $\Sigma(x - \bar{x})^2 = 24{,}00{,}000$. Discuss the significance of the difference of the sample means.*

**Sol. Null hypothesis $H_0$.** There is no significant difference between the sample means.

$$H_0 : \bar{x}_1 = \bar{x}_2 ; H_1 : \bar{x}_1 \neq \bar{x}_2$$

To calculate sample variance

$$s_1^2 = \frac{1}{n_1} \Sigma(X_1 - \bar{X}_1)^2 = \frac{784000}{1000} = 784$$

$$s_2^2 = \frac{1}{n_2} \Sigma(X_2 - \bar{X}_2)^2 = \frac{1}{1500}(2400000) = 1600$$

$$\bar{x}_1 = \frac{\Sigma x_1}{n_1} = \frac{49000}{1000} = 49 \; ; \; \bar{x}_2 = \frac{\Sigma x_2}{n_2} = \frac{70500}{1500} = 47$$

Under the null hypothesis, the test statistic

$$z = \frac{\bar{x}_1 - \bar{x}_2}{\sqrt{\dfrac{s_1^2}{n_1} + \dfrac{s_2^2}{n_2}}} = \frac{49 - 47}{\sqrt{\dfrac{784}{1000} + \dfrac{1600}{1500}}} = 1.470.$$

**Conclusion.** As the calculated value of $|z| = 1.47 < 1.96$, the significant value of $z$ at 5% level of significance, $H_0$ is accepted. *i.e.,* there is no significant difference between the sample means.

**Example 4.** *From the data given below, compute the standard error of the difference of the two sample means and find out if the two means significantly differ at 5% level of significance.*

| | *No. of items* | *Mean* | *S.D.* |
|---|---|---|---|
| *Group I* | *50* | *181.5* | *3.0* |
| *Group II* | *75* | *179* | *3.6* |

**Sol. Null hypothesis $H_0$.** There is no significant difference between the samples.

$$\overline{x}_1 = \overline{x}_2 ;\ H_1 : \overline{x}_1 \neq \overline{x}_2$$

$$\text{Under } H_0,\ z = \frac{\overline{x}_1 - \overline{x}_2}{\sqrt{\frac{s_1^2}{n_1} + \frac{s_2^2}{n_2}}} = \frac{181.5 - 179.0}{\sqrt{\frac{9}{50} + \frac{(3.6)^2}{75}}} = 4.2089.$$

**Conclusion.** As $|z| >$ the tabulated value of $z$ at 5% level of significance $H_0$ is rejected *i.e.,* there is significant difference between the samples.

**Example 5.** *A random sample of 200 villages from Coimbatore district gives the mean population per village at 485 with a S.D. of 50. Another random sample of the same size from the same district gives the mean population per village at 510 with a S.D. of 40. Is the difference between the mean values given by the two samples statistically significant ? Justify your answer.*

**Sol.** Here $n_1 = 200$, $n_2 = 250$, $\overline{x}_1 = 485$, $\overline{x}_2 = 510$, $s_1 = 50$, $s_2 = 40$

**Null hypothesis $H_0$.** There is no significant difference between the mean values (*i.e.,*) $\overline{x}_1 = \overline{x}_2$ ; H : $\overline{x}_1 \neq \overline{x}_2$ (Two tailed test)

$$\text{Under } H_0, \text{ the test statistic is given by } z = \frac{\overline{x}_1 - \overline{x}_2}{\sqrt{\frac{s_1^2}{n_1} + \frac{s_2^2}{n_2}}} = \frac{485 - 510}{\sqrt{\frac{50^2}{200} + \frac{40^2}{200}}} = -5.52$$

$\therefore \quad |z| = 5.52.$

**Conclusion.** As the calculated value of $|z| > 1.96$, the significant value of $z$ at 5% level of significance, $H_0$ is rejected. *i.e.,* there is significant difference between the mean values of two sample.

## TEST YOUR KNOWLEDGE

1. Intelligence tests on two groups of boys and girls gave the following results. Examine if the difference is significant.

| | *Mean* | *S.D.* | *Size* |
|---|---|---|---|
| *Girls* | *70* | *10* | *70* |
| *Boys* | *75* | *11* | *100* |

2. Two random samples of sizes 1000 and 2000 farms gave an average yield of 2000 kg and 2050 kg respectively. The variance of wheat farms in the country may be taken as 100 kg. Examine whether the two samples differ significantly in yield ?
3. A sample of heights of 6400 soldiers has a mean of 67.85 inches and a S.D. of 2.56 inches. While another sample of heights of 1600 sailors has a mean of 68.55 inches with S.D. of 2.52 inches. Do the data indicate that the sailors are on the average taller than soldiers ?

4. In a survey of buying habits, 400 women shoppers are chosen at random in supermarket A. Their average weekly food expenditure is ₹ 250 with a S.D. of ₹ 40. For 500 women shoppers chosen at supermarket B, the average weekly food expenditure is ₹ 220 with a S.D. of ₹ 45 test at 1% level of significance whether the average food expenditures of the two groups are equal.
5. The number of accident per day were studied for 144 days in town A and for 100 days in town B and the following information was obtained.

| | *Mean number of accident* | *S.D.* |
|---|---|---|
| Town A | 4.5 | 1.2 |
| Town B | 5.4 | 1.5 |

Is the difference between the mean accidents of the two towns statistically significant ?
6. An examination was given to 50 students of a college A and to 60 students of college B. For A, the mean grade was 75 with S.D. of 9 and for B, the mean grade was 79 with S.D. of 7. Is there any significant difference between the performance of the students of college A and those of college B ?
7. A random sample of 200 measurements from a large population gave a mean value of 50 and S.D. of 9. Determine the 95% confidence interval for the mean of the population ?
8. The means of two large samples of 1000 and 2000 members are 168.75 cms and 170 cms respectively. Can the samples be regarded as drawn from the same population of standard deviation 6.25 cms ?
9. An IQ test is given to two groups of students and the results are as follows :

| | *Mean* | *SD* | *Size* |
|---|---|---|---|
| Group A | 68 | 2 | 64 |
| Group B | 67 | 3 | 81 |

Examine whether the differences between the mean scores is significant at 5% level of significance.

**Answers**

1. No significant difference 2. Highly significant 3. Highly significant
4. Highly significant 5. Highly significant 6. Not significant
7. 49.584, 50.416 8. Not significant
9. The sample mean differs significantly.

## 5.13. TEST OF SIGNIFICANCE FOR THE DIFFERENCE OF STANDARD DEVIATIONS

If $s_1$ and $s_2$ are the standard deviations of two independent samples then under the null hypothesis $H_0 : \sigma_1 = \sigma_2$, *i.e.*, the sample standard deviations don't differ significantly, the statistic

$$z = \frac{s_1 - s_2}{\sqrt{\dfrac{\sigma_1^2}{2n_1} + \dfrac{\sigma_2^2}{2n_2}}},$$ where $\sigma_1$ and $\sigma_2$ are population standard deviations.

when population standard deviations are not known then $z = \dfrac{s_1 - s_2}{\sqrt{\dfrac{s_1^2}{2n_1} + \dfrac{s_2^2}{2n_2}}}$.

## ILLUSTRATIVE EXAMPLES

**Example 1.** *Random samples drawn from two countries gave the following data relating to the heights of adult males.*

| | *Country A* | *Country B* |
|---|---|---|
| *Mean height (in inches)* | *67.42* | *67.25* |
| *Standard deviation* | *2.58* | *2.50* |
| *Number in samples* | *1000* | *1200* |

(*i*) *Is the difference between the means significant ?*

(*ii*) *Is the difference between the standard deviations significant ?*

**Sol.** Given : $n_1 = 1000$, $n_2 = 1200$, $\bar{x}_1 = 67.42$ ; $\bar{x}_2 = 67.25$, $s_1 = 2.58$, $s_2 = 2.50$

Since the samples size are large we can take $\sigma_1 = s_1 = 2.58$ ; $\sigma_2 = s_2 = 2.50$.

(*i*) **Null Hypothesis.** $H_0 = \mu_1 = \mu_2$ *i.e.*, sample means do not differ significantly.

Alternative hypothesis : $H_1 : \mu_1 \neq \mu_2$ (two tailed test)

$$z = \frac{\bar{x}_1 - \bar{x}_2}{\sqrt{\dfrac{s_1^2}{n_1} + \dfrac{s_2^2}{n_2}}} = \frac{67.42 - 67.25}{\sqrt{\dfrac{(2.58)^2}{1000} + \dfrac{(2.50)^2}{1200}}} = 1.56$$

since $|z| < 1.96$ we accept the null hypothesis at 5% level of significance.

(*ii*) We set up the null hypothesis.

$H_0 : \sigma_1 = \sigma_2$ *i.e.*, the sample S.D.'s do not differ significantly.

Alternative Hypothesis : $H_1 = \sigma_1 \neq \sigma_2$ (two tailed)

$\therefore$ The test statistic is given by

$$z = \frac{s_1 - s_2}{\sqrt{\dfrac{\sigma_1^2}{2n_1} + \dfrac{\sigma_2^2}{2n_2}}} = \frac{s_1 - s_2}{\sqrt{\dfrac{s_1^2}{2n_1} + \dfrac{s_2^2}{2n_2}}} \quad (\because \ \sigma_1 = s_1, \sigma_2 = s_2 \text{ for large samples})$$

$$= \frac{2.58 - 2.50}{\sqrt{\dfrac{(2.58)^2}{2 \times 1000} \times \dfrac{(2.50)^2}{2 \times 1200}}} = \frac{0.08}{\sqrt{\dfrac{6.6564}{2000} + \dfrac{6.25}{2400}}} = 1.0387$$

Since $|z| < 1.96$ we accept the null hypothesis at 5% level of significance.

**Example 2.** *Intelligence test of two groups of boys and girls gives the following results :*

| *Girls* | *mean = 84* | *S.D. = 10* | *N = 121* |
|---|---|---|---|
| *Boys* | *mean = 81* | *S.D. = 12* | *N = 81* |

(*a*) *Is the difference in mean scores significant ?*

(*b*) *Is the difference between the standard deviations significant ?*

**Sol.** Given : $n_1 = 121, n_2 = 81, \bar{x}_1 = 84, \bar{x}_2 = 81, s_1 = 10, s_2 = 12$

(*a*) **Null hypothesis.** $H_0 = \mu_1 = \mu_2$ *i.e.*, sample means do not differ significantly.

Alternative hypothesis : $H_1 = \mu_1 \neq \mu_2$ (two tailed)

The test statistic is $z = \dfrac{\bar{x}_1 - \bar{x}_2}{\sqrt{\dfrac{s_1^2}{n_1} + \dfrac{s_2^2}{n_2}}} = \dfrac{84 - 81}{\sqrt{\dfrac{(10)^2}{121} + \dfrac{(12)^2}{81}}} = 0.1859$

Since $|z| < 1.96$ we accept the null hypothesis at 5% level of significance.

(*b*) We set up the null hypothesis $H_0 = \sigma_1 = \sigma_2$ *i.e.*, the sample S.D.'s do not differ significantly. Alternative hypothesis : $H_1 = \sigma_1 \neq \sigma_2$ (two tailed)

The test statistic is $z = \dfrac{s_1 - s_2}{\sqrt{\dfrac{\sigma_1^2}{2n_1} + \dfrac{\sigma_2^2}{2n_2}}} = \dfrac{s_1 - s_2}{\sqrt{\dfrac{s_1^2}{2n_1} + \dfrac{s_2^2}{2n_2}}}$

($\because$ $\sigma_1 = s_1, \sigma_2 = s_2$ for large samples)

$$= \frac{10 - 12}{\sqrt{\dfrac{100}{2 \times 121} + \dfrac{144}{2 \times 81}}} = -1.7526 \quad \therefore \quad |z| = 1.7526$$

since $|z| = 1.75 < 1.96$ we accept the null hypothesis at 5% level of significance.

## TEST YOUR KNOWLEDGE

**1.** The mean yield of two sets of plots and their variability are as given examine.

(*i*) Whether the difference in the mean yield of the two sets of plots is significant.

(*ii*) Whether the difference in the variability in yields is significant.

| | *Set of 40 plots* | *Set of 60 plots* |
|---|---|---|
| Mean yield per plot | 1258 lb | 1243 lb |
| S.D. per plot | 34 | 28 |

**2.** The yield of wheat in a random sample of 1000 farms in a certain area has a S.D. of 192 kg. Another random sample of 1000 farms gives a S.D. of 224 kg. Are the S.Ds significantly different ?

### Answers

**1.** $z = 2.321$ Difference significant at 5% level ; $z = 1.31$ Difference not significant at 5% level

**2.** $z = 4.851$ The S.D.s are significantly different.

## 5.14. TEST OF SIGNIFICANCE OF SMALL SAMPLES

When the size of the sample is less than 30, then the sample is called small sample. For such sample it will not be possible for us to assume that the random sampling distribution of a statistic is approximately normal and the values given by the sample data are sufficiently close to the population values and can be used in their place for the calculation of the standard error of the estimate.

# t-TEST

## 5.15. STUDENT'S-t-DISTRIBUTION

This $t$-distribution is used when sample size is $\leq 30$ and the population standard deviation is unknown.

$t$-statistic is defined as $t = \dfrac{\bar{x} - \mu}{s/\sqrt{n}} \sim t(n-1\, d.f.)$ d.f.-degrees of freedom where $s = \sqrt{\dfrac{\Sigma(X - \bar{X})^2}{n-1}}$.

**The t-table**

The $t$-table given at the end is the probability integral of $t$-distribution. The $t$-distribution has a different values for each degrees of freedom and when the degrees of freedom are infinitely large, the $t$-distribution is equivalent to normal distribution and the probabilities shown in the normal distribution tables are applicable.

**Application of t-distribution**

Some of the applications of $t$-distribution are given below :

1. *To test if the sample mean* ($\bar{X}$) *differs significantly from the hypothetical value* $\mu$ *of the population mean.*
2. *To test the significance between two sample means.*
3. *To test the significance of observed partial and multiple correlation coefficients.*

**Critical value of t**

The critical value or significant value of $t$ at level of significance $\alpha$ degrees of freedom $\gamma$ for two tailed test is given by

$$P[\,|\,t\,|\, > t_{\gamma}(\alpha)] = \alpha$$
$$P[\,|\,t\,|\, \leq t_{\gamma}(\alpha)] = 1 - \alpha$$

The significant value of $t$ at level of significance $\alpha$ for a single tailed test can be got from those of two tailed test by referring to the values at $2\alpha$.

## 5.16. TEST I : t-TEST OF SIGNIFICANCE OF THE MEAN OF A RANDOM SAMPLE

To test whether the mean of a sample drawn from a normal population deviates significantly from a stated value when variance of the population is unknown.

$H_0$ : There is no significant difference between the sample mean $\bar{x}$ and the population mean $\mu$ *i.e.,* we use the statistic

$$t = \frac{\bar{X} - \mu}{s/\sqrt{n}}, \qquad \text{where } \bar{X} \text{ is mean of the sample.}$$

$$s^2 = \frac{1}{n-1}\sum_{i=1}^{n} (X_i - \bar{X})^2 \text{ with degrees of freedom } (n-1).$$

At given level of significance $\alpha_1$ and degrees of freedom $(n - 1)$. We refer to $t$-table $t_{\alpha}$ (two tailed or one tailed).

If calculated $t$ value is such that $|\,t\,| < t_{\alpha}$ the null hypothesis is accepted. $|\,t\,| > t_{\alpha}$ $H_0$ is rejected.

**Fiducial limits of population mean**

If $t_\alpha$ is the table of $t$ at level of significance $\alpha$ at $(n-1)$ degrees of freedom.

$$\left|\frac{\overline{X}-\mu}{s/\sqrt{n}}\right| < t_\alpha \text{ for acceptance of } H_0.$$

$$\bar{x} - t_\alpha\, s/\sqrt{n} < \mu < \bar{x} + t_\alpha\, s/\sqrt{n}$$

95% confidence limits (level of significance 5%) are $\overline{X} \pm t_{0.05}\, s/\sqrt{n}$.

99% confidence limits (level of significance 1%) are $\overline{X} \pm t_{0.01}\, s/\sqrt{n}$.

**Note.** Instead of calculating $s$, we calculate S for the sample.

Since $s^2 = \frac{1}{n-1}\sum_{i=1}^{n}(X_i - \overline{X})^2 \quad \therefore \quad S^2 = \frac{1}{n}\sum_{i=1}^{n}(X_i - \overline{X})^2.$ $\left[(n-1)s^2 = nS^2,\ s^2 = \frac{n}{n-1}S^2\right]$

## ILLUSTRATIVE EXAMPLES

**Example 1.** *A random sample of size 16 has 53 as mean. The sum of squares of the derivation from mean is 135. Can this sample be regarded as taken from the population having 56 as mean ? Obtain 95% and 99% confidence limits of the mean of the population.*

**Sol.** $H_0$ : There is no significant difference between the sample mean and hypothetical population mean.

$$H_0 : \mu = 56 \ ;\ H_1 : \mu \neq 56 \quad \text{(Two tailed test)}$$

$$t : \frac{\overline{X}-\mu}{s/\sqrt{n}} \sim t(n-1 \text{ d.f})$$

Given : $\overline{X} = 53,\ \mu = 56,\ n = 16,\ \Sigma(X - \overline{X})^2 = 135$

$$s = \sqrt{\frac{\Sigma(X-\overline{X})^2}{n-1}} = \sqrt{\frac{135}{15}} = 3 \ ;\ t = \frac{53-56}{3/\sqrt{16}} = \frac{-3\times 4}{3} = -4$$

$|\,t\,| = 4$ . $d.fv = 16 - 1 = 15$.

**Conclusion.** $t_{0.05} = 1.753$.

Since $|\,t\,| = 4 > t_{0.05} = 1.753$ *i.e.*, the calculated value of $t$ is more than the table value. The hypothesis is rejected. Hence the sample mean has not come from a population having 56 as mean.

95% confidence limits of the population mean.

$$\overline{X} \pm \frac{s}{\sqrt{n}}\, t_{0.05},\ 53 \pm \frac{3}{\sqrt{16}}\,(1.725) = 51.706 \ ;\ 54.293$$

99% confidence limits of the population mean.

$$\overline{X} \pm \frac{s}{\sqrt{n}}\, t_{0.01},\ 53 \pm \frac{3}{\sqrt{16}}\,(2.602) = 51.048 \ ;\ 54.951.$$

**Example 2.** *The life time of electric bulbs for a random sample of 10 from a large consignment gave the following data :*

| *Item* | *1* | *2* | *3* | *4* | *5* | *6* | *7* | *8* | *9* | *10* |
|---|---|---|---|---|---|---|---|---|---|---|
| *Life in '000 hrs.* | *4.2* | *4.6* | *3.9* | *4.1* | *5.2* | *3.8* | *3.9* | *4.3* | *4.4* | *5.6* |

*Can we accept the hypothesis that the average life time of bulb is 4000 hrs ?*

**Sol.** $H_0$ : There is no significant difference in the sample mean and population mean. *i.e.,* $\mu = 4000$ hrs.

Applying the *t*-test : $t = \dfrac{\overline{X} - \mu}{s/\sqrt{n}} \sim t(10 - 1 d.f)$

| $X$ | 4.2 | 4.6 | 3.9 | 4.1 | 5.2 | 3.8 | 3.9 | 4.3 | 4.4 | 5.6 |
|---|---|---|---|---|---|---|---|---|---|---|
| $X - \overline{X}$ | – 0.2 | 0.2 | – 0.5 | – 0.3 | 0.8 | – 0.6 | – 0.5 | – 0.1 | 0 | 1.2 |
| $(X - \overline{X})^2$ | 0.04 | 0.04 | 0.25 | 0.09 | 0.64 | 0.36 | 0.25 | 0.01 | 0 | 1.44 |

$$\overline{X} = \frac{\Sigma X}{n} = \frac{44}{10} = 4.4 \qquad \Sigma(X - \overline{X})^2 = 3.12$$

$$s = \sqrt{\frac{\Sigma(X - \overline{X})^2}{n-1}} = \sqrt{\frac{3.12}{9}} = 0.589 \; ; \; t = \frac{4.4 - 4}{\dfrac{0.589}{\sqrt{10}}} = 2.123$$

For $\gamma = 9$, $t_{0.05} = 2.26$.

**Conclusion.** Since the calculated value of $t$ is less than table $t_{0.05}$. $\therefore$ The hypothesis $\mu = 4000$ hrs is accepted.

*i.e.,* The average life time of bulbs could be 4000 hrs.

**Example 3.** *A sample of 20 items has mean 42 units and S.D. 5 units. Test the hypothesis that it is a random sample from a normal population with mean 45 units.*

**Sol.** $H_0$ : There is no significant difference between the sample mean and the population mean.

*i.e.,* $\mu = 45$ units

$H_1 : \mu \neq 45$ (Two tailed test)

Given : $n = 20, \overline{X} = 42, S = 5 \; ; \gamma = 19$ d.f.

$$s^2 = \frac{n}{n-1} S^2 = \left[\frac{20}{20-1}\right](5)^2 = 26.31 \quad \therefore \quad s = 5.129$$

Applying *t*-test $\quad t = \dfrac{\overline{X} - \mu}{s/\sqrt{n}} = \dfrac{42 - 45}{5.129/\sqrt{20}} = -2.615 \; ; \; |t| = 2.615$

The tabulated value of $t$ at 5% level for 19 d.f. is $t_{0.05} = 2.09$.

**Conclusion.** Since $|t| > t_{0.05}$, the hypothesis $H_0$ is rejected. *i.e.,* there is significant difference between the sample mean and population mean.

*i.e.,* The sample could not have come from this population.

**Example 4.** *The 9 items of a sample have the following values 45, 47, 50, 52, 48, 47, 49, 53, 51. Does the mean of these values differ significantly from the assumed mean 47.5.*

**Sol.** $H_0 : \mu = 47.5$

*i.e.,* there is no significant difference between the sample and population mean.

$H_1 : \mu \neq 47.5$ (two tailed test) ; Given : $n = 9$, $\mu = 47.5$

| $X$ | 45 | 47 | 50 | 52 | 48 | 47 | 49 | 53 | 51 |
|---|---|---|---|---|---|---|---|---|---|
| $X - \overline{X}$ | – 4.1 | – 2.1 | 0.9 | 2.9 | – 1.1 | – 2.1 | – 0.1 | 3.9 | 1.9 |
| $(X - \overline{X})^2$ | 16.81 | 4.41 | 0.81 | 8.41 | 1.21 | 4.41 | 0.01 | 15.21 | 3.61 |

$$\overline{X} = \frac{\Sigma x}{n} = \frac{442}{9} = 49.11 \; ; \; \Sigma(X - \overline{X})^2 = 54.89 \; ; \; s^2 = \frac{\Sigma(X - \overline{X})^2}{(n-1)} = 6.86 \quad \therefore \quad s = 2.619$$

Applying $t$-test
$$t = \frac{\overline{X} - \mu}{s/\sqrt{n}} = \frac{49.1 - 47.5}{2.619/\sqrt{8}} = \frac{(1.6)\sqrt{8}}{2.619} = 1.7279$$

$t_{0.05} = 2.31$ for $\gamma = 8$.

**Conclusion.** Since $| t | < t_{0.05}$, the hypothesis is accepted *i.e.,* there is no significant difference between their mean.

**Example 5.** *The following results are obtained from a sample of 10 boxes is biscuits.*

*Mean weight content = 490 gm*

*S.D. of the weight = 9 gm could the sample come from a population having a mean of 500 gm ?*

**Sol.** Given : $n = 10, \overline{X} = 490 \; ; \; S = 9$ gm, $\mu = 500$

$$s = \sqrt{\frac{n}{n-1} S^2} = \sqrt{\frac{10}{9} \times 9^2} = 9.486$$

$H_0$ : The difference is not significant *i.e.,* $\mu = 500$ ; $H_1 : \mu \neq 500$

Applying $t$-test
$$t = \frac{\overline{X} - \mu}{s/\sqrt{n}} = \frac{490 - 500}{9.486/\sqrt{10}} = -\,0.333$$

$t_{0.05} = 2.26$ for $\gamma = 9$.

**Conclusion.** Since $| t | = .333 > t_{0.05}$ the hypothesis $H_0$ is rejected *i.e.,* $\mu \neq 500$

$\therefore$ The sample could not have come from the population having mean 500 gm.

## TEST YOUR KNOWLEDGE

1. Ten individuals are chosen at random from a normal population of students and their marks found to be 63, 63, 66, 67, 68, 69, 70, 70, 71, 71. In the light of these data discuss the suggestion that mean mark of the population of students is 66.
2. The following values gives the lengths of 12 samples of egyptian cotton taken from a consignment : 48, 46, 49, 46, 52, 45, 43, 47, 47, 46, 45, 50. Test if the mean length of the consignment can be taken as 46.
3. A sample of 18 items has a mean 24 units and standard deviation 3 units. Test the hypothesis that it is a random sample from a normal population with mean 27 units.
4. A random sample of 10 boys had the I.Q's 70, 120, 110, 101, 88, 83, 95, 98, 107 and 100. Do these data support the assumption of a population mean I.Q of 160 ?
5. A filling machine is expected to fill 5 kg of powder into bags. A sample of 10 bags gave the following weights. 4.7, 4.9, 5.0, 5.1, 5.4, 5.2, 4.6, 5.1, 4.6 and 4.7. Test whether the machine is working properly.

**6.** A random sample of size 8 from a normal distribution gave the following observations.

6, 8, 11, 5, 9, 11, 10, 12

Can the sample be regarded as a sample drawn from a population with mean equal to 7 at 5% level of significance ?

**Answers**

**1.** accepted **2.** accepted **3.** rejected

**4.** accepted **5.** accepted **6.** Accepted.

## 5.17. TEST II : t-TEST FOR DIFFERENCE OF MEANS OF TWO SMALL SAMPLES (FROM A NORMAL POPULATION)

This test is used to test whether the two samples $x_1, x_2, \ldots\ldots, x_{n_1}, y_1, y_2, \ldots\ldots, y_{n_2}$ of sizes $n_1, n_2$ have been drawn from two normal populations with mean $\mu_1$ and $\mu_2$ respectively under the assumption that the population variance are equal. ($\sigma_1 = \sigma_2 = \sigma$).

$H_0$ : The samples have been drawn from the normal population with means $\mu_1$ and $\mu_2$ *i.e.*, $H_0 : \mu_1 \neq \mu_2$.

Let $\overline{X}, \overline{Y}$ be their means of the two sample.

Under this $H_0$ the test of statistic $t$ is given by $t = \dfrac{(\overline{X} - \overline{Y})}{s\sqrt{\dfrac{1}{n_1} + \dfrac{1}{n_2}}} \sim t(n_1 + n_2 - 2 \text{ d.f.})$

**Note 1.** If the two sample standard deviations $s_1, s_2$ are given then we have $s^2 = \dfrac{n_1 s_1^2 + n_2 s_2^2}{n_1 + n_2 - 2}$.

**Note 2.** If $n_1 = n_2 = n$, $t = \dfrac{\overline{X} - \overline{Y}}{\sqrt{\dfrac{s_1^2 + s_2^2}{n - 1}}}$ can be used as a test statistic.

**Note 3.** If the pairs of values are in some way associated (correlated) we can't use the test statistic as given in note 2. In this case we find the differences of the associated pairs of values and apply for single mean *i.e.*, $t = \dfrac{\overline{X} - \mu}{s/\sqrt{n}}$ with degrees of freedom $n - 1$.

The test statistic is $t = \dfrac{\overline{d}}{s/\sqrt{n}}$ or $t = \dfrac{\overline{d}}{s/\sqrt{n-1}}$, where $\overline{d}$ is the mean of paired difference

*i.e.*, $d_i = x_i - y_i$

$\overline{d_i} = \overline{X} - \overline{Y}$, where $(x_i, y_i)$ are the paired data $i = 1, 2, \ldots\ldots, n$.

## ILLUSTRATIVE EXAMPLES

**Example 1.** *Two samples of sodium vapour bulbs were tested for length of life and the following results were got* :

| | *Size* | *Sample mean* | *Sample S.D.* |
|---|---|---|---|
| *Type I* | 8 | *1234 hrs* | *36 hrs* |
| *Type II* | 7 | *1036 hrs* | *40 hrs* |

*Is the difference in the means significant to generalise that type I is superior to type II regarding length of life.*

**Sol.** $H_0 : \mu_1 = \mu_2$ *i.e.*, two types of bulbs have same lifetime.

$H_1 : \mu_1 > \mu_2$ *i.e.*, type I is superior to type II

$$s^2 = \frac{n_1 s_2{}^2 + n_2 s_2{}^2}{n_1 + n_2 - 2} = \frac{8 \times (36)^2 + 7(40)^2}{8 + 7 - 2} = 1659.076 \quad \therefore \quad s = 40.7317$$

The $t$-statistic
$$t = \frac{\overline{X}_1 - \overline{X}_2}{s\sqrt{\frac{1}{n_1} + \frac{1}{n_2}}} = \frac{1234 - 1036}{40.7317\sqrt{\frac{1}{8} + \frac{1}{7}}} = 18.1480 \sim t(n_1 + n_2 - 2 \text{ d.f.})$$

$t_{0.05}$ at d.f. 13 is 1.77 (one tailed test)

**Conclusion.** Since calculated $|\ t\ | > t_{0.05}$ $H_0$ is rejected *i.e.*, $H_1$ is accepted.

$\therefore$ Type I is definitely superior to type II.

where $\overline{X} = \sum_{i=1}^{n_1} \frac{X_i}{n_i}$, $\quad \overline{Y} = \sum_{j=1}^{n_2} \frac{Y_j}{n_2}$ ; $\quad s^2 = \frac{1}{n_1 + n_2 - 2}\ [\Sigma(X_i - \overline{X})^2 + (Y_j - \overline{Y})^2]$

is an unbiased estimate of the population variance $\sigma^2$.

$t$ follows $t$ distribution with $n_1 + n_2 - 2$ degrees of freedom.

**Example 2.** *Samples of sizes 10 and 14 were taken from two normal populations with S.D. 3.5 and 5.2. The sample means were found to be 20.3 and 18.6. Test whether the means of the two populations are the same at 5% level.*

**Sol.** $H_0 : \mu_1 = \mu_2$ *i.e.*, the means of the two populations are the same.

$H_1 : \mu_1 \neq \mu_2$.

Given $\overline{X}_1 = 20.3$, $\overline{X}_2 = 18.6$ ; $n_1 = 10$, $n_2 = 14$, $s_1 = 3.5$, $s_2 = 5.2$

$$s^2 = \frac{n_1 s_1^2 + n_2 s_2^2}{n_1 + n_2 - 2} = \frac{10(3.5)^2 + 14(5.2)^2}{10 + 14 - 2} = 22.775 \quad \therefore \quad s = 4.772$$

$$t = \frac{\overline{X}_1 - \overline{X}_2}{s\sqrt{\frac{1}{n_1} + \frac{1}{n_2}}} = \frac{20.3 - 18.6}{\left(\sqrt{\frac{1}{10} + \frac{1}{14}}\right) 4.772} = 0.8604$$

The value of $t$ at 5% level for 22 d.f. is $t_{0.05} = 2.0739$.

**Conclusion.** Since $|\ t\ | = 0.8604 < t_{0.05}$ the hypothesis is accepted. *i.e.*, there is no significant difference between their means.

**Example 3.** *The height of 6 randomly chosen sailors are in inches are 63, 65, 68, 69, 71 and 72. Those of 9 randomly chosen soldiers are 61, 62, 65, 66, 69, 70, 71, 72 and 73. Test whether the sailors are on the average taller than soldiers.*

**Sol.** Let $X_1$ and $X_2$ be the two samples denoting the heights of sailors and soldiers.

Given the sample size $n_1 = 6$, $n_2 = 9$, $H_0 : \mu_1 = \mu_2$.

*i.e.*, the mean of both the population are the same.

$H_1 : \mu_1 > \mu_2$ (one tailed test)

**Calculation of two sample mean :**

| $X_1$ | 63 | 65 | 68 | 69 | 71 | 72 |
|---|---|---|---|---|---|---|
| $X_1 - \overline{X}_1$ | – 5 | – 3 | 0 | 1 | 3 | 4 |
| $(X_1 - \overline{X}_1)^2$ | 25 | 9 | 0 | 1 | 9 | 16 |

$$\overline{X}_1 = \frac{\Sigma X_1}{n_1} = 68 \ ; \quad \Sigma(X_1 - \overline{X}_1)^2 = 60$$

| $X_2$ | 61 | 62 | 65 | 66 | 69 | 70 | 71 | 72 | 73 |
|---|---|---|---|---|---|---|---|---|---|
| $X_2 - \overline{X}_2$ | – 6.66 | – 5.66 | – 2.66 | 1.66 | 1.34 | 2.34 | 3.34 | 4.34 | 5.34 |
| $(X_2 - \overline{X}_2)^2$ | 44.36 | 32.035 | 7.0756 | 2.7556 | 1.7956 | 5.4756 | 11.1556 | 18.8356 | 28.5156 |

$$\overline{X}_2 = \frac{\Sigma X_2}{n_2} = 67.66 \ ; \quad \Sigma(X_2 - \overline{X}_2)^2 = 152.0002$$

$$s^2 = \frac{1}{n_1 + n_2 - 2}\,[\Sigma(X_1 - \overline{X}_1)^2 + \Sigma(X_2 - \overline{X}_2)^2]$$

$$= \frac{1}{6 + 9 - 2}\,[60 + 152.0002] = 16.3077 \quad \therefore \quad s = 4.038$$

Under $H_0$,
$$t = \frac{\overline{X}_1 - \overline{X}_2}{s\sqrt{\frac{1}{n_1} + \frac{1}{n_2}}} = \frac{68 - 67.666}{4.0382\sqrt{\frac{1}{6} + \frac{1}{9}}} = 0.3031 \sim t(n_1 + n_2 - 2 \text{ d.f.})$$

The value of $t$ at 10% level of significance ($\because$ the test is one tailed) for 13 d.f. is 1.77.

**Conclusion.** Since $|\ t\ | = 0.3031 < t_{0.05} = 1.77$ the hypothesis $H_0$ is accepted.

*i.e.*, there is no significance difference between their average.

*i.e.*, the sailors are not on the average taller than the soldiers.

**Example 4.** *A certain stimulus administered to each of 12 patients resulted in the following increases of blood pressure : 5, 2, 8, – 1, 3, 0, – 2, 1, 5, 0, 4, 6. Can it be concluded that the stimulus will in general be accompanied by an increase in blood pressure ?*

**Sol.** To test whether the mean increase in blood pressure of all patients to whom the stimulus is administered will be positive. We have to assume that this population is normal with mean μ and S.D. σ which are unknown.

$$H_0 : \mu = 0 \ ; \ H_1 : \mu_1 > 0$$

The test statistic under $H_0$

$$t = \frac{\overline{d}}{s/\sqrt{n-1}} \sim t(n - 1 \text{ degrees of freedom})$$

$$\overline{d} = \frac{5 + 2 + 8 + (-1) + 3 + 0 + 6 + (-2) + 1 + 5 + 0 + 4}{12} = 2.583$$

$$s^2 = \frac{\Sigma d^2}{n} - \bar{d}^2 = \frac{1}{12}\,[5^2 + 2^2 + 8^2 + (-1)^2 + 3^2 + 0^2 + 6^2$$
$$+ (-2)^2 + 1^2 + 5^2 + 0^2 + 4^2] - (2.583)^2$$
$$= 8.744 \quad \therefore \quad s = 2.9571$$

$$t = \frac{\bar{d}}{s/\sqrt{n-1}} = \frac{2.583}{2.9571/\sqrt{12-1}} = \frac{2.583\sqrt{11}}{2.9571} = 2.897 \sim t(n-1 \text{ d.f.})$$

**Conclusion.** The tabulated value of $t_{0.05}$ at 11 d.f. is 2.2.

$\because \quad |t| > t_{0.05}$, $H_0$ is rejected.

*i.e.*, the stimulus does not increase the blood pressure. The stimulus in general will be accompanied by increase in blood pressure.

**Example 5.** *Memory capacity of 9 students was tested before and after a course of meditation for a month. State whether the course was effective or not from the data below (in same units)*

| *Before* | *10* | *15* | *9* | *3* | *7* | *12* | *16* | *17* | *4* |
|---|---|---|---|---|---|---|---|---|---|
| *After* | *12* | *17* | *8* | *5* | *6* | *11* | *18* | *20* | *3* |

**Sol.** Since the data are correlated and concerned with the same set of students we use paired $t$-test.

$H_0$ : Training was not effective $\mu_1 = \mu_2$

$H_1 : \mu_1 \neq \mu_2$ (Two tailed test).

| *Before training (X)* | *After training (Y)* | $d = X - Y$ | $d^2$ |
|---|---|---|---|
| 10 | 12 | − 2 | 4 |
| 15 | 17 | − 2 | 4 |
| 9 | 8 | 1 | 1 |
| 3 | 5 | − 2 | 4 |
| 7 | 6 | 1 | 1 |
| 12 | 11 | 1 | 1 |
| 16 | 18 | − 2 | 4 |
| 17 | 20 | − 3 | 9 |
| 4 | 3 | 1 | 1 |
| | | $\Sigma d = -7$ | $\Sigma d^2 = 29$ |

$$\bar{d} = \frac{\Sigma d}{n} = \frac{-7}{9} = -0.7778\ ;\ s^2 = \frac{\Sigma d^2}{n} - (\bar{d})^2 = \frac{29}{9} - (-0.7778)^2 = 2.617$$

$$t = \frac{\bar{d}}{s/\sqrt{n-1}} = \frac{-0.7778}{\sqrt{2.6172}/\sqrt{8}} = \frac{-0.7778 \times \sqrt{8}}{1.6177} = -1.359$$

The tabulated value of $t_{0.05}$ at 8 d.f. is 2.31.

**Conclusion.** Since $|t| = 1.359 < t_{0.05}$, $H_0$ is accepted *i.e.*, training was not effective in improving performance.

**Example 6.** *The following figures refer to observations in live independent samples.*

| *Sample I* | *25* | *30* | *28* | *34* | *24* | *20* | *13* | *32* | *22* | *38* |
|---|---|---|---|---|---|---|---|---|---|---|
| *Sample II* | *40* | *34* | *22* | *20* | *31* | *40* | *30* | *23* | *36* | *17* |

*Analyse whether the samples have been drawn from the populations of equal means.*

**Sol.** $H_0$ : The two samples have been drawn from the population of equal means. *i.e.*, there is no significant difference between their means

*i.e.*, $\mu_1 = \mu_2$

$H_1 : \mu_1 \neq \mu_2$ (Two tailed test)

Given $n_1$ = Sample I size = 10 ; $n_2$ = Sample II size = 10

To calculate the two sample mean and sum of squares of deviation from mean. Let $X_1$ be the sample I and $X_2$ be the sample II.

| $X_1$ | 25 | 30 | 28 | 34 | 24 | 20 | 13 | 32 | 22 | 38 |
|---|---|---|---|---|---|---|---|---|---|---|
| $X_1 - \overline{X}_1$ | – 1.6 | 3.4 | 1.4 | 7.4 | – 2.6 | – 6.6 | – 13.6 | 5.4 | 4.6 | 11.4 |
| $(X_1 - \overline{X}_1)^2$ | 2.56 | 11.56 | 1.96 | 54.76 | 6.76 | 43.56 | 184.96 | 29.16 | 21.16 | 129.96 |
| $X_2$ | 40 | 34 | 22 | 20 | 31 | 40 | 30 | 23 | 36 | 17 |
| $X_2 - \overline{X}_2$ | 10.7 | 4.7 | – 7.3 | – 9.3 | 1.7 | 10.7 | 0.7 | – 6.3 | 6.7 | – 12.3 |
| $(X_2 - \overline{X}_2)^2$ | 114.49 | 22.09 | 53.29 | 86.49 | 2.89 | 114.49 | 0.49 | 39.67 | 44.89 | 151.29 |

$$\overline{X}_1 = \sum_{i=1}^{10} \frac{X_1}{n_1} = 26.6 \qquad \overline{X}_2 = \sum_{i=1}^{10} \frac{X_2}{n_2} = \frac{293}{10} = 29.3$$

$$\Sigma(X_1 - \overline{X}_1)^2 = 486.4 \qquad \Sigma(X_2 - \overline{X}_2)^2 = 630.08$$

$$s^2 = \frac{1}{n_1 + n_2 - 2}[\Sigma(X_1 - \overline{X}_1)^2 + \Sigma(X_2 - \overline{X}_2)^2]$$

$$= \frac{1}{10 + 10 - 2}[486.4 + 630.08] = 62.026 \qquad \therefore \quad s = 7.875$$

Under $H_0$ the test statistic is given by

$$t = \frac{\overline{X}_1 - \overline{X}_2}{s\sqrt{\frac{1}{n_1} + \frac{1}{n_2}}} = \frac{26.6 - 29.3}{7.875\sqrt{\frac{1}{10} + \frac{1}{10}}} = -0.7666 \sim t(n_1 + n_2 - 2 \text{ d.f.})$$

$|t| = 0.7666.$

**Conclusion.** The tabulated value of $t$ at 5% level of significance for 18 d.f. is 2.1. Since the calculated value $|t| = 0.7666 < t_{0.05}$, $H_0$ is accepted.

*i.e.*, there is no significant difference between their means.

*i.e.*, the two samples have been drawn from the populations of equal means.

## TEST YOUR KNOWLEDGE

**1.** The mean life of 10 electric motors was found to be 1450 hrs with S.D. of 423 hrs. A second sample of 17 motors chosen from a different batch showed a mean life of 1280 hrs with a S.D. of 398 hrs. Is there a significant difference between means of the two samples.

**2.** The marks obtained by a group of 9 regular course students and another group of 11 part time course students in a test are given below

| | | | | | | | | | | | |
|---|---|---|---|---|---|---|---|---|---|---|---|
| *Regular* | : | 56 | 62 | 63 | 54 | 60 | 51 | 67 | 69 | 58 | | |
| *Part-time* | : | 62 | 70 | 71 | 62 | 60 | 56 | 75 | 64 | 72 | 68 | 66 |

Examine whether the marks obtained by regular students and part-time students differ significantly at 5% and 1% level of significance.

**3.** A group of 10 boys fed on diet A and another group of 8 boys fed on a different diet B recorded the following increase in weight (kgs).

| | | | | | | | | | | |
|---|---|---|---|---|---|---|---|---|---|---|
| *Diet A* : | 5 | 6 | 8 | 1 | 12 | 4 | 3 | 9 | 6 | 10 |
| *Diet B* : | 2 | 3 | 6 | 8 | 10 | 1 | 2 | 8 | | |

Does it show the superiority of diet A over the diet B ?

**4.** Two independent samples of sizes 7 and 9 have the following values :

| | | | | | | | | | |
|---|---|---|---|---|---|---|---|---|---|
| *Sample A* : | 10 | 12 | 10 | 13 | 14 | 11 | 10 | | |
| *Sample B* : | 10 | 13 | 15 | 12 | 10 | 14 | 11 | 12 | 11 |

Test whether the difference between the mean is significant.

**5.** To compare the prices of a certain product in two cities, 10 shops when related at random in each town. The price was noted below :

| | | | | | | | | | | |
|---|---|---|---|---|---|---|---|---|---|---|
| *City 1* : | 61 | 63 | 56 | 63 | 56 | 63 | 59 | 56 | 44 | 61 |
| *City 2* : | 55 | 54 | 47 | 59 | 51 | 61 | 57 | 54 | 64 | 58 |

Test whether the average prices can be said to be the same in two cities.

**6.** The average number of articles produced by two machines per day are 200 and 250 with standard deviation 20 and 25 respectively on the basis of records of 25 days production. Can you regard both the machines equally efficient at 5% level of significance.

**7.** Two salesman represent a firm in a certain company. One of them claims that he makes large sales than the other. A sample survey was made and the following results were obtained :

| *No. of sales* | : | 1st Salesman (18) | 2nd Salesman (20) |
|---|---|---|---|
| *Average sales* | : | ₹ 210 | ₹ 175 |
| *S.D.* | : | ₹ 25 | ₹ 20 |

Find if the average sales differ significantly.

### Answers

| | | | |
|---|---|---|---|
| **1.** accepted | **2.** rejected | **3.** accepted | **4.** accepted |
| **5.** accepted | **6.** rejected | **7.** rejected. | |

## 5.18. SNEDECOR'S VARIANCE RATIO TEST OR F-TEST

In testing the significance of the difference of two means of two samples, we assumed that the two sample came from the same population or population with equal variance. The object of the F-test is to discover whether two independent estimates of population variance differ significantly or whether the two samples may be regarded as drawn from the normal populations having the same variance. Hence before applying the $t$-test for the significance of the difference of two means, we have to test for the equality of population variance by using F-test.

Let $n_1$ and $n_2$ be the sizes of two samples with variance $s_1^2$ and $s_2^2$. The estimate of the population variance based on these samples are $s_1^2 = \frac{n_1 s_1^2}{n_1 - 1}$ and $s_2^2 = \frac{n_2 s_2^2}{n_2 - 1}$. The degrees of freedom of these estimates are $\nu_1 = n_1 - 1$, $\nu_2 = n_2 - 1$.

To test whether these estimates $s_1^2$ and $s_2^2$ are significantly different or if the samples may be regarded as drawn from the same population or from two populations with same variance $\sigma^2$. We setup the null hypothesis $H_0 : \sigma_1^2 = \sigma_2^2 = \sigma^2$

*i.e.*, the independent estimates of the common population do not differ significantly.

To carry out the test of significance of the difference of the variances we calculate the test statistic (Nr) $F = \frac{s_1^2}{s_2^2}$, the Numerator, is greater than the Denominator (Dr) *i.e.*, $s_1^2 > s_2^2$.

**Conclusion.** If the calculated value of F exceeds $F_{0.05}$ for $(n_1 - 1)$, $(n_2 - 1)$ degrees of freedom given in table we conclude that the ratio is significant at 5% level.

*i.e.*, we conclude that the sample could have come from two normal population with same variance.

The assumptions on which F-test is based are :

1. *The populations for each sample must be normally distributed.*
2. *The samples must be random and independent.*
3. *The ratio of $\sigma_1^2$ to $\sigma_2^2$ should be equal to 1 or greater than 1. That is why we take the larger variance in the Numerator of the ratio.*

**Applications.** *F-test is used to test*

*(i) whether two independent samples have been drawn from the normal populations with the same variance $\sigma^2$.*

*(ii) Whether the two independent estimates of the population variance are homogeneous or not.*

## ILLUSTRATIVE EXAMPLES

**Example 1.** *In two independent samples of sizes 8 and 10 the sum of squares of deviations of the sample values from the respective sample means were 84.4 and 102.6. Test whether the difference of variances of the populations is significant or not.*

**Sol. Null hypothesis $H_0$.** $\sigma_1^2 = \sigma_2^2 = \sigma^2$ *i.e.*, there is no significant difference between population variance.

$$\text{Under } H_0 : F = \frac{s_1^2}{s_2^2} \sim F(\nu_1, \nu_2 \text{ d.f})$$

where $\nu_1 = n_1 - 1$, $n_1$ = Sample I size = 8 ; $\nu_2 = n_2 - 1$, $n_2$ = Sample II size = 10

$\Sigma(X_1 - \overline{X}_1)^2 = 84.4$ ; $\Sigma(X_2 - \overline{X}_2)^2 = 102.6$

$$s_1^2 = \frac{\Sigma(X_1 - \overline{X}_1)^2}{n_1 - 1} = \frac{84.4}{7} = 12.057 \text{ ; } s_2^2 = \frac{\Sigma(X_2 - \overline{X}_2)^2}{n_2 - 1} = \frac{102.6}{9} = 11.4$$

$$F = \frac{s_1^2}{s_2^2} \quad \because \quad s_1^2 > s_2^2 \quad \therefore \quad F = \frac{12.057}{11.4} = 1.0576.$$

**Conclusion.** The tabulated value of F at 5% level of significance for (7, 9) d.f is 3.29

$\therefore$ $F_{0.05} = 3.29$ and $|F| = 1.0576 > 3.29 = F_{0.05}$ $\Rightarrow$ $H_0$ is accepted.

$\therefore$ There is no significant difference between the variance of the populations.

**Example 2.** *Two random samples are drawn from 2 normal populations are as follows :*

| A | 17 | 27 | 18 | 25 | 27 | 29 | 13 | 17 |
|---|---|---|---|---|---|---|---|---|
| B | 16 | 16 | 20 | 27 | 26 | 25 | 21 | |

*Test whether the samples are drawn from the same normal population.*

**Sol.** To test if two independent samples have been drawn from the same population we have to test (*i*) equality of the means by applying the *t*-test and (*ii*) equality of population variance by applying F-test.

Since the *t*-test assumes that the sample variances are equal, we shall first apply the F-test.

**F-test. Null hypothesis $H_0$.** $\sigma_1^2 = \sigma_2^2$ *i.e.*, the population variance do not differ significantly.

**Alternative hypothesis.** $H_1 : \sigma_1^2 \neq \sigma_2^2$

Test statistic : $F = \frac{s_1^2}{s_2^2}$, (if $s_1^2 > s_2^2$)

**Computations for $s_1^2$ and $s_2^2$**

| $X_1$ | $X_1 - \overline{X}_1$ | $(X_1 - \overline{X}_1)^2$ | $X_2$ | $X_2 - \overline{X}_2$ | $(X_2 - \overline{X}_2)^2$ |
|---|---|---|---|---|---|
| 17 | – 4.625 | 21.39 | 16 | – 2.714 | 7.365 |
| 27 | 5.735 | 28.89 | 16 | – 2.714 | 7.365 |
| 18 | – 3.625 | 13.14 | 20 | 1.286 | 1.653 |
| 25 | 3.375 | 11.39 | 27 | 8.286 | 68.657 |
| 27 | 5.735 | 28.89 | 26 | 7.286 | 53.085 |
| 29 | 7.735 | 54.39 | 25 | 6.286 | 39.513 |
| 13 | – 8.625 | 74.39 | 21 | 2.286 | 5.226 |
| 17 | – 4.625 | 21.39 | | | |

$$\overline{X}_1 = 21.625 \; ; n_1 = 8 \; ; \Sigma(X_1 - \overline{X}_1)^2 = 253.87$$

$$\overline{X}_2 = 18.714 \; ; n_2 = 7 \; ; \Sigma(X_2 - \overline{X}_2)^2 = 182.859$$

$$s_1^2 = \frac{\Sigma(X_1 - \overline{X}_1)^2}{n_1 - 1} = \frac{253.87}{7} = 36.267 \; ;$$

$$s_2^2 = \frac{\Sigma(X_2 - \overline{X}_2)^2}{n_2 - 1} = \frac{182.859}{6} = 30.47$$

$$F = \frac{s_1^2}{s_2^2} = \frac{36.267}{30.47} = 1.190.$$

**Conclusion.** The table value of F for $\nu_1 = 7$ and $\nu_2 = 6$ degrees of freedom at 5% level is 4.21. The calculated value of F is less than the tabulated value of F. $\therefore$ $H_0$ is accepted. Hence we conclude that the variability in two populations is same.

**t-test : Null hypothesis.** $H_0 : \mu_1 = \mu_2$ *i.e.,* the population means are equal.

**Alternative hypothesis.** $H_1 : \mu_1 \neq \mu_2$

**Test of statistic**

$$s^2 = \frac{\Sigma(X_1 - \overline{X}_1)^2 + \Sigma(X_2 - \overline{X}_2)^2}{n_1 + n_2 - 2} = \frac{253.87 + 182.859}{8 + 7 - 2} = 33.594 \quad \therefore \quad s = 5.796$$

$$t = \frac{\overline{X}_1 - \overline{X}_2}{s\sqrt{\frac{1}{n_1} + \frac{1}{n_2}}} = \frac{21.625 - 18.714}{5.796\sqrt{\frac{1}{8} + \frac{1}{7}}} = 0.9704 \sim t(n_1 + n_2 - 2) \text{ d.f.}$$

**Conclusion.** The tabulated value of $t$ at 5% level of significance for 13 d.f. is 2.16.

The calculated value of $t$ is less than the tabulated value. $H_0$ is accepted *i.e.,* there is no significant difference between the population mean. *i.e.,* $\mu_1 = \mu_2$. $\therefore$ We conclude that the two samples have been drawn from the same normal population.

**Example 3.** *Two independent sample of sizes 7 and 6 had the following values :*

| *Sample A* | *28* | *30* | *32* | *33* | *31* | *29* | *34* |
|---|---|---|---|---|---|---|---|
| *Sample B* | *29* | *30* | *30* | *24* | *27* | *28* | |

*Examine whether the samples have been drawn from normal populations having the same variance.*

**Sol.** $H_0$ : The variance are equal. *i.e.,* $\sigma_1^2 = \sigma_2^2$

*i.e.,* the samples have been drawn from normal populations with same variance.

$$H_1 : \sigma_1^2 \neq \sigma_2^2$$

Under null hypothesis, the test statistic $F = \frac{s_1^2}{s_2^2} (s_1^2 > s_2^2)$

**Computations for $s_1^2$ and $s_2^2$**

| $X_1$ | $X_1 - \overline{X}_1$ | $(X_1 - \overline{X}_1)^2$ | $X_2$ | $X_2 - \overline{X}_2$ | $(X_2 - \overline{X}_2)^2$ |
|---|---|---|---|---|---|
| 28 | – 3 | 9 | 29 | 1 | 1 |
| 30 | – 1 | 1 | 30 | 2 | 4 |
| 32 | 1 | 1 | 30 | 2 | 4 |
| 33 | 2 | 4 | 24 | – 4 | 16 |
| 31 | 0 | 0 | 27 | – 1 | 1 |
| 29 | – 2 | 4 | 28 | 0 | 0 |
| 34 | 3 | 9 | | | |
| | | 28 | | | 26 |

$$\overline{X}_1 = 31, \quad n_1 = 7 ; \quad \Sigma(X_1 - \overline{X}_1)^2 = 28$$

$$\overline{X}_2 = 28, \quad n_2 = 6 ; \quad \Sigma(X_2 - \overline{X}_2)^2 = 26$$

$$s_1^2 = \frac{\Sigma(X_1 - \overline{X}_1)^2}{n_1 - 1} = \frac{28}{6} = 4.666 ; \quad s_2^2 = \frac{\Sigma(X_2 - \overline{X}_2)^2}{n_2 - 1} = \frac{26}{5} = 5.2$$

$$F = \frac{s_1^2}{s_2^2} = \frac{5.2}{4.666} = 1.1158. \qquad (\because \ s_2^2 > s_1^2)$$

**Conclusion.** The tabulated value of F at $\nu_1 = 6 - 1$ and $\nu_2 = 7 - 1$ d.f. for 5% level of significance is 4.39.

Since the tabulated value of F is less than the calculated value, $H_0$ is accepted *i.e.,* there is no significant difference between the variance. *i.e.,* the samples have been drawn from the normal population with same variance.

**Example 4.** *The two random samples reveal the following data :*

| *Sample no.* | *Size* | *Mean* | *Variance* |
|---|---|---|---|
| *I* | *16* | *440* | *40* |
| *II* | *25* | *460* | *42* |

*Test whether the samples come from the same normal population.*

**Sol.** A normal population has two parameters namely the mean $\mu$ and the variance $\sigma^2$. To test whether the two independent samples have been drawn from the same normal population, we have to test

(*i*) the equality of means (*ii*) the equality of variance.

Since the *t*-test assumes that the sample variance are equal, we first apply F-test.

**F-test. Null hypothesis.** $\sigma_1^2 = \sigma_2^2$

The population variance do not differ significantly.

**Alternative hypothesis.** $\sigma_1^2 \neq \sigma_2^2$

Under the null hypothesis the test statistic is given by $F = \frac{s_1^2}{s_2^2}$, $(s_1^2 > s_2^2)$

Given : $n_1 = 16, n_2 = 25$ ; $s_1^2 = 40, s_2^2 = 42$

$$\therefore \qquad F = \frac{s_1^2}{s_2^2} = \frac{\dfrac{n_1 s_1^2}{n_1 - 1}}{\dfrac{n_2 s_2^2}{n_2 - 1}} = \frac{16 \times 40}{15} \times \frac{24}{25 \times 42} = 0.9752.$$

**Conclusion.** The calculated value of F is 0.9752. The tabulated value of F at 16 – 1, 25 – 1 d.f. for 5% level of significance is 2.11.

Since the calculated value is less than that of the tabulated value, $H_0$ is accepted. *i.e.,* the population variance are equal.

**t-test. Null hypothesis.** $H_0 : \mu_1 = \mu_2$ *i.e.,* the population means are equal.

**Alternative hypothesis.** $H_1 : \mu_1 \neq \mu_2$ under null hypothesis the test statistic

Given : $n_1 = 16, n_2 = 25, \overline{X}_1 = 440, \overline{X}_2 = 460$

$$s^2 = \frac{n_1 s_1^2 + n_2 s_2^2}{n_1 + n_2 - 2} = \frac{16 \times 40 + 25 \times 42}{16 + 25 - 2} = 43.333 \quad \therefore \quad s = 6.582$$

$$t = \frac{\overline{X}_1 - \overline{X}_2}{s\sqrt{\dfrac{1}{n_1} + \dfrac{1}{n_2}}} = \frac{440 - 460}{6.582\sqrt{\dfrac{1}{16} + \dfrac{1}{25}}} = -\,9.490 \text{ for } (n_1 + n_2 - 2) \text{ d.f.}$$

**Conclusion.** The calculated value of | $t$ | is 9.490. The tabulated value of $t$ at 39 d.f. for 5% level of significance is 1.96.

Since the calculated value is greater than the tabulated value, $H_0$ is rejected. *i.e.,* there is significant difference between means. *i.e.,* $\mu_1 \neq \mu_2$.

Since there is significant difference between means, and no significant difference between variance, we conclude that the samples do not come from the same normal population.

**Example 5.** *Two random samples drawn from two normal populations have the variable values as below :*

| *Sample I* | *19* | *17* | *16* | *28* | *22* | *23* | *19* | *24* | *26* | | | |
|---|---|---|---|---|---|---|---|---|---|---|---|---|
| *Sample II* | *28* | *32* | *40* | *37* | *30* | *35* | *40* | *28* | *41* | *45* | *30* | *36* |

*Obtain the estimate of the variance of the population and test whether the two population have the same variance.*

**Sol.** $\overline{X}_1 = \dfrac{\Sigma X_1}{n_1} = 21.55$ ; $n_1 = 9$ ; $\overline{X}_2 = \dfrac{\Sigma X_2}{n_2} = 35.166$ ; $n_2 = 12$

| $X_1$ | $d_1 = X_1 - 17$ | $d_1^2$ | $X_2$ | $d_2 = X_2 - 28$ | $d_2^2$ |
|---|---|---|---|---|---|
| 19 | 2 | 4 | 28 | 0 | 0 |
| 17 | 0 | 0 | 32 | 4 | 16 |
| 16 | – 1 | 1 | 40 | 12 | 144 |
| 28 | 11 | 121 | 37 | 9 | 81 |

| | | | | | |
|---|---|---|---|---|---|
| 22 | 5 | 25 | 30 | 2 | 4 |
| 23 | 6 | 36 | 35 | 7 | 49 |
| 19 | 2 | 4 | 40 | 12 | 144 |
| 24 | 7 | 49 | 28 | 0 | 0 |
| 26 | 9 | 81 | 41 | 13 | 169 |
| | | | 45 | 17 | 289 |
| | | | 30 | 2 | 4 |
| | | | 36 | 8 | 64 |
| | | $\Sigma d_1^2 = 321$ | | | $\Sigma d_2^2 = 964$ |

$$s_1^2 = \frac{\Sigma(X_1 - \overline{X}_1)^2}{n_1 - 1} = \frac{\Sigma d_1^2 - n_1(\overline{X}_1 - A)^2}{n_1 - 1} = \frac{321 - 9(21.55 - 17)^2}{9 - 1} = 16.834$$

$$s_2^2 = \frac{\Sigma(X_2 - \overline{X}_2)^2}{n_2 - 1} = \frac{\Sigma d_2^2 - n_2(X_2 - A)^2}{n_2 - 1} = \frac{964 - 12(35.166 - 28)^2}{12 - 1} = 31.616$$

$$F = \frac{s_2^2}{s_1^2} = \frac{31.616}{16.834} = 1.878. \qquad (\because \; s_2^2 > s_1^2)$$

**Conclusion.** The calculated value of F is 1.878. The tabulated value of F for $v_2 = 12 - 1 = 11$, $v_1 = 9 - 1 = 8$ d.f at 5% level of significance is 3.315. Since the calculated value of $|F|$ is less than the tabulated value, $H_0$ is accepted. *i.e.,* there is no significant difference between the population variance. *i.e.,* the two populations has the same variance.

## TEST YOUR KNOWLEDGE

**1.** From the following two sample values find out whether they have come from the same population :

| *Sample 1* | 17 | 27 | 18 | 25 | 27 | 29 | 27 | 23 | 17 |
|---|---|---|---|---|---|---|---|---|---|
| *Sample 2* | 16 | 16 | 20 | 16 | 20 | 17 | 15 | 21 | |

**2.** The daily wages in Rupees of skilled workers in two cities are as follows :

| | *Size of sample of workers* | *S.D. of wages in the sample* |
|---|---|---|
| *City A* | 16 | 25 |
| *City B* | 13 | 32 |

**3.** The standard deviation calculated from two random samples of sizes 9 and 13 are 2.1 and 1.8 respectively. May the samples be regrated as drawn from normal populations with the same standard deviation ?

**4.** Two independent samples of size 8 and 9 had the following values of the variables :

| *Sample I* | 20 | 30 | 23 | 25 | 21 | 22 | 23 | 24 | |
|---|---|---|---|---|---|---|---|---|---|
| *Sample II* | 30 | 31 | 32 | 34 | 35 | 29 | 28 | 27 | 26 |

Do the estimates of the population variance differ significantly ?

**Answers**

**1.** rejected **2.** accepted **3.** accepted **4.** accepted.

## 5.19. CHI-SQUARE ($\chi^2$) TEST

When a coin is tossed 200 times, the theoretical considerations lead us to expect 100 heads and 100 tails. But in practice, these results are rarely achieved. The quantity $\chi^2$ (a Greek letter, pronounced as chi-square) describes the magnitude of discrepancy between theory and observation. If $\chi = 0$, the observed and expected frequencies completely coincide. The greater the discrepancy between the observed and expected frequencies, the greater is the value of $\chi^2$. Thus $\chi^2$ **affords a measure of the correspondence between theory and observation.**

If $O_i$ $(i = 1, 2, ......, n)$ is a set of observed (experimental) frequencies and $E_i$ $(i = 1, 2, ......, n)$ is the corresponding set of expected (theoretical or hypothetical) frequencies, then, $\chi^2$ **is defined as**

$$\chi^2 = \sum_{i=1}^{n} \left[ \frac{(O_i - E_i)^2}{E_i} \right]$$

where $\Sigma O_i = \Sigma E_i = N$ (total frequency) and degrees of freedom $(d.f.) = (n - 1)$.

**Note.** (*i*) If $\chi^2 = 0$, the observed and theoretical frequencies agree exactly.

(*ii*) If $\chi^2 > 0$ they do not agree exactly.

### 5.19.1. Degree of Freedom

While comparing the calculated value of $\chi^2$ with the table value, we have to determine the degrees of freedom.

If we have to choose any four numbers whose sum is 50, we can exercise our independent choice for any three numbers only, the fourth being 50 minus the total of the three numbers selected. Thus, though we were to choose any four numbers, our choice was reduced to three because of one condition imposed. There was only one restraint on our freedom and our degrees of freedom were $4 - 1 = 3$. If two restrictions are imposed, our freedom to choose will be further curtailed and degrees of freedom will be $4 - 2 = 2$.

In general, the number of degrees of freedom is the total number of observations less the number of independent constraints imposed on the observations. Degrees of freedom (*d.f.*) are usually denoted by $\nu$ (the letter 'nu' of the Greek alphabet).

Thus, $\nu = n - k$, where $k$ is the number of independent constraints in a set of data of $n$ observations.

**Note.** (*i*) For a $p \times q$ contingency table ($p$ columns and $q$ rows), $\nu = (p - 1)(q - 1)$

(*ii*) In the case of a contingency table, the expected frequency of any class

$$= \frac{\text{Total of row in which it occurs} \times \text{Total of columns in which it occurs}}{\text{Total number of observations}}$$

$\chi^2$ test is one of the simplest and the most general test known. It is applicable to a very large number of problems in practice which can be summed up under the following heads :

(*i*) as a test of goodness of fit.

(*ii*) as a test of independence of attributes.

(*iii*) as a test of homogeneity of independent estimates of the population variance.

(*iv*) as a test of the hypothetical value of the population variance $\sigma^2$.

(*v*) as a list to the homogeneity of independent estimates of the population correlation coefficient.

### 5.19.2. Conditions for Applying $\chi^2$ Test

Following are the conditions which should be satisfied before $\chi^2$ test can be applied.

(*a*) N, the total number of frequencies should be large. It is difficult to say what constitutes largeness, but as an arbitrary figure, we may say that **N should be at least 50,** however, few the cells.

(*b*) No theoretical cell-frequency should be small. Here again, it is difficult to say what constitutes smallness, but 5 should be regarded as the very minimum and **10 is better.** If small theoretical frequencies occur (*i.e.*, < 10), the difficulty is overcome by grouping two or more classes together before calculating (O – E). **It is important to remember that the number of degrees of freedom is determined with the number of classes after regrouping.**

(*c*) The constraints on the cell frequencies, if any, should be linear.

**Note.** If any one of the theoretical frequency is less than 5, then we apply a corrected given by F Yates, which is usually known as 'Yates correction for continuity', we add 0.5 to the cell frequency which is less than 5 and adjust the remaining cell frequency suitably so that the marginal total is not changed.

### 5.19.3. The $\chi^2$ Distribution

For large sample sizes, the sampling distribution of $\chi^2$ can be closely approximated by a continuous curve known as the chi-square distribution. The probability function of $\chi^2$ distribution is given by

$$f(\chi^2) = c(\chi^2)^{(\nu/2-1)}\, e^{-x^2/2}$$

where $e = 2.71828$, $\nu$ = number of degrees of freedom ; $c$ = a constant depending only on $\nu$.

Symbolically, the degrees of freedom are denoted by the symbol $\nu$ or by d.f. and are obtained by the rule $\nu = n - k$, where $k$ refers to the number of independent constraints.

In general, when we fit a binomial distribution the number of degrees of freedom is one less than the number of classes ; when we fit a Poisson distribution the degrees of freedom are 2 less than the number of classes, because we use the total frequency and the arithmetic mean to get the parameter of the Poisson distribution. When we fit a normal curve the number of degrees of freedom are 3 less than the number of classes, because in this fitting we use the total frequency, mean and standard deviation.

If the data is given in a series of "$n$" number then degrees of freedom = $n - 1$.

In the case of Binomial distribution d.f. = $n - 1$

In the case of Poisson distribution d.f. = $n - 2$

In the case of Normal distribution d.f. = $n - 3$.

### 5.19.4. $\chi^2$ Test as a Test of Goodness of Fit

$\chi^2$ test enables us to ascertain how well the theoretical distributions such as Binomial, Poisson or Normal etc. fit empirical distributions, *i.e.*, distributions obtained from sample data.

If the **calculated value of $\chi^2$ is less than the table value** at a specified level (generally 5%) of significance, the **fit is considered to be good** *i.e.*, the divergence between actual and expected frequencies is attributed to fluctuations of simple sampling. If the calculated value of $\chi^2$ is greater than the table value, the fit is considered to be poor.

## ILLUSTRATIVE EXAMPLES

**Example 1.** *The following table gives the number of accidents that took place in an industry during various days of the week. Test if accidents are uniformly distributed over the week.*

| *Day* | *Mon* | *Tue* | *Wed* | *Thu* | *Fri* | *Sat* |
|---|---|---|---|---|---|---|
| *No. of accidents* | *14* | *18* | *12* | *11* | *15* | *14* |

**Sol. Null hypothesis $H_0$.** The accidents are uniformly distributed over the week.

Under this $H_0$, the expected frequencies of the accidents on each of these days $= \dfrac{84}{6} = 14$

| *Observed frequency $O_i$* | 14 | 18 | 12 | 11 | 15 | 14 |
|---|---|---|---|---|---|---|
| *Expected frequency $E_i$* | 14 | 14 | 14 | 14 | 14 | 14 |
| *$(O_i - E_i)^2$* | 0 | 16 | 4 | 9 | 1 | 0 |

$$\chi^2 = \frac{\Sigma(O_i - E_i)^2}{E_i} = \frac{30}{14} = 2.1428.$$

**Conclusion.** Table value of $\chi^2$ at 5% level for (6 – 1 = 5 d.f.) is 11.09.

Since the calculated value of $\chi^2$ is less than the tabulated value, $H_0$ is accepted *i.e.*, the accidents are uniformly distributed over the week.

**Example 2.** *A die is thrown 270 times and the results of these throws are given below :*

| *No. appeared on the die* | *1* | *2* | *3* | *4* | *5* | *6* |
|---|---|---|---|---|---|---|
| *Frequency* | *40* | *32* | *29* | *59* | *57* | *59* |

*Test whether the die is biased or not.*

**Sol. Null hypothesis $H_0$.** Die is unbiased.

Under this $H_0$, the expected frequencies for each digit is $\dfrac{276}{6} = 46$

To find the value of $\chi^2$

| *$O_i$* | 40 | 32 | 29 | 59 | 57 | 59 |
|---|---|---|---|---|---|---|
| *$E_i$* | 46 | 46 | 46 | 46 | 46 | 46 |
| *$(O_i - E_i)^2$* | 36 | 196 | 289 | 169 | 121 | 169 |

$$\chi^2 = \frac{\Sigma(O_i - E_i)^2}{E_i} = \frac{980}{46} = 21.30.$$

**Conclusion.** Tabulated value of $\chi^2$ at 5% level of significance for $(6 - 1 = 5)$ d.f. is 11.09. Since the calculated value of $\chi^2 = 21.30 > 11.07$ the tabulated value, $H_0$ is rejected.

*i.e.,* die is not unbiased or die is biased.

**Example 3.** *The following table shows the distribution of digits in numbers chosen at random from a telephone directory :*

| *Digits* | *0* | *1* | *2* | *3* | *4* | *5* | *6* | *7* | *8* | *9* |
|---|---|---|---|---|---|---|---|---|---|---|
| *Frequency* | *1026* | *1107* | *997* | *966* | *1075* | *933* | *1107* | *972* | *964* | *853* |

*Test whether the digits may be taken to occur equally frequently in the directory.*

**Sol. Null hypothesis $H_0$.** The digits taken in the directory occur equally frequency.

*i.e.,* there is no significant difference between the observed and expected frequency.

Under $H_0$, the expected frequency is given by $= \frac{10,000}{10} = 1000$

To find the value of $\chi^2$

| $O_i$ | 1026 | 1107 | 997 | 996 | 1075 | 1107 | 933 | 972 | 964 | 853 |
|---|---|---|---|---|---|---|---|---|---|---|
| $E_i$ | 1000 | 1000 | 1000 | 1000 | 1000 | 1000 | 1107 | 1000 | 1000 | 1000 |
| $(O_i - E_i)^2$ | 676 | 11449 | 9 | 1156 | 5625 | 11449 | 4489 | 784 | 1296 | 21609 |

$$\chi^2 = \frac{\Sigma(O_i - E_i)^2}{E_i} = \frac{58542}{1000} = 58.542.$$

**Conclusion.** The tabulated value of $\chi^2$ at 5% level of significance for 9 d.f. is 16.919. Since the calculated value of $\chi^2$ is greater than the tabulated value, $H_0$ is rejected.

*i.e.,* there is significant difference between the observed and theoretical frequency.

*i.e.,* the digits taken in the directory do not occur equally frequently.

**Example 4.** *Records taken of the number of male and female births in 800 families having four children are as follows :*

| *No. of male births* | *0* | *1* | *2* | *3* | *4* |
|---|---|---|---|---|---|
| *No. of female births* | *4* | *3* | *2* | *1* | *0* |
| *No. of families* | *32* | *178* | *290* | *236* | *94* |

*Test whether the data are consistent with the hypothesis that the binomial law holds and the chance of male birth is equal to that of female birth, namely $p = q = 1/2$.*

**Sol.** $H_0$ : The data are consistent with the hypothesis of equal probability for male and female births. *i.e.,* $p = q = 1/2$.

We use binomial distribution to calculate theoretical frequency given by :

$$N(r) = N \times P(X = r)$$

where N is the total frequency. N($r$) is the number of families with $r$ male children :

$$P(X = r) = {}^nC_r p^r q^{n-r}$$

where $p$ and $q$ are probability of male and female birth, $n$ is the number of children.

$$N(0) = \text{No. of families with 0 male children} = 800 \times {}^4C_0 \left(\frac{1}{2}\right)^4 = 800 \times 1 \times \frac{1}{2^4} = 50$$

$$N(1) = 800 \times {}^4C_1 \left(\frac{1}{2}\right)^1 \left(\frac{1}{2}\right)^3 = 200 \text{ ; } N(2) = 800 \times {}^4C_2 \left(\frac{1}{2}\right)^2 \left(\frac{1}{2}\right)^2 = 300$$

$$N(3) = 800 \times {}^4C_3 \left(\frac{1}{2}\right)^1 \left(\frac{1}{2}\right)^3 = 200 \text{ ; } N(4) = 800 \times {}^4C_4 \left(\frac{1}{2}\right)^0 \left(\frac{1}{2}\right)^4 = 50$$

| *Observed frequency* $O_i$ | 32 | 178 | 290 | 236 | 94 |
|---|---|---|---|---|---|
| *Expected frequency* $E_i$ | 50 | 200 | 300 | 200 | 50 |
| $(O_i - E_i)^2$ | 324 | 484 | 100 | 1296 | 1936 |
| $\frac{(O_i - E_i)^2}{E_i}$ | 6.48 | 2.42 | 0.333 | 6.48 | 38.72 |

$$\chi^2 = \frac{\Sigma(O_i - E_i)^2}{E_i} = 54.433.$$

**Conclusion.** Table value of $\chi^2$ at 5% level of significance for $5 - 1 = 4$ d.f. is 9.49.

Since the calculated value of $\chi^2$ is greater than the tabulated value, $H_0$ is rejected. *i.e.,* the data are not consistent with the hypothesis that the binomial law holds and that the chance of a male birth is not equal to that of a female birth.

**Note.** Since the fitting is binomial, the degrees of freedom $\nu = n - 1$ *i.e.,* $\nu = 5 - 1 = 4$.

**Example 5.** *Verify whether Poisson distribution can be assumed from the data given below :*

| *No. of defects* | *0* | *1* | *2* | *3* | *4* | *5* |
|---|---|---|---|---|---|---|
| *Frequency* | *6* | *13* | *13* | *8* | *4* | *3* |

**Sol.** $H_0$ : Poisson fit is a good fit to the data.

$$\text{Mean of the given distribution} = \frac{\Sigma f_i x_i}{\Sigma f_i} = \frac{94}{47} = 2$$

To fit a Poisson distribution we require $m$. Parameter $m = \bar{x} = 2$.

By Poisson distribution the frequency of $r$ success is

$$N(r) = N \times e^{-m} \cdot \frac{m^r}{r!}, \text{ N is the total frequency.}$$

$$N(0) = 47 \times e^{-2} . \frac{(2)^0}{0!} = 6.36 \approx 6 ; N(1) = 47 \times e^{-2} . \frac{(2)^1}{1!} = 12.72 \approx 13$$

$$N(2) = 47 \times e^{-2} . \frac{(2)^2}{2!} = 12.72 \approx 13 ; N(3) = 47 \times e^{-2} . \frac{(2)^3}{3!} = 8.48 \approx 9$$

$$N(4) = 47 \times e^{-2} . \frac{(2)^4}{4!} = 4.24 \approx 4 ; N(5) = 47 \times e^{-2} . \frac{(2)^5}{5!} = 1.696 \approx 2.$$

| $X$ | 0 | 1 | 2 | 3 | 4 | 5 |
|---|---|---|---|---|---|---|
| $O_i$ | 6 | 13 | 13 | 8 | 4 | 3 |
| $E_i$ | 6.36 | 12.72 | 12.72 | 8.48 | 4.24 | 1.696 |
| $\frac{(O_i - E_i)^2}{E_i}$ | 0.2037 | 0.00616 | 0.00616 | 0.02716 | 0.0135 | 1.0026 |

$$\chi^2 = \frac{\Sigma(O_i - E_i)^2}{E_i} = 1.2864.$$

**Conclusion.** The calculated value of $\chi^2$ is 1.2864. Tabulated value of $\chi^2$ at 5% level of significance for $\gamma = 6 - 2 = 4$ d.f. is 9.49. Since the calculated value of $\chi^2$ is less than that of tabulated value. $H_0$ is accepted *i.e.,* Poisson distribution provides a good fit to the data.

**Example 6.** *The theory predicts the proportion of beans in the four groups, $G_1$, $G_2$, $G_3$, $G_4$ should be in the ratio 9 : 3 : 3 : 1. In an experiment with 1600 beans the numbers in the four groups were 882, 313, 287 and 118. Does the experimental result support the theory.*

**Sol.** $H_0$ . The experimental result support the theory. *i.e.,* there is no significant difference between the observed and theoretical frequency under $H_0$, the theoretical frequency can be calculated as follows :

$$E(G_1) = \frac{1600 \times 9}{16} = 900 ; E(G_2) = \frac{1600 \times 3}{16} = 300 ;$$

$$E(G_3) = \frac{1600 \times 3}{16} = 300 ; E(G_4) = \frac{1600 \times 1}{16} = 100$$

To calculate the value of $\chi^2$.

| *Observed frequency $O_i$* | 882 | 313 | 287 | 118 |
|---|---|---|---|---|
| *Expected frequency $E_i$* | 900 | 300 | 300 | 100 |
| $\frac{(O_i - E_i)^2}{E_i}$ | 0.36 | 0.5633 | 0.5633 | 3.24 |

$$\chi^2 = \frac{\Sigma(O_i - E_i)^2}{E_i} = 4.7266.$$

**Conclusion.** Table value of $\chi^2$ at 5% level of significance for 3 d.f. is 7.815. Since the calculated value of $\chi^2$ is less than that of the tabulated value. Hence $H_0$ is accepted.
*i.e.,* the experimental result support the theory.

## TEST YOUR KNOWLEDGE

**1.** The following table gives the frequency of occupance of the digits 0, 1, ......, 9 in the last place in four logarithm of numbers 10–99. Examine if there is any peculiarity.

| *Digits* | 0 | 1 | 2 | 3 | 4 | 5 | 6 | 7 | 8 | 9 |
|---|---|---|---|---|---|---|---|---|---|---|
| *Frequency* | 6 | 16 | 15 | 10 | 12 | 12 | 3 | 2 | 9 | 5 |

**2.** The sales in a supermarket during a week are given below. Test the hypothesis that the sales do not depend on the day of the week, using a significant level of 0.05.

| *Days* | Mon | Tues | Wed | Thurs | Fri | Sat |
|---|---|---|---|---|---|---|
| *Sales (in ₹ 1000)* | 65 | 54 | 60 | 56 | 71 | 84 |

**3.** A survey of 320 families with 5 children each revealed the following information :

| *No. of boys* | 5 | 4 | 3 | 2 | 1 | 0 |
|---|---|---|---|---|---|---|
| *No. of girls* | 0 | 1 | 2 | 3 | 4 | 5 |
| *No. of families* | 14 | 56 | 110 | 88 | 40 | 12 |

Is this result consistent with the hypothesis that male and female birth are equally probable ?

**4.** 4 coins were tossed at a time and this operation is repeated 160 times. It is found that 4 heads occur 6 times, 3 heads occur 43 times, 2 heads occur 69 times, one head occur 34 times. Discuss whether the coin may be regarded as unbiased ?

**5.** Fit a Poisson distribution to the following data and best the goodness of fit :

| $x$ | 0 | 1 | 2 | 3 | 4 |
|---|---|---|---|---|---|
| $f$ | 109 | 65 | 22 | 3 | 1 |

**6.** In the accounting department of bank, 100 accounts are selected at random and estimated for errors. The following results were obtained :

| *No. of errors* | 0 | 1 | 2 | 3 | 4 | 5 | 6 |
|---|---|---|---|---|---|---|---|
| *No. of accounts* | 35 | 40 | 19 | 2 | 0 | 2 | 2 |

Does this information verify that the errors are distributed according to the Poisson probability law ?

**7.** A sample analysis of examination results of 500 students, it was found that 280 students have failed, 170 have secured a third class, 90 have secured a second class and the rest, a first class. Do these figures support the general belief that above categories are in the ratio 4 : 3 : 2 : 1 respectively ?

**8.** A set of 5 similar coins are tossed 320 times and the following results were obtained.

| *No. of Heads* | 0 | 1 | 2 | 3 | 4 | 5 |
|---|---|---|---|---|---|---|
| *Frequency* | 6 | 27 | 72 | 112 | 71 | 32 |

Fit a Binomial distribution and test the goodness of fit at 5% level of significance.

(*M.G.U. Jan. 2007*)

**9.** Fit a Poisson distribution to the following data and lost for its goodness of fit at level of signification 0.05.

| $x$ | 0 | 1 | 2 | 3 | 4 |
|---|---|---|---|---|---|
| $f$ | 319 | 252 | 124 | 46 | 13 |

(*M.G.U. Nov. 2009*)

### Answers

**1.** no **2.** accepted **3.** accepted **4.** unbiased

**5.** Poisson law fits the data **6.** may be **7.** yes

**8.** Mean = 2.97, $(.594 + .406)^5\ 320$.

**9.** $P(x) = e^{-.915119363} \frac{(.915119363)^x}{x\,!}$, N = 754 $NP(x) = 302 \frac{(.915119363)^x}{x\,!}$, $x = 0, 1, 2, 3, 4$, theoretical frequencies are 302, 277, 127, 39, 9 respectively $\chi^2 = \sum_i \frac{(0_i - E_i)}{E_i} = 6.318$.

$\chi^2$ at 5% level of significance for 3 d.o.f. is 7.815 ; But the calculated value is 6.318, which is less than 7.815. Hence the Poisson distribution provides a good fit to the data.

## ADDITIONAL PROBLEMS

**1.** A random sample of size $n = 100$ is taken from a population with $\sigma = 5.1$. Given that the sample mean $\bar{x} = 21.6$. Construct a 95% confidence interval for $\mu$, the population mean.

**2.** A random sample of size 11 from a normal population is formed to have variance 12.3. Find a 95% confidence interval for $\sigma^2$.

**3.** Fit a Poisson Distribution to the following data :

| $x$ | : | 0 | 1 | 2 | 3 | 4 | 5 | 6 | 7 |
|---|---|---|---|---|---|---|---|---|---|
| $f$ | : | 48 | 92 | 125 | 100 | 87 | 35 | 13 | 6 |

Test for goodness of fit at 5% level of significance.

### Answers

**1.** [20.6, 22.6] **2.** $6 < \sigma^2 < 37.88$ **3.** $P(x) = e^{-2.54} \frac{(2.54)^x}{x\,!}$.

# APPENDIX—I

## Table 1 : NORMAL TABLE
### AREAS UNDER THE STANDARD NORMAL

$$\text{CURVE} = \frac{1}{\sqrt{2\pi}} \int_0^z e^{-\frac{z^2}{2}} dz$$

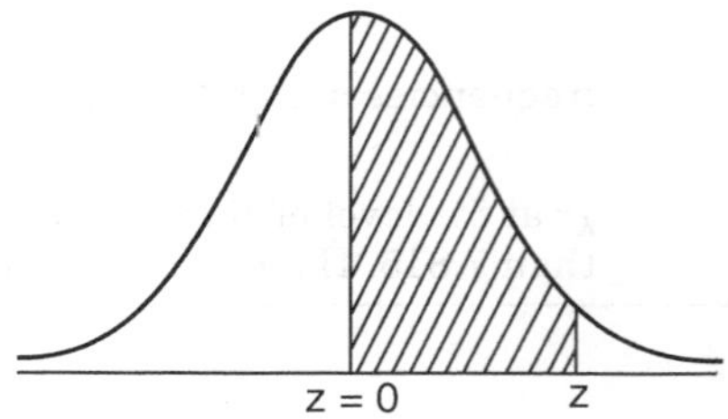


| z | .00 | .01 | .02 | .03 | .04 | .05 | .06 | .07 | .08 | .09 |
|---|---|---|---|---|---|---|---|---|---|---|
| 0.0 | .0000 | .0040 | .0080 | .0120 | .0160 | .0199 | .0239 | .0279 | .0319 | .0359 |
| 0.1 | .0398 | .0438 | .0478 | .0517 | .0557 | .0596 | .0636 | .0675 | .0714 | .0754 |
| 0.2 | .0793 | .0832 | .0871 | .0910 | .0948 | .0987 | .1026 | .1064 | .1103 | .1141 |
| 0.3 | .1179 | .1217 | .1255 | .1293 | .1331 | .1368 | .1406 | .1443 | .1480 | .1517 |
| 0.4 | .1554 | .1591 | .1628 | .1664 | .1700 | .1736 | .1772 | .1808 | .1844 | .1879 |
| 0.5 | .1915 | .1950 | .1985 | .2019 | .2054 | .2088 | .2123 | .2157 | .2190 | .2224 |
| 0.6 | .2257 | .2291 | .2324 | .2357 | .2389 | .2422 | .2454 | .2485 | .2517 | .2549 |
| 0.7 | .2580 | .2611 | .2642 | .2673 | .2704 | .2734 | .2764 | .2794 | .2823 | .2852 |
| 0.8 | .2881 | .2910 | .2939 | .2967 | .2995 | .3023 | .3051 | .3078 | .3106 | .3133 |
| 0.9 | .3159 | .3186 | .3212 | .3238 | .3264 | .3289 | .3315 | .3340 | .3365 | .3389 |
| 1.0 | .3413 | .3438 | .3461 | .3485 | .3508 | .3531 | .3554 | .3577 | .3599 | .3621 |
| 1.1 | .3643 | .3665 | .3686 | .3708 | .8729 | .3749 | .3770 | .3790 | .3810 | .3830 |
| 1.2 | .3849 | .3869 | .3888 | .3907 | .3925 | .3944 | .3962 | .3980 | .3997 | .4015 |
| 1.3 | .4032 | .4049 | .4066 | .4082 | .4099 | .4115 | .4131 | .4147 | .4162 | .4177 |
| 1.4 | .4192 | .4207 | .4222 | .4236 | .4251 | .4255 | .4279 | .4292 | .4306 | .4319 |
| 1.5 | .4332 | .4345 | .4357 | .4370 | .4382 | .4394 | .4406 | .4418 | .4429 | .4441 |
| 1.6 | .4452 | .4463 | .4474 | .4484 | .4495 | .4505 | .4515 | .4525 | .4535 | .4545 |
| 1.7 | .4554 | .4564 | .4573 | .4582 | .4591 | .4599 | .4608 | .4616 | .4625 | .4633 |
| 1.8 | .4641 | .4649 | .4656 | .4664 | .4671 | .4678 | .4686 | .4693 | .4699 | .4706 |
| 1.9 | .4713 | .4719 | .4726 | .4732 | .4738 | .4744 | .4750 | .4756 | .4761 | .4767 |
| 2.0 | .4772 | .4778 | .4783 | .4788 | .4793 | .4798 | .4803 | .4808 | .4812 | .4817 |
| 2.1 | .4821 | .4826 | .4830 | .4834 | .4838 | .4842 | .4846 | .4850 | .4854 | .4857 |
| 2.2 | .4861 | .4864 | .4868 | .4871 | .4875 | .4878 | .4881 | .4884 | .4887 | .4890 |
| 2.3 | .4893 | .4896 | .4898 | .4901 | .4904 | .4906 | .4909 | .4911 | .4913 | .4916 |
| 2.4 | .4918 | .4920 | .4922 | .4925 | .4927 | .4929 | .4931 | .4932 | .4934 | .4936 |
| 2.5 | .4938 | .4940 | .4941 | .4943 | .4945 | .4946 | .4948 | .4949 | .4951 | .4952 |
| 2.6 | .4953 | .4955 | .4956 | .4957 | .4959 | .4930 | .4961 | .4962 | .4963 | .4964 |
| 2.7 | .4965 | .4966 | .4967 | .4968 | .4969 | .4970 | .4971 | .4972 | .4973 | .4974 |
| 2.8 | .4974 | .4975 | .4976 | .4977 | .4977 | .4978 | .4979 | .4979 | .4980 | .4981 |
| 2.9 | .4981 | .4982 | .4982 | .4983 | .4984 | .4984 | .4985 | .4985 | .4986 | .4986 |
| 3.0 | .4987 | .4987 | .4987 | .4988 | .4988 | .4989 | .4999 | .4989 | .4990 | .4990 |
| 3.1 | .4990 | .4991 | .4991 | .4991 | .4992 | .4992 | .4992 | .4992 | .4993 | .4993 |

# Table 2 : SIGNIFICANT VALUES $t_v$ ($\alpha$) OF t-DISTRIBUTION (TWO TAIL AREAS) [ | t | > $t_v(\alpha)$] = $\alpha$

| *d.f.* | *Probability (Level of Significance)* | | | | | |
|---|---|---|---|---|---|---|
| (v) | *0.50* | *0.10* | *0.05* | *0.02* | *0.01* | *0.001* |
| 1 | 1.00 | 6.31 | 12.71 | 31.82 | 63.66 | 636.62 |
| 2 | 0.82 | 0.92 | 4.30 | 6.97 | 6.93 | 31.60 |
| 3 | 0.77 | 2.32 | 3.18 | 4.54 | 5.84 | 12.94 |
| 4 | 0.74 | 2.13 | 2.78 | 3.75 | 4.60 | 8.61 |
| 5 | 0.73 | 2.02 | 2.57 | 3.37 | 4.03 | 6.86 |
| 6 | 0.72 | 1.94 | 2.45 | 3.14 | 3.71 | 5.96 |
| 7 | 0.71 | 1.90 | 2.37 | 3.00 | 3.50 | 5.41 |
| 8 | 0.71 | 1.80 | 2.31 | 2.90 | 3.36 | 5.04 |
| 9 | 0.70 | 1.83 | 2.26 | 2.82 | 3.25 | 4.78 |
| 10 | 0.70 | 1.81 | 2.23 | 2.76 | 3.17 | 4.59 |
| 11 | 0.70 | 1.80 | 2.20 | 2.72 | 3.11 | 4.44 |
| 12 | 0.70 | 1.78 | 2.18 | 2.68 | 3.06 | 4.32 |
| 13 | 0.69 | 1.77 | 2.16 | 2.05 | 3.01 | 4.22 |
| 14 | 0.69 | 1.76 | 2.15 | 2.62 | 2.98 | 4.14 |
| 15 | 0.69 | 1.75 | 2.13 | 2.60 | 2.95 | 4.07 |
| 16 | 0.69 | 1.75 | 2.12 | 2.58 | 2.92 | 4.02 |
| 17 | 0.69 | 1.74 | 2.11 | 2.57 | 2.90 | 3.97 |
| 18 | 0.69 | 1.73 | 2.10 | 2.55 | 2.88 | 3.92 |
| 19 | 0.69 | 1.73 | 2.09 | 2.54 | 2.86 | 3.88 |
| 20 | 0.69 | 1.73 | 2.09 | 2.53 | 2.85 | 3.85 |
| 21 | 0.69 | 1.72 | 2.08 | 2.52 | 2.83 | 3.83 |
| 22 | 0.69 | 1.72 | 2.07 | 2.51 | 2.42 | 3.79 |
| 23 | 0.69 | 1.71 | 2.07 | 2.50 | 2.81 | 3.77 |
| 24 | 0.69 | 1.71 | 2.06 | 2.49 | 2.80 | 3.75 |
| 25 | 0.68 | 1.71 | 2.06 | 2.49 | 2.79 | 3.73 |
| 26 | 0.68 | 1.71 | 2.06 | 2.48 | 2.78 | 3.71 |
| 27 | 0.68 | 1.70 | 2.05 | 2.47 | 2.77 | 3.69 |
| 28 | 0.68 | 1.70 | 2.05 | 2.47 | 2.76 | 3.67 |
| 29 | 0.68 | 1.70 | 2.05 | 2.46 | 2.76 | 3.66 |
| 30 | 0.68 | 1.70 | 2.04 | 2.46 | 2.75 | 3.65 |
| $\infty$ | 0.67 | 1.65 | 1.96 | 2.33 | 2.58 | 3.29 |

## Table 3 : F-Distribution
## Values of F for F-Distributions with 0.05 of the Area in the Right Tail

| | *Degrees of freedom for numerator* | | | | | | | | | | | | | | | | | | |
|---|---|---|---|---|---|---|---|---|---|---|---|---|---|---|---|---|---|---|---|
| | *1* | *2* | *3* | *4* | *5* | *6* | *7* | *8* | *9* | *10* | *12* | *15* | *20* | *24* | *30* | *40* | *60* | *120* | *∞* |
| 1 | 161 | 200 | 216 | 225 | 230 | 234 | 237 | 239 | 241 | 242 | 244 | 246 | 248 | 249 | 250 | 251 | 252 | 253 | 254 |
| 2 | 18.5 | 19.0 | 19.2 | 19.2 | 19.3 | 19.3 | 19.4 | 19.4 | 19.4 | 19.4 | 19.4 | 19.4 | 19.4 | 19.5 | 19.5 | 19.5 | 19.5 | 19.5 | 19.5 |
| 3 | 10.1 | 9.55 | 9.28 | 9.12 | 9.01 | 9.94 | 8.89 | 8.85 | 8.81 | 8.79 | 8.74 | 8.70 | 8.66 | 8.64 | 8.62 | 8.59 | 8.57 | 8.55 | 8.53 |
| 4 | 7.71 | 6.94 | 6.59 | 6.39 | 6.26 | 6.16 | 6.09 | 6.04 | 6.00 | 5.96 | 5.91 | 5.86 | 5.80 | 5.77 | 5.75 | 5.72 | 5.69 | 5.66 | 5.63 |
| 5 | 6.61 | 5.79 | 5.41 | 5.19 | 5.05 | 4.95 | 4.88 | 4.82 | 4.77 | 4.74 | 4.68 | 4.62 | 4.56 | 4.53 | 4.50 | 4.46 | 4.43 | 4.40 | 4.37 |
| 6 | 5.99 | 5.14 | 4.76 | 4.53 | 4.39 | 4.28 | 4.21 | 4.15 | 4.10 | 4.06 | 4.00 | 3.94 | 3.87 | 3.84 | 3.81 | 3.77 | 3.74 | 3.70 | 3.67 |
| 7 | 5.59 | 4.74 | 4.35 | 4.12 | 3.97 | 3.87 | 3.79 | 3.73 | 3.68 | 3.64 | 3.57 | 3.51 | 3.44 | 3.41 | 3.38 | 3.34 | 3.30 | 3.27 | 3.23 |
| 8 | 5.32 | 4.46 | 4.07 | 3.84 | 3.69 | 3.58 | 3.50 | 3.44 | 3.39 | 3.35 | 3.28 | 3.22 | 3.15 | 3.12 | 3.08 | 3.04 | 3.01 | 2.97 | 2.93 |
| 9 | 5.12 | 4.26 | 3.86 | 3.63 | 3.48 | 3.37 | 3.29 | 3.23 | 3.18 | 3.14 | 3.07 | 3.01 | 2.94 | 2.90 | 2.86 | 2.83 | 2.79 | 2.75 | 2.71 |
| 10 | 4.96 | 4.10 | 3.71 | 3.48 | 3.33 | 3.22 | 3.14 | 3.07 | 3.02 | 2.98 | 2.91 | 2.85 | 2.77 | 2.74 | 2.70 | 2.66 | 2.62 | 2.58 | 2.54 |
| 11 | 4.84 | 3.98 | 3.59 | 3.36 | 3.20 | 3.09 | 3.01 | 2.95 | 2.90 | 2.85 | 2.79 | 2.72 | 2.65 | 2.61 | 2.57 | 2.53 | 2.49 | 2.45 | 2.40 |
| 12 | 4.75 | 3.89 | 3.49 | 3.26 | 3.11 | 3.00 | 2.91 | 2.85 | 2.80 | 2.75 | 2.69 | 2.62 | 2.54 | 2.51 | 2.47 | 2.43 | 2.38 | 2.34 | 2.30 |
| 13 | 4.67 | 3.81 | 3.41 | 3.18 | 3.03 | 2.92 | 2.83 | 2.77 | 2.71 | 2.67 | 2.60 | 2.53 | 2.46 | 2.42 | 2.38 | 2.34 | 2.30 | 2.25 | 2.21 |
| 14 | 4.60 | 3.74 | 3.34 | 3.11 | 3.96 | 2.85 | 2.76 | 2.70 | 2.65 | 2.60 | 2.53 | 2.46 | 2.39 | 2.35 | 2.31 | 2.27 | 2.22 | 2.18 | 2.13 |
| 15 | 4.54 | 3.68 | 3.29 | 3.06 | 3.90 | 2.79 | 2.71 | 2.64 | 2.59 | 2.54 | 2.48 | 2.40 | 2.33 | 2.29 | 2.25 | 2.20 | 2.16 | 2.11 | 2.07 |
| 16 | 4.49 | 3.63 | 3.24 | 3.01 | 2.85 | 2.74 | 2.66 | 2.59 | 2.54 | 2.49 | 2.42 | 2.35 | 2.28 | 2.24 | 2.19 | 2.15 | 2.11 | 2.06 | 2.01 |
| 17 | 4.45 | 3.59 | 3.20 | 2.96 | 2.81 | 2.70 | 2.61 | 2.55 | 2.49 | 2.45 | 2.38 | 2.31 | 2.23 | 2.19 | 2.15 | 2.10 | 2.06 | 2.01 | 1.96 |
| 18 | 4.41 | 3.55 | 3.16 | 2.93 | 2.77 | 2.66 | 2.58 | 2.51 | 2.46 | 2.41 | 2.34 | 2.27 | 2.19 | 2.15 | 2.11 | 2.06 | 2.02 | 1.97 | 1.92 |
| 19 | 4.38 | 3.52 | 3.13 | 2.90 | 2.74 | 2.63 | 2.54 | 2.48 | 2.42 | 2.38 | 2.31 | 2.23 | 2.16 | 2.11 | 2.07 | 2.03 | 1.98 | 1.93 | 1.88 |
| 20 | 4.35 | 3.49 | 3.10 | 2.87 | 2.17 | 2.60 | 2.51 | 2.45 | 2.39 | 2.35 | 2.28 | 2.20 | 2.12 | 2.08 | 2.04 | 1.99 | 1.95 | 1.90 | 1.84 |
| 21 | 4.32 | 3.47 | 3.07 | 2.84 | 2.68 | 2.57 | 2.49 | 2.42 | 2.37 | 2.32 | 2.25 | 2.18 | 2.10 | 2.05 | 2.01 | 1.96 | 1.92 | 1.87 | 1.81 |
| 22 | 4.30 | 3.44 | 3.05 | 2.82 | 2.66 | 2.55 | 2.46 | 2.40 | 2.34 | 2.30 | 2.23 | 2.15 | 2.07 | 2.03 | 1.98 | 1.94 | 1.89 | 1.84 | 1.78 |
| 23 | 4.28 | 3.42 | 3.03 | 2.80 | 2.64 | 2.53 | 2.44 | 2.37 | 2.32 | 2.27 | 2.20 | 2.13 | 2.05 | 2.01 | 1.96 | 1.91 | 1.86 | 1.81 | 1.76 |
| 24 | 4.26 | 3.40 | 3.01 | 2.78 | 2.62 | 2.51 | 2.42 | 2.36 | 2.30 | 2.25 | 2.18 | 2.11 | 2.03 | 1.98 | 1.94 | 1.98 | 1.84 | 1.79 | 1.73 |
| 25 | 4.24 | 3.39 | 2.99 | 2.76 | 2.60 | 2.94 | 2.40 | 2.34 | 2.28 | 2.24 | 2.16 | 2.29 | 2.01 | 1.96 | 1.92 | 1.87 | 1.82 | 1.77 | 1.71 |
| 30 | 4.17 | 3.32 | 2.92 | 2.69 | 2.53 | 2.42 | 2.33 | 2.27 | 2.21 | 2.16 | 2.09 | 2.01 | 1.93 | 1.89 | 1.84 | 1.79 | 1.74 | 1.64 | 1.62 |
| 40 | 4.08 | 3.23 | 2.84 | 2.61 | 2.45 | 2.34 | 2.25 | 2.18 | 2.12 | 2.08 | 2.00 | 1.92 | 1.84 | 1.79 | 1.74 | 1.69 | 1.64 | 1.58 | 1.51 |
| 60 | 4.00 | 3.15 | 2.76 | 2.53 | 2.37 | 2.25 | 2.17 | 2.10 | 2.04 | 1.99 | 1.92 | 1.84 | 1.75 | 1.70 | 1.65 | 1.59 | 1.53 | 1.47 | 1.39 |
| 120 | 3.92 | 3.07 | 2.68 | 2.45 | 2.29 | 2.18 | 2.09 | 2.02 | 1.96 | 1.91 | 1.83 | 1.75 | 1.66 | 1.61 | 1.55 | 1.50 | 1.43 | 1.35 | 1.25 |
| ∞ | 3.84 | 3.00 | 2.60 | 2.37 | 2.21 | 2.10 | 2.01 | 1.94 | 1.88 | 1.83 | 1.75 | 1.67 | 1.57 | 1.52 | 1.46 | 1.39 | 1.32 | 1.22 | 1.00 |

## Table 4 : CHI-SQUARE
**Significant Values $\chi^2$ ($\alpha$) of Chi-Square Distribution Right Tail Areas for Given Probability $\alpha$,**

**$P = P_r (\chi^2 > \chi^2 (\alpha)) = \alpha$**

**And is Degrees of Freedom (d.f.)**

| *Degree of freedom (ν)* | *Probability (Level of Significance)* | | | | | | |
|---|---|---|---|---|---|---|---|
| | *0 = .99* | *0.95* | *0.50* | *0.10* | *0.05* | *0.02* | *0.01* |
| 1 | .000157 | .00393 | .455 | 2.706 | 3.841 | 5.214 | 6.635 |
| 2 | .0201 | .103 | 1.386 | 4.605 | 5.991 | 7.824 | 9.210 |
| 3 | .115 | .352 | 2.366 | 6.251 | 7.815 | 9.837 | 11.341 |
| 4 | .297 | .711 | 3.357 | 7.779 | 9.488 | 11.668 | 13.277 |
| 5 | .554 | 1.145 | 4.351 | 9.236 | 11.070 | 13.388 | 15.086 |
| 6 | .872 | 2.635 | 5.348 | 10.645 | 12.592 | 15.033 | 16.812 |
| 7 | 1.239 | 2.167 | 6.346 | 12.017 | 14.067 | 16.622 | 18.475 |
| 8 | 1.646 | 2.733 | 7.344 | 13.362 | 15.507 | 18.168 | 20.090 |
| 9 | 2.088 | 3.325 | 8.343 | 14.684 | 16.919 | 19.679 | 21.669 |
| 10 | 2.558 | 3.940 | 9.340 | 15.987 | 18.307 | 21.161 | 23.209 |
| 11 | 3.053 | 4.575 | 10.341 | 17.275 | 19.675 | 22.618 | 24.725 |
| 12 | 3.571 | 5.226 | 11.340 | 18.549 | 21.026 | 24.054 | 26.217 |
| 13 | 4.107 | 5.892 | 12.340 | 19.812 | 22.362 | 25.472 | 27.688 |
| 14 | 4.660 | 6.571 | 13.339 | 21.064 | 23.685 | 26.873 | 29.141 |
| 15 | 4.229 | 7.261 | 14.339 | 22.307 | 24.996 | 28.259 | 30.578 |
| 16 | 5.812 | 7.962 | 15.338 | 23.542 | 26.296 | 29.633 | 32.000 |
| 17 | 6.408 | 8.672 | 15.338 | 24.769 | 27.587 | 30.995 | 33.409 |
| 18 | 7.015 | 9.390 | 17.338 | 25.989 | 28.869 | 32.346 | 34.805 |
| 19 | 7.633 | 10.117 | 18.338 | 27.204 | 30.144 | 33.687 | 36.191 |
| 20 | 8.260 | 10.851 | 19.337 | 28.412 | 31.410 | 35.020 | 37.566 |
| 21 | 8.897 | 11.591 | 20.337 | 29.615 | 32.671 | 36.343 | 38.932 |
| 22 | 9.542 | 12.338 | 21.337 | 30.813 | 33.924 | 37.659 | 40.289 |
| 23 | 10.196 | 13.091 | 22.337 | 32.007 | 35.172 | 38.968 | 41.638 |
| 24 | 10.856 | 13.848 | 23.337 | 32.196 | 36.415 | 40.270 | 42.980 |
| 25 | 11.524 | 14.611 | 24.337 | 34.382 | 37.65 | 41.566 | 44.314 |
| 26 | 12.198 | 15.379 | 25.336 | 35.363 | 38.885 | 41.856 | 45.642 |
| 27 | 12.879 | 16.151 | 26.336 | 36.741 | 40.113 | 41.140 | 46.963 |
| 28 | 13.565 | 16.928 | 27.336 | 37.916 | 41.337 | 45.419 | 48.278 |
| 29 | 14.256 | 17.708 | 28.336 | 39.087 | 42.557 | 46.693 | 49.588 |
| 30 | 14.933 | 18.493 | 29.336 | 40.256 | 43.773 | 47.962 | 50.892 |

**Note.** For degrees of freedom (ν) greater than 30, the quantity $\sqrt{2\chi^2} - \sqrt{2\nu - 1}$ may be used as a normal variate with unit variance.

# APPENDIX—II

## SOME IMPORTANT CURVES

Cissoid (Imp.)

$y^2(2a - x) = x^3$

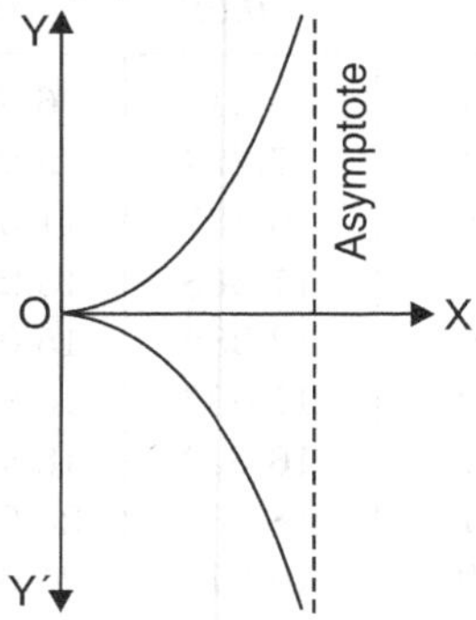


Catenary

$y = a \cosh \frac{x}{a}$

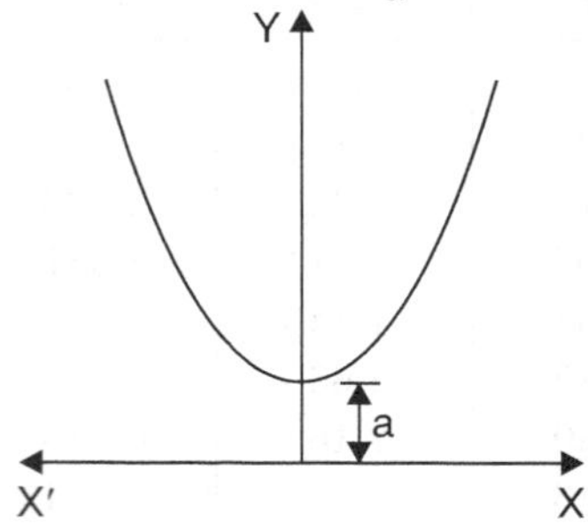


Cubical Parabola

$a^2 y = x^3$

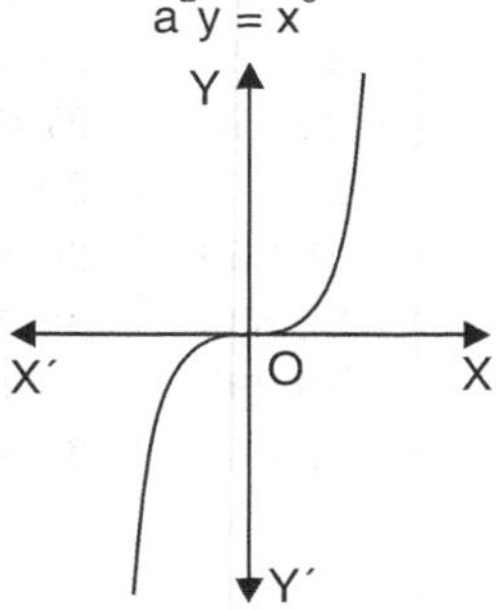


Semicubical Parabola

$ay^2 = x^3$

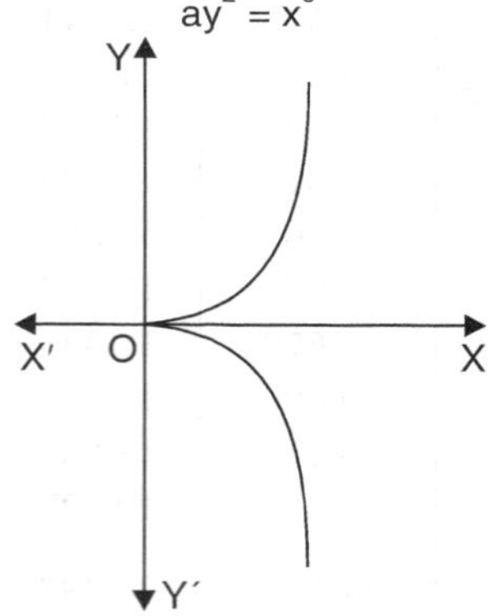


Strophoid

$y^2(a - x) = x^2(a + x)$

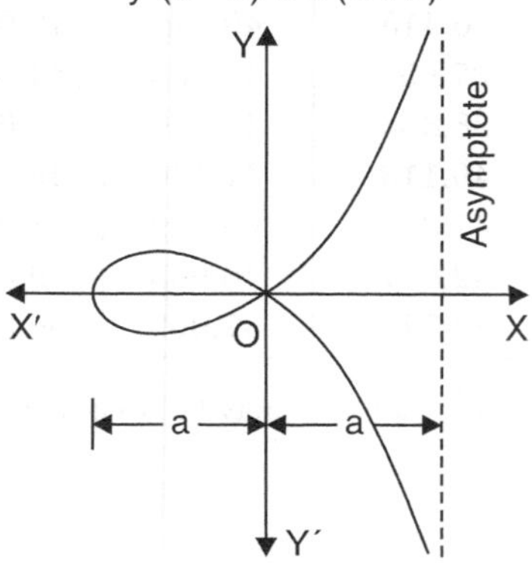


Folium of Descartes

$x^3 + y^3 = 3axy$

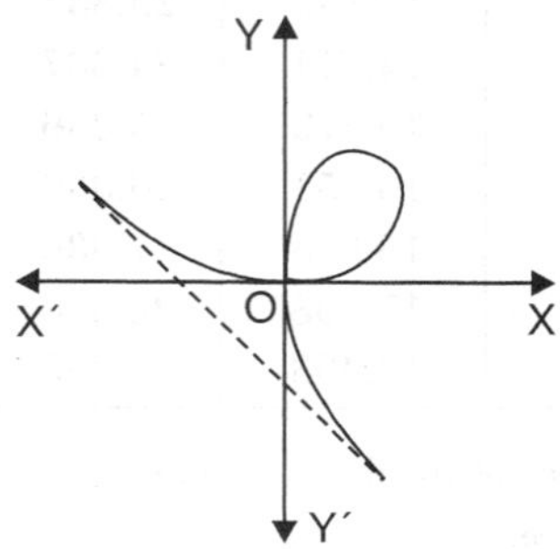

Hypocycloid (Imp.)

$x^{2/3} + y^{2/3} = a^{2/3}$

$x = a\cos^3\theta \quad y = a\sin^3\theta$

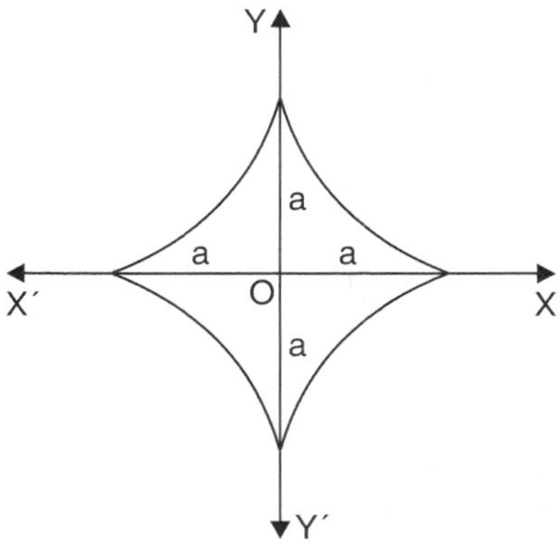


Witon of Agnesi

$xy^2 = 4a^2(2a - x)$

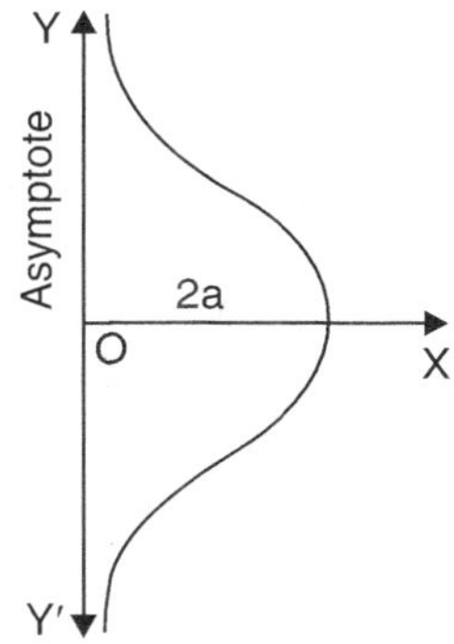


Cardioid (Imp.)

$r = a(1 + \cos\theta)$

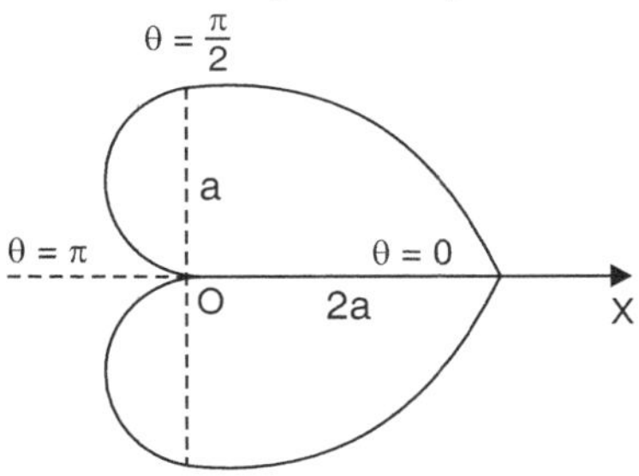


Cardioid (Imp.)

$r = a(1 - \cos\theta)$

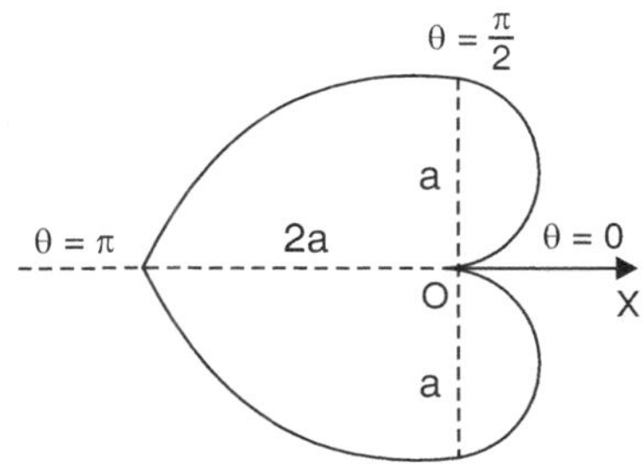


Cycloid (Most Imp.)

$x = a(\theta + \sin\theta)$

$y = a(1 - \cos\theta)$

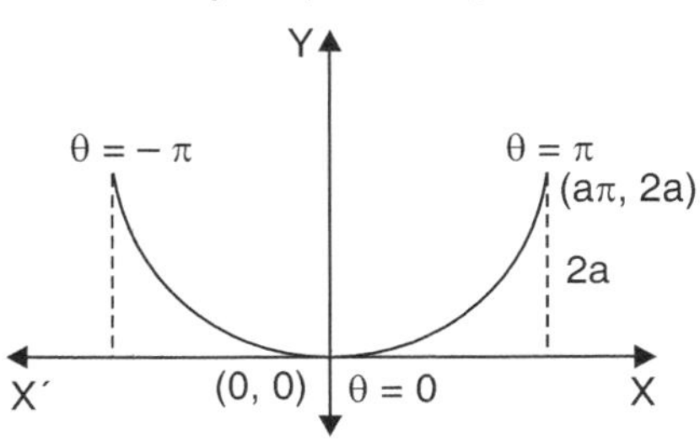


Cycloid

$x = a(\theta - \sin\theta)$

$y = a(1 + \cos\theta)$

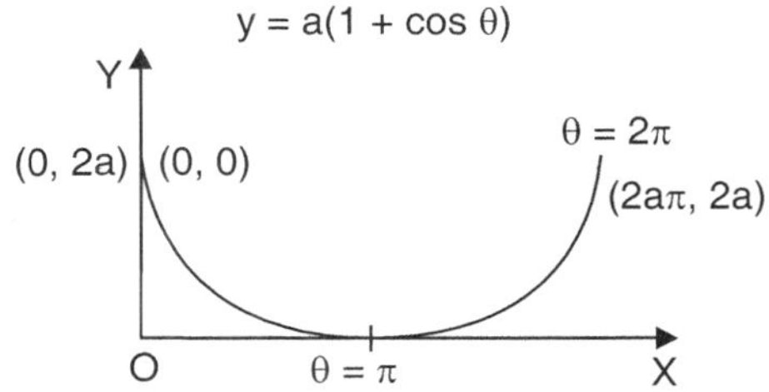

Cycloid (Imp.)
$x = a(\theta - \sin\theta)$
$y = a(1 - \cos\theta)$

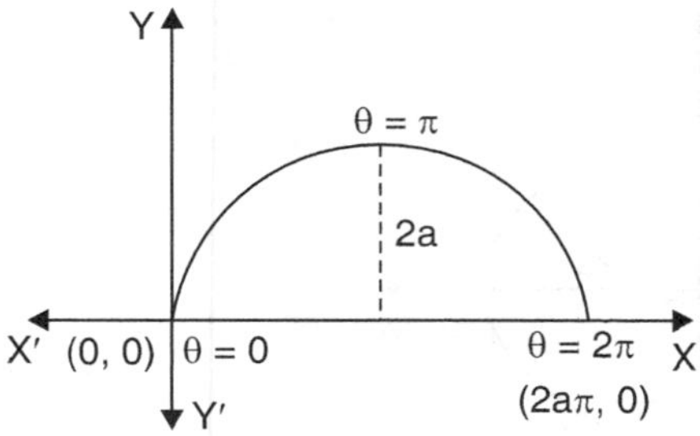


Cycloid
$x = a(\theta + \sin\theta)$
$y = a(1 + \cos\theta)$

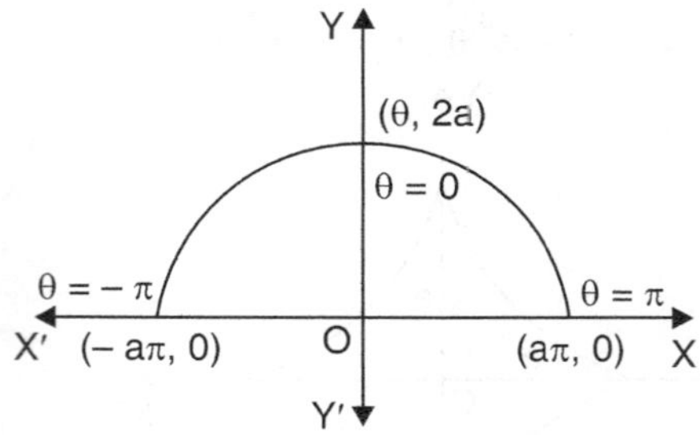


Lemniscate
$r^2 = a^2 \cos 2\theta$

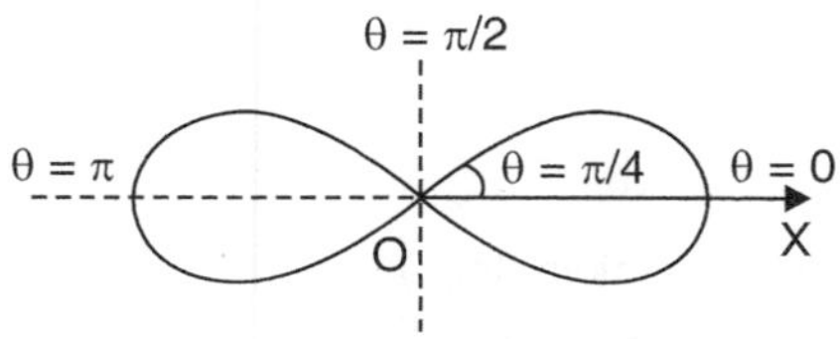


The three leaved rose
$r = a \sin 3\theta$

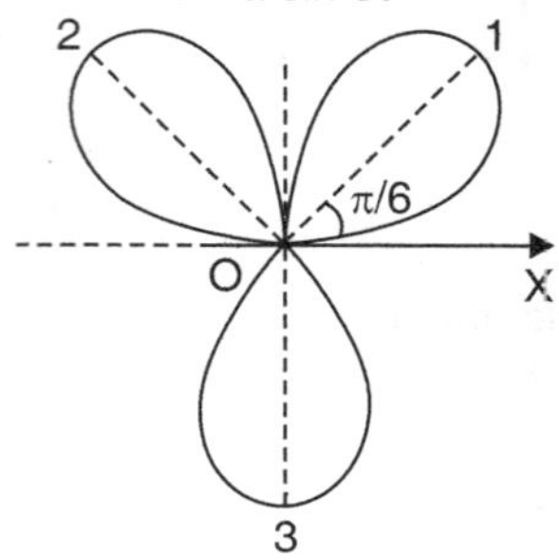

# APPENDIX—III

## CONVERSION FACTORS

| *To convert* | *into* | *Multiple by* | |
|---|---|---|---|
| **LINEAR MEASURE** | | | |
| Inch | Millimetre | 25.40 | 0.03937 |
| Inch | Centimetre | 2.54 | 0.3937 |
| Inch | Metre | 0.0254 | 39.37 |
| Feet | Metre | 0.3048 | 3.281 |
| Yard | Metre | 0.9144 | 1.0936 |
| Mile | Kilometre | 1.6093 | 0.62137 |
| Furlong | Metre | 201.1678 | 0.004971 |
| Miles | Nautical miles (int.) | 0.858975 | 1.15078 |
| **WEIGHT MEASURE** | | | |
| Ounces | Grammes | 28.3495 | 0.035274 |
| Pounds | Kilogrammes | 0.4536 | 2.20462 |
| Cwt. | Quintal (100 kg.) | 0.50802 | 1.9684 |
| Ton | Kilogrammes | 1016.05 | 0.0009842 |
| U.S. Ton | Kilogrammes | 907.18 | 0.0011 |
| Ton (2240 lb) | Metric ton (Tonne) | 1.01605 | 0.9842 |
| Maunds | Ton | 0.036735 | 27.2222 |
| Tola | Ounce | 0.411429 | 2.43056 |
| Tola | Gramme | 11.6628 | 0.087535 |
| **SQUARE MEASURE** | | | |
| Square inches | Square millimetres | 645.16 | 0.00155 |
| Square inches | Square centimetres | 6.4516 | 0.155 |
| Square feet | Square metre | 0.0929 | 10.764 |
| Square Yard | Square metre | 0.836 | 1.196 |
| Acre | Square metre | 4046.9 | 0.00025 |
| Square mile | Square kilometre | 2.59 | 0.3861 |
| Acre (4840 sq.yd.) | Hectare (10,000 sq. m) | 0.40468 | 2.4711 |
| **CUBIC MEASURE** | | | |
| Cubic inch | Cubic centimetre | 16.387 | 0.061 |
| Cubic feet | Cubic metre | 0.02832 | 35.315 |
| Cubic Yard | Cubic metre | 0.76455 | 1.308 |
| Cubic foot | Gallon (Imp.) | 6.2288 | 0.16054 |

| To obtain | From | Multiple by | |
|---|---|---|---|
| Cubic foot | Litres (1000 cc) | 28.3161 | 0.0353156 |
| Gollon (Imp.) | Litres | 4.54596 | 0.219976 |
| Pint (0.124 Imp. Gln) | Litres | 0.568 | 1.76 |
| U.S. Gallon | Litres | 3.78533 | 0.264178 |
| **PRESSURES AND DENSITIES** | | | |
| Pounds per sq in. | Kg. per sq. cm. | 0.070307 | 14.2233 |
| Pounds per sq. ft. | Kg. per sq. metre | 4.88243 | 0.204816 |
| Tonnes per sq. ft. | Tonnes per sq. metre | 10.937 | 0.091436 |
| Atmospheres | Pounds per sq. in. | 14.6959 | 0.06804 |
| Inch of Hg | Pounds per sq. in. | 0.491154 | 2.036 |
| Inch of Hg | Pounds per sq. in. | 0.0345316 | 28.959 |
| Pounds per sq. ft. | mm. of Hg. | 0.035913 | 2.78450 |
| Pounds per sq. in. | Feet of water | 2.30672 | 0.433516 |
| Feet of water | Kg. per sq. cm | 0.0304792 | 32.81 |
| Pounds per cu. m. | Grammes per cc | 27.6799 | 0.0361273 |
| Pounds per cft. | Kg. per cu. m. | 16.02 | 0.052422 |
| **MISCELLANEOUS** | | | |
| Pounds per foot | Kg. per metre | 1.48816 | 0.67197 |
| Miles per hour | Feet per metre | 1.46667 | 0.68182 |
| Feet per Second | Km per hour | 1.09728 | 0.91134 |
| H.P. (550 ft. lb/sec.) | Metric H.P. | 1.01387 | 0.98632 |